RANGE ROVER

40 Years of the 4 x 4 Icon

The Range Rover attracted an upper-crust image from the start, and the creation of State Review vehicles like this one for the British Royal Family was only to be expected.

RANGE ROVER

40 Years of the 4 x 4 Icon

JAMES TAYLOR

THE CROWOOD PRESS

First published in 2010 by
The Crowood Press Ltd
Ramsbury, Marlborough
Wiltshire SN8 2HR

www.crowood.com

This impression 2016

British Library Cataloguing-in-Publication Data
A catalogue record for this book is available from the British Library.

ISBN 978 1 84797 184 5

Typeset in Bembo by Bookcraft, Stroud, Gloucestershire
Printed and bound in India by Replika Press Pvt. Ltd.

Contents

Introduction and Acknowledgements   6

 1   The Background to Success   7
 2   The Birth of an Idea   14
 3   The Life and Times of the Original Range Rover   24
 4   Building the Original Range Rover   44
 5   Developing the 38A   52
 6   The Life and Times of the Second-generation Range Rover   62
 7   Building the 38A Range Rover   78
 8   Developing the Third-generation Range Rover   86
 9   The Life and Times of the Third-generation Range Rover   101
10   Building the L322   117
11   Range Rover Sport: Design and Development   124
12   The Life and Times of the Range Rover Sport   132
13   Building the Range Rover Sport   144
14   First-generation Range Rovers and the Aftermarket   148
15   Later Range Rovers and the Aftermarket   160

Appendix: VIN Codes   170
Index   174

Introduction and Acknowledgements

I saw my first Range Rover over the summer of 1970 in Oxford. I remember it was Tuscan Blue, and I remember the gentle but powerful sound of its V8 engine. Eight years later, I bought my first example, a rather well-used 1971 model which I took to Morocco for a long holiday to celebrate the end of university life. On my return to the UK, it had to go, because the salary of the civil servant I had become couldn't support its upkeep – but I was hooked.

Since then, I have owned two others and become a motoring writer, and I have been lucky enough to drive dozens of examples of all three generations and of the Range Rover Sport as well, thanks to the generosity of Land Rover's press office. I am no less impressed by today's Range Rover than I was by the first-generation models all those years ago, but I have had to accept that a motoring writer's income will not support one any more than a civil servant's could. One day, though…

I am very far from being alone in my enthusiasm for the Range Rover family. Over the years, I have met or corresponded with dozens of fellow enthusiasts who have provided information, access to their vehicles, photographs and all manner of other help in understanding the Range Rover story. To list them all here would be impossible, but they need to know how much their contributions have helped in the writing of this book.

Most important, perhaps, is that my writing activities have allowed me to meet many of the key people at Land Rover who have been involved with the Range Rover family. Enthusiasts all, their explanations and reminiscences have done a great deal to shape this book. Sadly, some of them are no longer with us, but I must record my grateful appreciation to all of the following:

George Adams, Malcolm Ainsley, Pip Archer, David Bache, Bill Baker, Graham Bannock, Tom Barton, Gordon Bashford, John Bilton, Gerry Boucher, Mike Broadhead, Roger Crathorne, Stuart Frith, Mike Gould, John Hall, Grant Horne, Charlie Hughes, Spen King, Paul Markwick, Bill Martin-Hurst, Geof Miller, Bill Morris, Tony Poole, Mike Sampson, Frank Shaw, Graham Silvers, David Sneath, George Thomson, Richard Woolley and Don Wyatt.

Lastly, there are more than 350 photographs in this book, and although some of them are my own I am happy to acknowledge that the majority are used by the kind permission of others. Many of the pictures of pre-1986 models were supplied to the media for editorial use when the vehicles were new. The negatives of these images are now held by the British Motor Industry Heritage Trust in the Heritage Motor Centre at Gaydon, and copies of the pictures are available to purchase. For the later pictures – and also some of the earlier ones as well – I am very grateful to Jaguar Land Rover, and in particular to Roger Crathorne in the Press Office. Special thanks also go to my long-term colleague and friend, photographer Nick Dimbleby, who took many of the pictures here for Land Rover.

James Taylor
Oxfordshire
December 2009

CHAPTER ONE

The Background to Success

Up until June 1970, a Land Rover was a Land Rover was a Land Rover. There were short-wheelbase and long-wheelbase models, there were several different body styles, and there was even a choice of engines. But there was nothing that could not be immediately recognized as a direct descendant of the iconic 1948 original.

And then there was the Range Rover.

It did not look like a Land Rover, it did not drive like a Land Rover, and it certainly did not accelerate like a Land Rover. But it did handle rough terrain like a Land Rover: in fact, it did the job better. It added comfortable seats and decent road performance to the Land Rover's all-terrain ability to create a new kind of vehicle and Land Rover, as a brand, has never looked back since.

It is arguable that many of the elements of the Range Rover had already been pioneered in the International Scout of 1961, the Jeep Wagoneer of 1963, and the Ford Bronco of 1965. However, as anybody who has driven any of those vehicles will readily concede, the Range Rover was a much more accomplished design. It is also important to remember that the Range Rover was not intended as a copy of any of these vehicles, of course. In fact, Spen King's original idea was pretty much a pure engineering concept; where it might fit into the global car marketplace was not his problem.

It was a real problem for those whose responsibility was marketing this new vehicle, though. They had never had to handle anything like it before, and for the very first sales brochure they came up with the description of it as 'a car for all reasons'. It was a rather desperate attempt to define what this new model was all about, but it could hardly have been more accurate.

The customers loved the vehicle's versatility, they loved the images that the name Range Rover suggested, and they loved both the practicality and the feeling of superiority that its elevated driving position delivered. But they liked its simplicity less, and from the beginning they demanded more luxury features, more equipment and more convenience gadgets to satisfy their idea of the complete car. So its makers responded – slowly at first, but spurred on to some extent by the success of aftermarket conversions – and by the end of the 1980s the Range Rover had become a fully-fledged luxury car with all the prestige associated with such possessions.

Today, the Range Rover name conjures up images of a versatile, practical and expensive luxury vehicle with the ability to take its occupants almost anywhere they could reasonably want to go on the planet. It is load-carrier, passenger-carrier, high-performance car and rugged off-road transport all rolled into one. But above all, it has become a status symbol.

Three generations of Range Rover pictured at the headquarters of Land Rover North America in 2005. On the left is the second-generation 38A model; in the centre is the third-generation L322, which had just been freshened up for the 2006 model-year; and on the right is a late-model County from the first generation.

It has also completely transformed the Land Rover brand and what that brand represents. The name that had started out in 1948 meaning a rugged commercial vehicle with off-road ability had by the turn of the century become more associated with luxury passenger-carriers embodying a vast breadth of capabilities. Yet within those capabilities, the original strengths of the Land Rover, especially its off-road ability and its ruggedness, still shine through.

Without the Range Rover, and the cheaper imitations it provoked, Land Rover would probably never have developed the Discovery, which arrived in 1989 to make the

The Range Rover's glamour spilled over onto other models, and from 2005 the companion model Range Rover Sport, which shared its chassis with the contemporary Discovery, brought a more sporting image to the brand.

The so-called Command Driving Position was always a major factor in the Range Rover's success. This view of the road from a 38A model was taken in Australia.

ABOVE: *From the end of the 1980s, Land Rover made sure that the Range Rover kept abreast or ahead of all the key trends in the luxury-car market. This is one of the first satellite navigation installations offered for the second-generation model from 1997.*

LEFT: *Customers demanded more and more luxury and convenience equipment, and the Range Rover became established in the luxury-car market. This is the interior of a 1993-model US-specification County LWB, the long-wheelbase variant of the first-generation Range Rover. The wood and leather created a traditionally British interior ambience which appealed strongly to customers.*

Central to the vehicle's appeal was its ability to deal effortlessly with terrain that would cause difficulties for conventional vehicles. Here, a late first-generation model demonstrates its sure-footedness on snow in Switzerland.

basic Range Rover qualities available to family buyers. Nor would it have developed the Freelander, which took many of those qualities down to an even more affordable level in 1998. And there would certainly never have been a Range Rover Sport, which added high performance and a sporting demeanour to the basic package.

The qualities of the Range Rover have even affected the original Land Rover, which is now far less utilitarian than it ever was before, embodies the Range Rover's trademark permanent four-wheel drive, and offers levels of equipment and luxury in its top models that would have been unthinkable before 1970. But perhaps the most telling comment on the way the Range Rover has shaped the company that developed it is a statement from that company's Managing Director, Matthew Taylor, in September 2003. He said, 'it is the Range Rover, even more than the original Land Rover, that is now the inspiration for this company's future.'

Range Rover Manufacturers

It is just about possible to make out the continuity in the story of the Range Rover's manufacturers, but the story is a long and complicated one.

When the first plans were being drawn up in 1965–1966 for the vehicle that would eventually be called the Range Rover, the designers and engineers were working for the Rover Company, a small independent British carmaker based at

From the earliest days, the Range Rover's ability as a towing vehicle was highly appreciated.

Despite increasing levels of luxury, the second-generation model was no less capable than the first across difficult terrain. Height-adjustable air suspension compensated for its longer wheelbase, allowing the driver to raise the body and chassis clear of obstructions which might otherwise have grounded the vehicle.

ABOVE: The third-generation model's rough-terrain ability was even greater, thanks to an array of sophisticated traction control systems. This early L322 claws it way steadily through wet mud on a slope, even though the tyre treads are already badly clogged.

Solihull in the West Midlands. The Rover Company built Rover cars and Land Rovers, and the Range Rover was seen as a vehicle which would embody desirable characteristics of both vehicle types.

Mergers elsewhere in the British motor industry persuaded Rover management that the time was right to form an alliance with a larger manufacturer. So in December 1966, the company merged with the Leyland group, which was primarily a maker of buses and trucks but also owned car manufacturer Standard-Triumph. Less than two years later, the British government brokered a merger between Leyland and the British Motor Corporation to produce a large company with the potential to

Customers always appreciated the feeling of security that a Range Rover provided in all conditions. These pictures show third-generation models in heavy snow and crossing a river. Note in the second picture the wheel articulation which allowed all four wheels to maintain contact with the ground to provide the maximum grip and traction.

The chassis of the first Range Rover was also used for the first-generation Discovery, which gave Land Rover a competitor in the family 4 × 4 market that had sprung up in the wake of the Range Rover's success.

face competition from large European combines such as Volkswagen.

The Range Rover was still not in production by this stage, but it did figure in Rover's forward production schedule, and Sir Donald Stokes, head of the new British Leyland Motor Corporation, thought it had great potential. So he was very keen that it should meet its target launch date of June 1970.

This was really the first time that British Leyland had any impact on the Range Rover project, but from this time onwards, Rover's existence within the BL group would have an increasingly large impact. First, it was BL's decision to pull Rover cars out of North America in 1971; as the Range Rover was viewed more as a car than as a Land Rover (even though it was marketed as made by Land Rover, which was not then a separate company), that immediately cancelled plans to take it into the North American market.

It was also during 1971 that organizational changes merged the Rover and Triumph engineering teams to create Rover-Triumph. This was supposedly BL's Large Cars Division, soon renamed the Specialist Cars Division, and at one point pushed into an alliance with Jaguar to create Jaguar-Rover-Triumph – a relationship from which Jaguar did everything in their power to remain aloof. Land Rovers and Range Rovers sat uncomfortably alongside the Rover cars' side of the house.

As the various component companies within BL were brought under more centralized control, finances were centralized, too. So although the Range Rover was selling strongly and bringing in big profits, those profits were ploughed into a central fund which was allocated amongst BL companies according to their needs. The loss-making

Austin-Morris Volume Cars Division had the greatest need, and as a result there was very little to plough back into improving Range Rovers. It meant that there was almost no money to develop the model further for the rest of the 1970s.

As 1974 drew to a close, BL ran into a cash-flow crisis and turned to the government for help. The government responded by partially nationalizing the company, and immediately asked its industrial adviser, Don Ryder, to look into BL's affairs and to

Timeline		
1965	First thoughts	Rover Company Ltd
1966		Rover Company Ltd, owned by Leyland
1968		Rover Company, owned by British Leyland
1970	First Range Rover launched	
1974		Rover Company, under partially nationalized British Leyland
1978		Land Rover Ltd, under partially nationalized British Leyland
1989		Land Rover Ltd, under Rover Group, owned by British Aerospace
1994		Land Rover Ltd, under Rover Group, owned by BMW
1994	Second Range Rover launched	
2000		Land Rover Ltd, under Premier Automotive Group of Ford Motor Company
2001	Third Range Rover launched	
2003		Jaguar Land Rover, under Premier Automotive Group of Ford Motor Company
2008		Jaguar Land Rover, owned by Tata Motors of India

Range Rovers always appealed to the rich and famous, and Land Rover publicity capitalized on the association. These pictures show Arsenal and England goal-keeper David Seaman collecting the half-millionth Range Rover from the assembly lines, and a Range Rover Sport lent to the Lions rugby team as part of Land Rover's sponsorship deal during 2005.

make recommendations. The Ryder Report was published in 1975, and among its recommendations was that an independent business unit should be created to look after Land Rovers and Range Rovers. Although a great deal of the Ryder Report was later rejected, this recommendation was adopted and in 1978, Land Rover Ltd was established as an independently-managed company within British Leyland.

British Leyland's identity changed over the next decade – to Austin-Rover in 1982 and to the Rover Group in 1986 – and from 1989 the Rover Group and Land Rover with it became the property of British Aerospace. But Land Rover Ltd remained unchanged until 1994. In March that year, when the Rover Group

LEFT: *Celebrities come no more celebrated than the British Royal Family, and ever since 1975 Land Rover has provided a specially-converted Range Rover for Her Majesty the Queen to use as a parade vehicle. This is the unique L322-based model, with a BMW V8 engine, that was delivered in 2006.*

was sold to the German BMW car company, the first-generation Range Rover was still in production.

The second-generation model, introduced in September 1994, had been wholly designed in the days of the Rover Group even though it was introduced during BMW ownership of the company. It was still in production six years later when BMW split the Rover Group into two and sold the car division to a business consortium and the Land Rover division to Ford.

So although the third-generation Range Rover incorporated a great deal of BMW technology, it was announced as a 2002 model under Ford ownership. Over the next couple of years, Ford merged the Land Rover engineering teams with the Jaguar engineering teams (it had owned Jaguar since late 1989) to create Jaguar Land Rover. Then Ford's own financial problems in the mid-2000s persuaded it to sell Jaguar Land Rover as a going concern to Tata Motors of India in 2008.

CHAPTER TWO

The Birth of an Idea

The first Range Rover came together as the result of a series of happy coincidences within the old Rover Company in the first half of the 1960s. Behind two of the key events that led to the creation of the new vehicle was the appointment in 1963 of William Martin-Hurst as Managing Director, a role which he took over on the death of Maurice Wilks, his brother-in-law. Wilks had joined Rover more than thirty years earlier as engineering chief, and he had been the man responsible for the hugely successful Land Rover that had kept the Rover Company profitable during the 1950s.

Martin-Hurst brought with him a new and more radical approach. Formerly at Teddington Aircraft Controls, where he had pushed through a number of enlightened schemes, he had become Rover's Production Director in 1960 but it was already clear that he was being groomed for the top job. Although the winds of change were already blowing at Rover, notably in the development of the revolutionary new 2000 saloon which would be introduced in 1963, the company still had the rather cautious culture of a small, family-run concern. Martin-Hurst envisaged expansion.

To that end, he appointed an assistant to carry out what would now be the work of a whole market research department. He also listened carefully to what the heads of Rover's overseas branches told him – and in particular, he listened to what he was being told from its North American branch. Rover had never had much of a presence in North America, but Martin-Hurst believed that it could have, and he was prepared to put the effort into achieving that. He was also an active supporter of new thinking within

Rover, and as a result he was open to the new ideas from the New Vehicle Projects department. This 'think-tank' department had been established some years earlier by Maurice Wilks as a way of focusing and developing ideas for future vehicles outside the mainstream of the engineering and design disciplines.

The original idea for the vehicle that would become the Range Rover some five years later came from Spen King, who was then running New Vehicle Projects. The way Spen tells it, the idea occurred to him when he drove one of the company's new Rover 2000 saloons across a ploughed field. The ride comfort was so superior to that of a Land Rover that he began to think in terms of using the long-travel coil-spring suspension of the car on a four-wheel drive vehicle to create a kind of super-Land Rover. At that stage, he could have had no idea how successful his idea would later become.

King's enthusiasm for the idea was swiftly turned into some sketches. Gordon Bashford, who was the chassis designer on King's team and had been with Rover since the 1930s, drew up an overall package for the vehicle. At this stage, the two men saw it as a five-seater estate car, with road performance that would eclipse anything then available with a Land Rover badge but with off-road ability that would be equal or close to that of current Land Rovers.

King wanted the vehicle to be simple and strong, and so he went for a two-door body design. The separate chassis-and-body structure was a given for an off-road vehicle, but Bashford's idea of hanging unstressed aluminium alloy body panels on a steel 'skeleton' for the body was new. It also reflected the use of unstressed

panels hung on the monocoque base-unit of the Rover 2000. To get the road performance they wanted, King and Bashford incorporated the 3-litre 6-cylinder engine that was the most

Progressively minded William ('Bill') Martin-Hurst created the conditions in which the Rover Company was able to develop the Range Rover.

Gordon Bashford had been the 'packaging' designer behind Rover's post-war saloon cars and had drawn up the chassis of the original Land Rover in 1948. He turned Spen King's ideas into the Land Rover 100-inch Station Wagon.

Spen King

Charles Spencer ('Spen') King was one of Rover's bright young engineers. He had been recruited to the company in the late 1940s after doing an engineering apprenticeship with Rolls-Royce, and his first jobs at Rover were associated with the company's attempts to build a gas turbine-powered car using technology that Rover had encountered when working on Frank Whittle's jet aircraft engine during the 1939–1945 war. He had worked on subsequent gas turbine car prototypes, and had contributed to the suspension design of the Rover 2000 as well.

As it happened, King was also a nephew of the Wilks brothers who had turned Rover into a hugely respected independent motor manufacturer. Spencer Wilks, then Chairman, was the older of those brothers and Maurice Wilks, who had died in 1963, was the 'father' of the Land Rover on which the Rover Company now depended so heavily. Peter Wilks, son of another Wilks brother and cousin to King, was by this stage Technical Director at Rover. Nick Wilks, who assisted Geof Miller with the competitor vehicle evaluations in 1966, was also a member of the family and was the son of Spencer Wilks.

Even though King was the inspiration behind the Range Rover and the guiding light in its early days, he was at Rover long

Spen King was the brains and the inspiration behind the Range Rover, but he was promoted out of the company some two years before it entered production.

enough only to see the second 100-inch Station Wagon. In 1968, as a consequence of re-organization when Rover became part of British Leyland, he was promoted to take charge of engineering at Triumph and was therefore not around to see his idea developed into a production reality.

powerful Rover had in production at that stage. Off-road ability would come from a standard Land Rover selectable four-wheel drive system.

As these initial concept drawings were coming together over the summer of 1965, so two other important events in that happy chain of coincidences were occurring within Rover. One was that Martin-Hurst's assistant, a young economist called Graham Bannock, reported on his findings after a tour of North America. In his role as the company's Market Research and Statistics chief, he concluded that there was an expanding market for four-wheel drive vehicles in North America. However, he stressed that this was very different from the traditional 'workhorse' market that Land Rover had always addressed. The new market was for four-wheel drives that could be used

in pursuit of leisure activities such as outdoor sports and caravanning. There were already some domestic American vehicles on sale that were capitalizing on it. To King and Bashford's delight, the report painted a picture of a buyer group that would be ideal for what was now being called the 100-inch Station Wagon.

Meanwhile, Martin-Hurst had been looking hard at Rover's chances of improving sales performance in North America. He had already appointed a dynamic new head of the Rover Company of North America. That new man, Bruce McWilliams, had pointed out that Land Rovers would sell better across the Atlantic if they had better road performance. As new and more powerful engines from Rover were still a few years in the future, he suggested buying-in an American V8 to save time.

Martin-Hurst's response had been to authorize him to find one that would do the job.

Although McWilliams had identified a strong contender from Chrysler, it was actually Martin-Hurst himself who found the engine that Rover would eventually buy. This was an advanced light-alloy small-block V8 used in Buick, Pontiac and Oldsmobile cars from General Motors and which went out of production in 1964 because GM had developed cheaper thin-wall iron-casting techniques. Its appeal to Rover was that it was small enough to fit into the engine bay of existing Rover cars as well as into Land Rovers, and by January 1965, Martin-Hurst had secured for Rover the rights to manufacture and develop it in the UK. Once it was clear that the V8 would be central to Rover's future plans, King and Bashford dropped the 3-litre engine from their schemes and incorporated the V8, which was a 3.5-litre engine, instead.

Initial Development

With the basic concept established, a new and powerful engine in place to power it, and a potentially large market identified, it was clear that the 100-inch Station Wagon project had legs. There was, however, one small problem. This was that Tom Barton, then Land Rover Chief Engineer, was not at all keen on the idea of using coil springs. His view was that if a Land Rover was too comfortable to drive, the driver would use it too hard in rough terrain and would damage it; he believed that the rough ride from traditional leaf springs prevented the driver from over-taxing the vehicle and so contributed to the Land Rover's legendary durability.

So initial development work on the 100-inch Station Wagon was not done within Land Rover engineering, but by a team seconded to New Vehicle Projects for the purpose. The first one seconded was Geof Miller, who had been running mainstream Land Rover development. Geof

The 3.5-litre V8 engine bought from Buick in America was fundamental to the Range Rover's success, giving it both high performance and refinement. It had actually entered production at Rover as a saloon car engine in 1967.

joined New Vehicle Projects in July 1966, and one of his first tasks was to set up a week-long vehicle evaluation exercise at Eastnor Castle, where Land Rover had been doing much of its off-road development testing since 1961. Spen King had realized that many of the people who might become involved with the 100-inch project had relatively little experience of off-road vehicles, and he wanted them to drive a selection of production Land Rovers, experimental Land Rovers and competitors' four-wheel drives. Among the experimental vehicles was a Land Rover that had been fitted with one of the new V8 engines, and its performance convinced the whole team that the

V8 would be the ideal engine for the new 100-inch Station Wagon.

That event, in November 1966, helped the company to focus on what the new vehicle would be expected to do, and therefore on what was going to be needed to achieve those aims. Refinement of the paper design followed, and Gordon Bashford remembered that once he had worked out the dimensional package to incorporate everything that was now needed, the wheelbase of the new design worked out at 99.9 inches. So he and Spen King agreed to round it up to 100 inches and that is how, in line with the Land Rover practice of naming vehicles after their wheelbase length, the new concept became known as the Land Rover 100-inch Station Wagon.

The team expanded: Miller was joined by Alan Wood and, in 1967, by Roger Crathorne. Nick Wilks (Maurice Wilks' nephew) had been involved with the competitor vehicle evaluations, but he now faded from the picture. Body styling would normally have fallen to Rover's Chief Stylist, David Bache, but he protested that he had too many other projects to occupy his time at that stage. So King and Bashford drew up the basic shape themselves, and persuaded Geoff Crompton in Bache's department to tidy it up for them in his spare time. It would be June 1967 before the Styling Department found

Geof Miller was a senior Land Rover engineer and was taken off mainstream development work in 1966 to run the 100-inch Station Wagon project.

time to work on the vehicle officially, and by that stage the basic shape had already imposed itself.

Meanwhile, the 100-inch Station Wagon was approved by the Rover Company management. In February 1967 – just a month before Rover was formally absorbed into the Leyland combine – three things happened. Geof Miller's project team set about constructing a first prototype; David Bache's Styling Department was formally asked to take on the styling task; and Rover's advertising agents engaged a market research company to investigate likely customer reactions to the 100-inch Station Wagon. In support of that research, Gordon Bashford drew up an outline description of the vehicle, which was codenamed 'Concept Oyster' for the benefit of the public whose opinions were being sought.

That first prototype was based on Gordon Bashford's drawings, and incorporated a Land Rover transmission with selectable four-wheel drive, and Land Rover axles and drum brakes, too. Geof Miller remembers that the original plan was to send the chassis out on test disguised under the body of a Vauxhall estate car, but in the event a body was ready in time, and was based on the King-Bashford-Crompton design.

The famous Eastnor 'safari' of November 1966 allowed many people at Rover to get to grips with what worked and what did not on an off-road vehicle. Geof Miller photographed the fleet of vehicles lined up; they included some experimental Land Rovers, as well as potential rivals to the 100-inch Station Wagon.

The culture at Rover in the 1960s was to build a prototype and then hand it over to the Drawing Office to be turned into production drawings afterwards! So Spen King had the first one, numbered 100/1, built in the Jig Shop.

The improved second prototype, seen on the left here, soon joined the first one. This picture was taken during ride height trials.

This view of the underside of 100/1 shows the standard Land Rover selectable two-wheel drive transmission with its high- and low-ratio gearing painted on the transfer box, and the original rear axle arrangement with both dampers facing backwards. This led to axle tramp, so for production one damper was moved to face forwards.

The Range Rover Gearbox

It was clear from an early stage that the existing '76mm' Land Rover gearbox and its associated transfer box were not strong enough to handle the torque of the V8 engine, but the first two prototypes were built in 1967 and 1968 with these components because there was nothing else available.

At that time, the Transmissions Department under Frank Shaw had been asked to draw up a new 4-speed gearbox for use with the V8 engine in the forthcoming 101 Forward Control military Land Rover. So it was inevitable that, when Spen King asked for a 4-speed gearbox to go behind the V8 engine in his new vehicle, the transmissions people should steer him towards using the new military gearbox. In the end, the Range Rover was announced with the LT95 transmission some two years before the 101 Forward Control was made public.

An interesting characteristic of this gearbox – and one which has never re-appeared on a Land Rover product – was that the transfer gears were mounted within the main gearbox casing so that there was no need for a separate transfer box.

Frank Shaw was never very satisfied with the LT95 gearbox. He always felt that there were too many compromises inherent in designing a gearbox to suit both a heavy-duty military vehicle and a refined estate-type 4 × 4, and wished he had insisted on developing two separate designs.

Rover stylist David Bache, seen here in the foreground, was asked to prepare the 100-inch Station Wagon for production. Behind him is Tony Poole, who was in day-to-day charge of the styling project.

This June 1967 scale model reflected Bache's first thoughts on the way the new vehicle should look…

…but it soon became clear that the best solution was to tidy up the original design. This scale mock-up explored alternative ways of doing so.

The Range Rover Prototypes

	Registration	Build date	Engine no	Remarks
100/1	SYE 157F	July 1967	Not known	Mid-Grey, RHD. Bronco-type front suspension, selectable four-wheel drive, drum brakes on Land Rover axles
100/2	ULH 696F	May 1968	Not known	Marine Blue, LHD. Improved front suspension, disc brakes, selectable four-wheel drive
100/3	AGN 316G	July 1969	Not known	Lincoln Green, LHD. First with production-style body. Trials with BL Competitions Department; later mocked-up as military radio car
100/4	AMV 287H	Aug 1969	2158/19	Sahara Dust, RHD. Scrapped after rig tests
100/5	WYK 315H	Oct 1969	2158/24A	Bahama Gold, LHD. Hot-climate tests in Sahara, then barrier-tested and scrapped
100/6	AOY 289H	Sep 1969	2158/24	Masai Red, RHD. Transmission test vehicle; hot-climate tests in Sahara. Original body destroyed in rollover accident; survives with replacement body
100/7	YVB 150H	Dec 1969	2158/26A	Amazon Green, LHD. Built on pilot assembly line

Buick shipped thirty-nine of its 215 cu in light-alloy V8 engines across to Rover when the licence-manufacturing deal had been signed. Rover gave these numbers prefixed with 2158 (215 cubic inches, 8 cylinders), and the engines in the Range Rover prototypes were almost certainly all from this batch. The engines would have been 'Roverized', using UK-made exhaust manifolds, electrical equipment and carburettors, but retained their Buick blocks and internal components.

This first vehicle, numbered 100/1, first ran in July 1967 and by September that year had been completed and registered as SYE 157F. It was painted grey and had three-abreast front seating, with black vinyl upholstery like that just introduced on Land Rovers. Roger Crathorne remembers that its chromed front bumper was a Ford Transit van item that he had been sent to buy from the parts counter of the local Ford dealer in Solihull. Later, it was badged as a Velar before being sent out on the roads for test.

David Bache's stylists had started work on a production body design in June, and much of the work was done by Tony Poole, who usually handled Land Rover styling projects. Some initial designs, probably by Bache himself, hinted at a more elaborate design with a flowing tail, more reminiscent of a conventional estate car. However, Spen King pointed out that this design was ill-suited to the 'skeleton' body structure proposed by Gordon Bashford and which King thought would greatly simplify the assembly from kit form that would be essential to get the new model into some overseas markets. So in the end, Bache's team tidied up the existing King-Bashford-Crompton design, their changes being subtle and yet decisive in producing a clean, distinctive shape.

It was during this phase that Tony Poole, working on the full-size clay model, was asked to put a name badge on the bonnet. No name had been chosen, but Poole was able to make up the name Road-Rover from some letters he had available. The resulting photograph subsequently led many historians to assume that the 100-inch Station Wagon was a later iteration of the cancelled Road-Rover project from the 1950s. Although there were some similarities of intent (the Road-Rover was intended as a rugged estate car mixing elements of Rover saloons and Land Rovers), all those involved with the 100-inch Station Wagon have insisted that there was no direct connection.

Testing and Interior Design

On test, the first prototype showed up a number of problems, and notable among them was severe steering kickback on some surfaces. This was traced to the method of locating the axle, which had unashamedly been copied from the Ford Bronco that Rover had bought for comparison trials. So Gordon Bashford's assistant, Joe Brown, drew up a modified design with a relocated Panhard rod, and this was incorporated into the second prototype. Vehicle 100/2 was completed in spring 1968 and featured left-hand drive, disc brakes, and a Boge Hydromat self-levelling strut at the rear. Painted dark blue, it had a variation of the original King-Bashford-Crompton body style because the production styling had only been signed off in January, by which time 100/2 was already in build.

The full-size mock-up was prepared for management viewing in September 1967. Stylist Tony Poole put the name Road-Rover on the bonnet to demonstrate where the model badging could go, but there was never any intention to call the vehicle a Road-Rover. Those are Rover 2000 wheel trims, again probably added purely to complete the model.

The third prototype, 100/3, was the first to have the production styling. As this rare colour picture shows, it was finished in a dark green that was not adopted for production, and had black bumpers with chrome wing mirrors.

The interior was still under development when 100/3 was built, and this picture shows the Land Rover-type spring-spoke steering wheel and the black upholstery that had been used to complete the vehicle.

One early idea was to have a rearward-facing bench seat in the load area. Here it is under development in the Styling Studio in March 1969.

This second prototype was right on target in most respects, but Geof Miller had already pointed out that the V8 engine was too powerful for the Land Rover clutch, gearbox, differentials and half-shafts which had been built into it. The best suggestion from Solihull's Transmissions Department was to use the stronger axles intended for long-wheelbase Land Rovers, but everyone agreed that would seriously compromise the handling. Fortunately, Geof remembered that the Land Rover engineers had looked at an experimental

transmission with permanent four-wheel drive some years earlier. The key factor was that by splitting the torque of the engine equally between front and rear axles instead of putting it all through the rear axle, much lighter axles could be used to the benefit of the ride and handling.

Spen King and Technical Director Peter Wilks thought it was worth a look, so Geof found it in the Experimental Department's stores and had it built into another Land Rover. Comparative trials between this vehicle and a V8-powered Land Rover with

the standard selectable transmission demonstrated the complete superiority of the permanent four-wheel drive system, so Frank Shaw's transmission engineers were asked to incorporate it into the new and stronger gearbox they were by this time designing for the 100-inch Station Wagon.

Meanwhile, that second prototype vehicle only represented one potential version of the 100-inch Station Wagon – the one that Spen King had envisaged. While the engineers had been busy building and testing prototypes, some thinking

The fourth prototype, built in summer 1969, was another step nearer the production models. It is pictured here during testing at Eastnor.

RIGHT: Prototype 100/6 was famously rolled by Rob Lyall, the Car Section's Ride and Handling Engineer. Subsequently rebuilt with a later production body, it is the only Range Rover prototype that still survives.

Geof Miller and his wife took 100/7 to Switzerland on holiday in 1970. Just visible in the rear is the prototype rearward-facing bench seat that obliged the spare wheel to go on the roof. The arrangement proved impractical and the rear bench never entered production.

had been going on to see where else the project might lead. Spen King's formal Product Proposal of July 1967 had incorporated a 4-cylinder alternative to the V8 engine (at this stage seen as the 2-litre ohc engine of the Rover 2000), an automatic-transmission model (using the Chrysler A727 3-speed transmission, which represented the best available in 1967), optional two-wheel drive (probably only with the 4-cylinder option), Land Rover drum brakes at the rear with discs at the front, and a self-levelling system at the rear on V8 models. The basic model was planned as a six-seater, with three abreast in both front and rear, and there would be four optional seats in the rear load area. There would also be both 'economy' and de luxe trim levels.

Interior styling got under way in the late summer of 1968, after the exterior had been done. Taking Spen King's thoughts on simplicity for overseas assembly very much on board, the stylists developed a straightforward modular facia design that would adapt easily to both RHD and LHD configurations. They then moved on to the door trims, again incorporating very simple internal release handles which could be operated by rear-seat passengers as well as those in the front.

The seats were the last job, and these presented a problem. The plan to sell the new model in the USA meant that safety belts would be needed for the front-seat passengers (belts were not yet mandatory in most markets, including the UK). However, the two-door configuration meant that the front seats had to tip forwards to give access for rear-seat passengers. Mounting the belts to the B-pillars would have put them in the way of rear-seat passengers trying to get in or out, while mounting them to the floor so that they ran up and over the seat backs would have caused difficulties when the seat backs were tipped forwards.

The solution was worked out between the stylists and Rover's safety engineers, and was to mount the belts to the seats themselves and to mount the seat bases very securely to the floor with tie-rods to the chassis as well. A simple tip-and-slide mechanism allowed the seats to slide fore and aft and to tip forwards. However, testing of the 'safety seats' had introduced delays into the programme and, as the team was now under pressure to deliver a finished interior, any thoughts of arranging backrest rake adjustment as well were abandoned for the time being. Ironically, when British Leyland came to sell the new model in Germany a few years later,

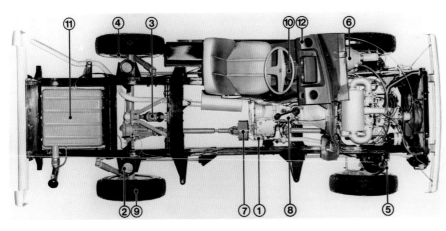

The original 1970 press picture of the Range Rover chassis explained its key features very well. The numbers are: (1) Centre differential (to avoid wind-up between the two permanently driven axles); (2) coil springs on beam axles (Land Rovers then had hard leaf-spring suspension); (3) Boge self-levelling strut (to maintain a constant ride height when laden and ensure unchanged handling qualities); (4) all-round disc brakes (Land Rovers then had all-round drums); (5) dual-pipe front braking system (to meet US safety regulations); (6) brake servo; (7) transmission parking brake; (8) four-speed, all-synchromesh gearbox; (9) radial tyres; (10) collapsible 'safety' steering column; (11) 19-gallon fuel tank; (12) impact-absorbing facia.

Coil springs and disc brakes were dangerously revolutionary thinking as far as the die-hard Land Rover people were concerned – but they were devastatingly effective.

Why Did the First Range Rover have Chassis Number 3?

Surviving records suggest that chassis number 1 (355-00001A) was the first pilot-production Range Rover to go down the assembly line, even though it was normal for vehicles not to go down the line in strict chassis-number order. As was normal practice at Solihull, when it left the assembly line it passed to the Despatch Department, which would normally have been responsible for 'despatching' it to a Land Rover dealer.

However, it was chassis number 3 (355-00003A) that was the first one actually to leave the assembly lines. The Rover Publicity Department wanted a blue vehicle and a red one to photograph for the first sales brochure, and as vehicle number 3 was blue, it was the first to be released. Geof Miller remembers that 'we collected it off the production line and towed it round to Engineering to finish it off. We were the only people who had the necessary correct interior trim – albeit handmade'.

The publicity team had to wait a little longer for a red one: chassis number 8 was the one they got, which was completed before chassis number 7 that was numerically the first red example.

Many years later, Land Rover Ltd tracked down that first Range Rover, which was then in the ownership of a Danish photographer. A deal was done: the owner settled for a brand-new Turbo D Range Rover in exchange for his old car, and the first Range Rover was handed over to the Heritage Motor Centre at Gaydon for its museum collection.

they found that backrest adjustment on the driver's seat was a compulsory requirement, and so the driver's seat had to be developed further before the vehicle could go on sale there.

Work on the seats was approaching a conclusion in November 1968, when Geof Miller summarized the state of play on the 100-inch Station Wagon project in a Technical Brochure. A 4-cylinder model (now with the 2.25-litre Land Rover engine) was still on the cards, but the automatic transmission option had been abandoned; so had the two-wheel drive and rear drum brake proposals, and instead of four individual seats in the rear there was to be the option of a rearward-facing bench seat.

However, the 4-cylinder engine and the additional rear seats (which the Styling Department was already working on) did not progress to production. That was mainly because of pressure from Rover's new owners at British Leyland, whose top management in the person of Sir Donald Stokes had developed an enthusiasm for the new Land Rover. Stokes wanted the vehicle on the market as soon as was humanly possible, and to that end the final development stages of the project were curtailed. There simply was no time to develop these additional features before production began and, once the new vehicle had been launched, demand was so great that enthusiasm for complicating the issue with extra variants fell away.

A Name and a Rush

Meanwhile, there had been discussions about what to call the new model. Tony Poole's accidental name of Road-Rover did find some acceptance, and the draughtsman responsible for the production body drawing issued on 7 May 1968 labelled it as for the '100-inch wheelbase Road-Rover'. To the engineers, it was still a 100-inch Station Wagon, but it was some time around November 1968 that Tony

ABOVE: *Production Range Rover number 1 was not the first to leave the Despatch Department. The publicity department wanted a brighter colour to feature in the sales brochure, and it was passed over in favour of number 3. In the end, the Olive Green seen here was not used on production models. The vehicle still survives, in enthusiast hands.*

RIGHT: *The press launch was held amid spectacular scenery in Cornwall. One of the twenty press demonstrators prepared for the event, NXC 235H was photographed there in June 1970.*

Poole came up with the definitive name. Geof Miller remembers that the Sales Department had circulated discussion lists with all kinds of outdoor and sporting names such as Jaguar, Cougar and Anaconda. Tony and others had been bouncing names like Rover Ranger back and forth, and Tony suddenly hit on Range Rover. It worked well, embodying ideas of wide open spaces, adventure and, above all, an almost snobbish superiority over the Land Rover.

On 18 December, that name was formally adopted at a meeting between the Sales and Engineering Departments. At the same meeting, the Sales Department formally registered their view that it was 'tragic' that the Range Rover was to have only two doors. There were concerns over escalating costs which would inevitably lead to higher showroom prices, and there was con-

Number 3, registered as YVB 153H, had the honour of becoming the 'official' first Range Rover. It has now been carefully restored and belongs to the Heritage Motor Centre at Gaydon.

firmation that the company planned to produce an emissions-controlled version for sale in North America, although this would have to follow on some months behind the mainstream models because US regulations demanded that compliance tests were carried out on a production car, not on a prototype. For the rest of the world, the meeting hoped that the Range Rover could be announced at the Geneva Motor Show in April 1970, and that it might have a production life of eight years.

At this stage, there were still only two prototypes in existence, and neither of them embodied the production styling or the permanent four-wheel drive of the production specification. Prototype 100/3, completed in April 1969, was the first to look like the eventual production model, and was also the first to have the new high-speed dual-purpose tyres that Michelin had developed specially for the vehicle. This was followed in fairly rapid succession by three more prototypes, two of which went on a hot-climate proving expedition in the Sahara in November–December 1969.

And that had to be enough. British Leyland had hoped to announce the Range Rover's introduction with the news that one was to participate in the *Daily Mirror* London–Mexico World Cup Rally in April 1970, but there was now no chance that production models would be ready in time. A pre-production assembly line was built at Solihull in December 1969, and was running in time to deliver one last prototype – number 100/7 – before Christmas, and three pilot-production cars before the end of the year. Production build-up then began in January 1970, and the launch date

was set as June 1970, with showroom sales beginning on 1 September.

Final details were developed as the pilot-production vehicles were being built. The original plan had been to use an automatic choke, but the SU-designed AED (Automatic Enrichment Device) that had been made available in Rover saloons with the V8 engine during 1969 had given a lot of trouble in service, so the decision was made to go with a manual choke. As this had not been planned in, there was nowhere to put the choke control on the dashboard, so it ended up being fitted through a bracket intended for the bonnet release cable: fortunately, there was a bracket on each side of the vehicle to simplify the production of RHD and LHD versions.

Another problem arose when it became clear that there were difficulties in making the large bonnet panel out of aluminium: the material would not 'draw' well into the castellation features that Bache's team had added to give character to the front end. So the bonnet had to be made of steel instead. Production was simplified by using a single colour for the pressed-steel wheels instead of the two originally planned, and of course early prototype tooling was remade to production standard. Notable among the modified tools was the one for the dashboard, which had been given a smooth finish for simplicity in prototype form but took on a grained finish for production. Most of the pilot-production vehicles were nevertheless built with 'smooth' dashboards, early vehicles that would be used for the dealer and media launches later being modified to production standard when the remodelled dashboard became available.

The first 25 RHD pilot-build vehicles were followed by three LHD examples, and all of these except for one were registered in the YVBxxx H sequence that also embraced prototype 100/7. Most of these vehicles were used for further engineering work, and many went out on the roads before the launch wearing a disguise which consisted of nothing more elaborate than badges reading 'Velar' instead of 'Range Rover'. Rover assumed – quite rightly, as it turned out – that the Croydon registrations they had deliberately chosen would prevent onlookers from associating the vehicles with the Rover factory! There was then a second batch of twenty pilot-build vehicles that were intended as the launch fleet, and these were all registered with Solihull numbers in the sequence NXCxxx H. Built in spring 1970, these had all been modified to the agreed production standard by the time of the launch itself.

The original plan had been to launch the Range Rover on a mini-safari in North Africa, and Geof Miller did a recce of the launch route around Marrakesh. However, the Sales Department had meanwhile decided to have a less elaborate launch, mainly because of the decision to supply vehicles only to the UK market for the first twelve months of production. So instead, the Range Rover launch event was held near Falmouth in Cornwall during June, with a press embargo of 17 June. For road driving, invitees were able to enjoy the spectacular local scenery, and for off-road driving, they used the Blue Hills Mine near St Agnes, a site that was regularly used for motorbike trials.

CHAPTER THREE

The Life and Times of the Original Range Rover

The earliest production Range Rovers were all two-door models, and were distinguished by painted rear quarter-panels. The 'By Land-Rover' oval badge used for the first few years is visible on the lower tailgate in the second picture.

Once the first examples of the Range Rover began to reach customers in September 1970, word quickly spread that this new vehicle was something very special. Some very warm and positive reviews from the motoring press played their part, and it was not long before the Range Rover had become a hot property. There was, quite simply, nothing else quite like it on the market. The European launch in early 1971 produced similar reactions, even though sales in many European countries were inhibited by high taxes on cars with large engines. However, the planned US launch was abandoned: Rover and Land Rover sales had never been great in that country, and it was in 1971 that Rover exports to the USA were discontinued. Land Rovers followed suit in 1974.

Meanwhile, the team at Solihull began to look at how the Range Rover might be developed over the next few years. Following the Sales Department's concern that the Range Rover was only available with two doors, the development team built a four-door prototype with one-piece, top-hinged tailgate in 1972. A van prototype was built at about the same time, and Geof Miller was involved in testing a roof-mounted rear spoiler in the desert to help keep sand away from the tailgate window. A less basic interior was also on the agenda, and the so-called 'HL' (High Line) prototype investigated what might be done.

Meanwhile, the Special Projects Department under George Mackie began to look at commercial conversions and adaptations of the Range Rover. Since 1957, this department

ABOVE: The original dashboard was assembled from hard plastic sections that did not fit together very well. Spaces for three optional auxiliary instruments were simply plugged with plastic discs. The plastic footwell mats are visible here, too.

ABOVE RIGHT: Acres of vinyl: this is the door trim of an early example. Palomino beige was the only colour available.

RIGHT: Slightly better – but not much! This is the interior of a 1974 model with carpeted transmission tunnel. The basic dashboard has not changed, but this example has the optional auxiliary instruments. It also has the new optional brushed-nylon seat facings, which were a major improvement over the original PVC type.

had been responsible for overseeing specialist conversions of Land Rovers and for ensuring that these conversions would not adversely affect the base vehicle's operability or durability. It now began to look at what could be done to make the Range Rover a more versatile platform.

Early investigations made clear that the Range Rover would make a first-class police patrol car, but that it was too small to meet the requirements of the fire and ambulance services who had traditionally been important customers for Land Rover conversions. So during 1971–1972 work focused on longer Range Rovers. Special Projects worked with the Birmingham company Spencer Abbott to produce a 110-inch wheelbase chassis that would suit ambulance conversions, and with fire appliance specialists Carmichael's of Worcester to produce an even longer chassis with an undriven third axle to suit the fire appliance and airfield emergency tender markets.

These conversions certainly expanded the Range Rover market, but they were only ever going to add small volumes to sales. With hindsight, it is arguable that they were an unnecessary distraction, not least because British Leyland was selling all the Range Rovers it could make and, by the middle of the 1970s, was struggling with long waiting lists for the standard vehicle. Demand was so high that sales continued to

increase even after the 1973–1974 Oil Crisis undermined demand for big-engined vehicles, and Range Rover sales actually increased by a massive 32 per cent.

Stifled Development

Behind this story of success, however, was a more worrying business story. If the Range Rover was to retain its lead in the market, it had to move

As productionized for the Range Rover, the 3.5-litre V8 engine had Zenith-Solex carburettors and a lower compression ratio than the car engines. The LT95 4-speed gearbox with its integral transfer box has been fitted to this engine.

Was the Range Rover as tough and as able off-road as a Land Rover? The engineers knew it was, but the public had yet to be convinced, and so two vehicles were lent to a British Army team for the Trans-Americas Expedition of 1971–1972. They drove the full length of the American continent, from Alaska to Cape Horn, and took a hundred days to fight through the swamps of the Darien Gap in Central America.

The first visible external changes arrived in 1973. First came a rear wash-wipe in January, and then the quarter-pillars were covered in vinyl in October. This second change gave the Range Rover its so-called 'floating roof' – a design feature carried over for all subsequent models.

on and to meet customer demands. Unfortunately, the money was not there to allow this. Poor sales by Austin and Morris, British Leyland's volume cars marques, meant that Range Rover profits were diverted to keep that side of the company afloat. British Leyland thinking was that while demand for Range Rovers exceeded supply, development could be minimized. It was a risky strategy: sooner or later, sales would inevitably

slow down and rivals would, equally inevitably, catch up.

So production changes to the Range Rover over the first nine years were minimal, and reflected only the essentials needed to keep it selling. Most importantly, they reflected customer demand, and it was already clear that customers wanted the Range Rover's car-like qualities to be emphasized. They were happy with its versatility and practicality; they

wanted more refinement and more luxury. From the middle of the 1973 season, marketing strategies began to reflect this change of emphasis.

Power-assisted steering was an early introduction, arriving in the middle of the 1973 season at the same time as carpet for the transmission tunnel. For 1974, cloth upholstery became a very welcome extra-cost alternative to the original PVC type which was cracking and splitting in service. Head restraints, though, were delayed until the 1976 season. Taller high-ratio gearing in the transfer box for 1977 made a slight improvement to fuel economy, which had come under the spotlight after the big increases in petrol prices after 1973, while a twin-pipe exhaust system reduced drive-by noise to meet new legislation in some countries.

The 1974 models also brought one lasting and ultimately very important change. This was a vinyl-covered rear quarter-pillar, which looked like a purely cosmetic change but was actually introduced because of production difficulties: the skin panels of the quarter-pillars often distorted, and Solihull needed a way of covering this up! In the end, it became one of the model's iconic characteristics, contributing to the 'floating roof' effect that was carried over to both subsequent generations of the Range Rover.

Solihull's engineers were not unaware of what Range Rover customers wanted, but they were unable to make headway without funds. They knew that there was demand for a four-door model, and after 1974 Land Rover's Special Projects Department granted its coveted approval to conversions from FLM Panelcraft, Wood & Pickett, Glenfrome, and others. They knew that there was a demand for more performance and better road handling, and were well aware of the work being done from 1975 by Schuler Presses. They knew, too, that many customers wanted better interior appointments, and that a thriving market had become established for

Small changes again: brushed-nylon upholstery and front seat head rests with a detachable cushion were standardized on the 1980 models.

bespoke interior conversions with leather upholstery, sports seats, air conditioning, deep-pile carpets and wood trim.

All these requests came together most noticeably in Range Rovers for the Gulf States, where both the traditionally wealthy upper classes and the newly oil-rich entrepreneurs demanded increasingly extravagant and showy personalized conversions. There were stretched wheelbases and extra doors, too, plus special elevating seats for those who indulged in the desert sport of falconry and needed to follow the flight of their valuable birds. By the end of the 1970s, these conversions were big business, and Land Rover began to make efforts to get it back under its own control (*see* Chapter 14).

There was hope on the horizon, but it seemed to take for ever to arrive. After the government bailed out British Leyland in 1975, Prime Minister Harold Wilson appointed his industrial adviser, Don Ryder, to look into BL's affairs and to make recommendations about its future. Although many of the Ryder Report's recommendations were later ignored, one important one did come through. This was that there should be substantial investment in the Land Rover marque, which was selling strongly world-wide and was highly respected. So in 1978 an investment plan was announced, and from July that year Land Rover Ltd was set up as a stand-alone business unit within BL, with Mike Hodgkinson as its Managing Director.

Kick-started

Not much became visible on Range Rovers for another year, but there was a feverish amount of new activity behind the scenes. The new Product Planning Department (an idea imported from Ford) began to look at four-door models, automatic transmission and improved interiors as a high priority, while Land Rover regained a degree of control over the Middle Eastern market by agreeing a common base specification for converted four-door models with FLM Panelcraft, Wood & Pickett, and Glenfrome.

The year 1979 was an important one. Under Stage 1 of the new Government funding, a huge extension to the existing North Works at Solihull was built so that Range Rover production could expand. The new 1980 models introduced that autumn had some cosmetic improvements which made a strong statement of intent, and it was in 1979 as well that the Swiss coachbuilder Monteverdi proposed a new four-door Range Rover design that was neater and more sophisticated than those available from other converters. Land Rover granted its approval and sold the Range Rover Monteverdi through its own showrooms to test the market. Equipped with leather upholstery and, in most cases, air conditioning, the Monteverdi was a rare and expensive top-of-the-range model that was not common in the UK, but it established the way forward for the Range Rover.

The links which Land Rover was establishing with the leading conversion specialists began to bear fruit, too. Wood & Pickett was asked to do a limited edition model with metallic paint and a luxury interior; its prototype appeared at the end of 1980 and went on the market in the first half of

The 1981 In Vogue special edition marked the beginning of the Range Rover's ascent into the luxury-car class. This example has the three-spoke alloy wheels that were intended to be standard; in practice, their manufacture was delayed and most In Vogue models had the standard steel wheels of the time.

Although there had been earlier 'approved' four-door conversions for the Middle East, the first four-door to be made available through Land Rover showrooms in Europe was the Monteverdi. It was luxuriously equipped and correspondingly expensive.

Diesel Range Rovers

By the end of the 1970s, it was clear that a diesel engine option would increase sales of the Range Rover in Continental Europe and in certain other countries where the standard 3.5-litre petrol V8 was a deterrent to sales on account of its thirst for fuel or because its cubic capacity attracted heavy taxation.

The first plan was to develop a turbocharged diesel derivative of the petrol V8, and Project Iceberg was initiated in 1980. It was run jointly with Perkins Engines, the UK diesel specialists, and by 1982 was looking feasible enough for Perkins to announce its impending availability at the Paris Motor Show. The engine was then developing about 125bhp.

However, there were problems, not least with developing a rotary fuel pump suitable for an 8-cylinder engine. The cost of the programme was escalating alarmingly at a time when the company was beginning to make losses, and in 1983 Land Rover's Managing Director Tony Gilroy had the Iceberg engine cancelled. There was, however, still a very clear need for a diesel engine in the Range Rover.

Some trials were carried out, supposedly with BMW 6-cylinder 2.4-litre and Peugeot 4-cylinder 2.5-litre turbocharged diesels, but in the end Land Rover favoured a proposal from VM, the Italian diesel specialists. This company was already providing its 2.4-litre 4-cylinder diesel for the Rover SD1 saloon car.

The 2.4-litre VM engine, built in Italy, was the first diesel available in a line-production Range Rover.

The initial BL powertrain strategy was to have the 2.4-litre 4-cylinder in the Rover, the 3-litre 5-cylinder VM in the Range Rover, and the 3.6-litre 6-cylinder in the Jaguar XJ6. Range Rover test vehicles were built with the 5-cylinder engine, and the six was also tried briefly, but in the end the 4-cylinder proved to be the best solution. So the VM 2.4-litre, uprated from its Rover saloon configuration by means of an intercooler, was made available in Range Rovers from April 1986. When VM developed a more powerful 2.5-litre variant, this replaced the earlier engine in Range Rovers from autumn 1989.

Meanwhile, Land Rover had already started work on its own new diesel engine. The plan this time was to develop the existing 4-cylinder block, newly enlarged from 2.25 litres to 2.5 litres, by replacing its indirect-injection cylinder head with a more efficient direct-injection type. The development was done in close collaboration with direct-injection specialists AVL in Austria, and with Bosch, who manufactured and had developed much of the necessary componentry.

Land Rover's 200Tdi diesel was powerful but lacked refinement. The later 300Tdi was more successful as a Range Rover powerplant.

The engine was originally intended for the Land Rover utility range, but proved so good that it was diverted to power the new Discovery model in 1989 and did not reach the utilities (renamed Defenders at the same time) until 1990. Known as the 200Tdi, this 111bhp engine was always less refined than the VM diesels and was not really in keeping with the Range Rover's relentless move into the luxury-car market. Nevertheless, it was made available with manual transmission in entry-level models from 1992, when it replaced the 2.5-litre VM diesel.

Considerable development on the original engine produced the much more refined 300Tdi of the same capacity and output in 1994. This was made available in Range Rovers up to and including Vogue SE level, and was even offered with the ZF automatic gearbox, but as a 4-cylinder its refinement was never quite up to what customers expected. The only real diesel solution for the Range Rover was a 6-cylinder, but that was held over until the introduction of the second-generation model in autumn 1994.

1981 as the Range Rover In Vogue, named after the prototype's use in a fashion shoot for *Vogue* magazine. Schuler Presses was asked to build twenty-five evaluation vehicles with their automatic transmission, and in fact a couple of these had also received a Monteverdi four-door conversion. The twenty-five Schulers (which also had the company's anti-lock brakes and quiet, chain-driven transfer box) were allocated to company staff and VIP owners for long-term test.

So by the middle of 1981 Land Rover was ready with its plans for the Range Rover's future. First on the agenda was a four-door body, in effect an improved derivative of the Monteverdi design that could be produced in volume. It went on sale in June 1981 and quickly began to out-sell the existing two-door models. Next came an automatic transmission, with the same Chrysler A727 3-speed gearbox that Schuler had adopted, but married to a new 2-speed gear-driven transfer gearbox developed by Land Rover. This was called the LT230 (that prefix stood for Leyland Transmissions, for reasons of political correctness) and would later be used right across the Land Rover product range. Automatic Range Rovers went on sale in autumn 1982, spearheaded by a second In Vogue limited edition. This time it was a four-door, and it was designed and built by Land Rover. Once again, it tested the market for metallic paint finishes, this time with two colour options.

Meanwhile, problems were brewing elsewhere in the company, and in due course these would affect the Range Rover's development. Changes in overseas funding arrangements for many of the countries in Land Rover's traditional African markets reduced the attractiveness of the British marque's products. Japanese manufacturers seized the opportunity to get their own 4 × 4s into those markets, piggy-backing on their existing car dealer networks. Land Rover's military sales were already beginning to suffer from the impact of the Mercedes-Benz G-Wagen, introduced in 1979. As a result, sales ran into a brick wall in the early 1980s and in the early 1980s Land Rover Ltd recorded its first-ever annual losses.

Plans were already in place for the Freight Rover division's Tony Gilroy to take over from Mike Hodgkinson as Land Rover's MD, and in 1983 he inherited Hodgkinson's initial plans for keeping the company afloat. Developing them further, he commissioned a thorough review of Land Rover's products and markets, and by 1985 had reached the conclusion that there was no future in trying to win back the lost utility-vehicle markets in Africa. Instead, Land Rover should expand into the developing European market and into the USA. At the forefront of that expansion should be the Range Rover, which would have to be developed further to become a luxury-car competitor.

Land Rover's own four-door arrived in autumn 1981 as a 1982 model. Note the carpeting and air conditioning vents in the dashboard of this example – items that added to the aura of luxury. The long, wand-like main gear lever was still both crude and an eyesore, though.

Automatic transmission added another tick in the luxury box in autumn 1982. This was the special edition in Vogue Automatic, a four-door available in metallic gold or metallic silver.

This view inside an automatic is almost certainly into one of the limited-edition models as it is also equipped with air conditioning.

The instrument binnacle was redesigned for the 1985 models introduced in summer 1984. This is a 1986-model Vogue built just over a year later, with wood trim on the doors, plus that season's neater centre console with the new and very welcome short-stick remote gearchange.

By the time of the 1986 models, the Range Rover was really looking the part of a luxury car. The setting for this publicity picture says something about the model's new pretensions.

This suitably dramatic picture of a 1987 Vogue illustrates the way the Range Rover looked when it was introduced to North America.

One negative side-effect of the Range Rover's new-found sophistication was already apparent, however, and that was increased showroom costs. Land Rover reacted quickly to feedback from both fleet users such as the police and from aftermarket converters that the higher prices were unwelcome. So from 1980, they introduced a special stripped-out model called the Fleet Line, which dispensed with power-assisted steering, had rubber mats instead of carpets, and had unique pleated Ambla (vinyl) seats. This kept costs down at home, which was where the Fleet Line was mostly sold.

Meanwhile, a not entirely dissimilar strategy had boosted Range Rover sales abroad. In some countries, import and licensing taxes made the vehicle prohibitively expensive but, as Land Rover discovered, a vehicle with the same specification classified as a van was not subject to these taxes. So from 1979, France, Denmark, the Netherlands and Portugal were among the countries to take Range Rover vans. There were several different varieties, but all of them dispensed with the rear bench seat. Some had plain rear side windows, and some had plain metal rear side panels. Small numbers were sold in the UK, too, although these were always built to special order.

LEFT: *With the new ZF automatic transmission came a neater transmission selector. This is the centre console of a 1987 model.*

ABOVE: *The US market demanded leather upholstery for 1988, and there was no reason not to use it in a new top model for other markets. Called the Vogue SE, it arrived in early spring 1988.*

A distinctive feature of the Vogue SE was alloy wheels that were painted to match the body. Lesser models had them enamelled in grey.

For the 1990 season, the injected 3.5-litre engine gave way to the more powerful 3.9-litre type that had been used in US-market Range Rovers a year earlier. The plenum chamber cover has '3.9' cast into it; the 3.5 had no such identification, but the later 4.2-litre engine had a special '4.2' plenum cover casting.

The Range Rover's twentieth birthday was celebrated a few months late with a limited-edition two-door model called the CSK.

Scaling the Heights

The 1984 and 1985 models brought some long-overdue improvements, those in 1984 being characterized by a 5-speed manual gearbox (the LT77, already seen in Rover and Triumph cars) instead of the clunky old 4-speed, while those of 1985 included a new top-model four-door. Branded in most territories as the Vogue (though Australia knew it as a Hi-Line), this had its own distinctive Silver Grey cloth upholstery, a loadspace cover, a better ICE system, headlamp washer jets and electric adjustment and demisting for the new door mirrors common to all the 1985 four-doors. This was luxury indeed for a Range Rover – but more was to come.

The real step-change began with the 1986 models, when a fuel-injected version of the 3.5-litre V8 engine arrived for Vogue variants. With this came a much-improved ZF automatic gearbox, with four speeds instead of three and a lock-up feature in the overdrive top gear. The extra 40bhp and increased transmission refinement made a huge difference, and demand for the Vogue made abundantly clear that Land Rover was now producing the model its customers wanted.

There were still two-door models, but these were increasingly seen as the poor man's variant – and in the UK and some other markets, they were actually withdrawn from sale when the 1987 models came onstream. These featured a wide choice of the metallic paint colours that had for

With the 3.9-litre engine came a new design of upholstery featuring larger panels with horizontal stitching. This is the leather version in a Vogue SE.

By this stage, the Range Rover had reached a high point in its development. This magnificent example is a 1994-model Vogue SE that has been retained by Land Rover at its Home of the Legend driving experience centre in the Solihull factory.

New in March 1994 for what were known as the 1995 models was the so-called 'soft dash' incorporating driver's and passenger's airbags. On the outside, it was matched by very visible covers over the new 'crush cans' at the front of the chassis.

The 'soft dash' was a much more integrated design than any earlier Range Rover dashboard, and is seen here on a Vogue SE model.

some years been expected in the luxury car market; most had the fuel-injected V8 engine; there was wood trim on the doors of top models; and all the petrol variants had a front apron spoiler that could be equipped with two rectangular driving lamps. It could also be removed to avoid damage if the vehicle was to be driven off-road.

The Vogue models reflected Land Rover's push towards entering the North American market, and the models that went on sale in the USA in March 1987 were closely similar to them. But there was a second line of development in train as well. The Range Rover was also being developed to gain sales in the European market, and to this end a diesel variant had been announced in April 1986.

Badged as a Range Rover Turbo D, the diesel variant featured a 2.4-litre 4-cylinder turbocharged indirect-injection diesel engine bought in from the Italian manufacturer VM. The same engine, in a different state of tune, had already been seen in Rover saloons from 1982. It was powerful, torquey, and relatively frugal, and it went down a storm in Italy and France. However, Land Rover was under no illusions about its refinement; though it was good by the standards of the day, it was no match for the injected petrol V8, and no diesel-powered Vogue model was listed.

However, the new Turbo D did make the carburettor V8 models an irrelevance in most territories. From

BELOW: The long-wheelbase Vogue LSE was introduced as a 1993 model and featured an enlarged 4.2-litre engine with height-adjustable air suspension. This feature would be carried over to later Range Rovers and would eventually spread to other models in the Land Rover range as well. Pictured is a 1994 model, with the 'cheese-cutter' alloy wheels and bodykit that distinguished these from those built in the preceding season.

This view under the front of an air-sprung Range Rover shows clearly one of the black rubber air 'springs' and the anti-roll bar that was standard on top models.

Limited Editions: UK Market

The first Autobiography custom-built versions of the Range Rover were announced in October 1993. All Autobiography vehicles were by definition individually finished, although there was also a special limited-run Autobiography limited edition in 1994 (*see* below). All Autobiography models, and most of the special and limited editions from mid-1993, were hand-finished by Land Rover Special Vehicles.

Model-year	Designation	Characteristics
1981 (Feb 1981)	In Vogue	1000 examples planned; probably 400 built. Based on two-door carburettor V8 model with 9.35:1 compression engine and high-geared (0.996:1) transfer box. Vogue Blue metallic paint (same as Denim Blue used on contemporary BL cars) with two-tone grey coachline decal. Air conditioning, polished wood door cappings, front stowage box, map pockets on front seat backs, carpeted loadspace and picnic hamper
1982 (Aug 1982)	Automatic In Vogue	500 examples. Based on four-door carburettor V8 model. Nevada Gold or Sierra Silver paint with twin decal coachlines (brown on Nevada Gold, grey on Sierra Silver). Grey enamel three-spoke alloy wheels with special centre caps. Front and rear armrests, rear head restraints, inlaid wood door cappings, and cool box in loadspace
1983 (Aug 1983)	In Vogue	325 examples. Based on four-door carburettor V8 with 5-speed manual gearbox or 3-speed automatic. Derwent Blue metallic paint with twin coachlines; grey enamel three-spoke alloy wheels. Front and rear armrests, rear head restraints, rear seat belts, walnut veneer door cappings, cool box and picnic hamper in loadspace, and digital radio-cassette with four speakers
1991 (Sep 1990)	CSK	200 examples. Based on two-door injected 3.9-litre V8 with recalibrated ECU for additional power, and 5-speed manual gearbox. Beluga Black paint with white coachline and CSK decals on scuttle sides. Five-spoke alloy wheels with black highlights, bright-finish bumpers and twin round driving lamps. Sorrell Beige leather perforated seat facings, leather steering wheel rim, American Walnut wood trim, numbered limited-edition plaque on radio panel. ABS, anti-roll bars, sports dampers and T-rated tyres
1992 (Jun 1992)	Range Rover in Brooklands Green	150 examples. Based on Vogue automatic. Brooklands Green paint with TWR bodykit and grey five-spoke alloy wheels. Top-specification ICE with six-disc CD autochanger and six speakers. (The limited edition was originally to be called the Brooklands, but a clash with the new Bentley Brooklands model persuaded Land Rover to change it to the cumbersome name given here.)
1994	Autobiography	25 examples. Based on 4.2-litre 100-inch wheelbase model as sold in the Gulf States. Gold '4.2' badge on tailgate
1996 (Oct 1995)	25th Anniversary	25 examples, plus one commemorative vehicle. Based on 3.9-litre Vogue SE. Oxford Blue with chrome bumpers and Anniversary badges on front wings. Lightstone leather upholstery with high-line radio and CD system

---

1986, by which time top models already had fuel injection, the 3.5-litre carburettor engine was equipped with twin SUs instead of the original Zenith-Strombergs, and a new camshaft boosted power to 144bhp. Most buyers, though, wanted the injected engine as part of the full Range Rover luxury package, or else they wanted the diesel engine as part of a more affordable derivative.

The 1988 model-year brought more luxury, although the US market tasted it before anyone else. For the first time, Range Rovers were available with an electric sunroof and with leather upholstery. Unsure quite how European customers would take to such extravagances, Land Rover held these improvements over until March 1988, launching them on a limited-edition top-of-the-range model called the Vogue SE. The company need hardly have worried: once again, this model was right on target and quickly sold out – so it was

no surprise to see a Vogue SE as an integral part of the 1989 model-range introduced in autumn 1988.

For most markets, the 1989 models featured the same three engines as before: 3.5-litre injected V8, 2.4-litre diesel, and (rarely) 3.5-litre carburettor V8. But the USA had an important preview of things to come. Tightening exhaust emissions regulations had sapped the power of the V8 engine badly in its US form, and since 1986 Land Rover had been

Fire! Police! Ambulance!

The Carmichael Commando with its three-axle chassis made an excellent first-response crash rescue vehicle. This example, dating from the mid-1980s but still based on the two-door body, entered service in Bahrain.

Typical of the early two-door motorway patrol Range Rovers is this 1981 example that belonged to London's Metropolitan Police.

The Range Rover was shown to police forces at a very early stage, and was taken on as a motorway patrol car by several forces during 1971. Police patrol Range Rovers soon became a common sight on Britain's motorways, as their combination of speed, carrying capacity and 'presence' made them ideal for the job. Four-doors superseded two-door models when they became available in the 1980s, and from 1992 the Tdi diesel models were the popular choice, usually fitted with the styled steel wheels introduced for the Land Rover Discovery.

Early examples were also kitted out as ambulances and as fire tenders for airport use, but it rapidly became apparent that the standard vehicle was too small for these tasks. So the Land Rover Special Projects Department got together with aftermarket specialists to develop the vehicle. Spencer Abbott of Birmingham was their partner on a 110-inch wheelbase conversion for ambulance use, and Carmichael's of Worcester led the development of a three-axle chassis (with undriven rear axle) which could be used as the basis of a fast-response airfield crash-rescue tender.

The main ambulance builders on the 110-inch wheelbase chassis were Lomas and Wadham Stringer, both established manufacturers. In due course, a 135-inch chassis was developed without Land Rover's participation, and some ambulances were built on this, though mainly for non-UK customers. Carmichael's offered their three-axle chassis with their own design of body as the Commando, and developed a

The Commando chassis formed the basis of the military TACR-2 airfield crash-rescue tender. This is an example bodied by Gloster Saro for the RAF, on the basis of a four-door Range Rover.

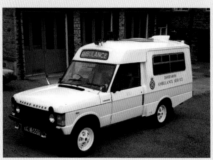

Most ambulance conversions were built on the extended 110-inch wheelbase chassis. This example was bodied by Wadham Stringer and belonged to the Derbyshire Ambulance Service.

companion four-door version when four-door Range Rovers became available. From the mid-1970s, the Commando chassis was also taken on by the Royal Air Force and Royal Navy as a crash-rescue tender. Known to the armed services as a TACR-2 (Truck, Airfield Crash Rescue, type 2), these vehicles had a number of differences from the 'civilian' Commandos and had bodywork built by Gloster Saro and HCB-Angus, as well as by Carmichael.

working on a larger-capacity version to counter this.

The greater capacity was achieved by enlarging the bore size, and the new 3.9-litre V8 was introduced on 1989 models for the USA. Despite the presence of a power-sapping catalytic converter, the engine developed a healthy 178bhp and delivered the extra punch that Land Rover needed without materially harming fuel consumption. A year later, it was standardized on all Range Rovers, although many markets managed

without the catalytic converter and as a result gained around 4bhp.

Meanwhile, the 1989 models for all markets had been fitted with a new transfer box. This was made by Borg Warner and used a chain drive instead of the gear drive which had always made Land Rover's own LT230 prone to whine at speed. It was an expensive but important step in achieving greater refinement and, as far as North America was concerned, was always associated with the 3.9-litre engine. Elsewhere, of course, it

was available for its first year with the last of the 3.5-litre engines.

Competing for business in the luxury car market of course forced Land Rover to follow trends to a certain extent, and it had been obvious for some time that the Range Rover would have to be available with an anti-lock braking system. Ordinary car-type systems did not work effectively off-road, however, and Solihull was keen not to compromise (as Mercedes-Benz did with its G-Wagen) by providing an 'off' switch for the

The North American Models

The Range Rover was introduced to the North American market in March 1987, by which time its basic design was nearly seventeen years old. The demands of the US market in particular (it was also sold in Canada) ensured that several new features were made available on US Range Rovers before they were released in other markets. Examples are leather upholstery and electrically adjustable front seats (March 1987 in the USA, March 1988 elsewhere), cruise control (October 1987 in the USA, October 1990 elsewhere), the electric sunroof (October 1987 in the USA, March 1988 elsewhere) and the 3.9-litre engine (October 1988 in the USA, October 1989 elsewhere).

Model-year	Designation	Characteristics
1987 (Mar–Oct 1987)	Range Rover	3.5-litre injected V8 with automatic transmission. Cloth upholstery standard, leather optional; air conditioning, six-way power adjustable front seats, ICE theft deterrent system and tow hitch plate
1988	Range Rover	Leather upholstery more widely available; delayed transmission lock-up; cruise control; new brake servo and pads; new air conditioning ducts; radio aerial in HRW element; optional electric sunroof
1989	Range Rover	3.9-litre injected V8 with 178bhp and catalytic converter; automatic transmission; Borg Warner chain-driven transfer box. New door trims, tan trim option, one-shot driver's window; improved air conditioning and ventilation; six-speaker ICE system; tailgate included in central locking; heated windscreen and washer jets; ignition headlamp over-ride
1990	Range Rover	All models with tan leather upholstery; ABS and ventilated front discs; high-mounted stoplight on top tailgate
	County	New micatallic paints and black option; chrome bumpers and body-colour wheels; new leather stitch pattern; cloth upholstery option; grey upholstery with some colours; County logo on front head rests; additional wood; upgraded ICE and speakers with 6-disc CD changer; electric sunroof and auto-dipping rear view mirror optional
	GDE	410-strong limited edition introduced in July 1990 and named after 1989 Great Divide Expedition; white with perforated beige leather upholstery and American Walnut wood trim; smoke grey five-spoke alloy wheels; bumper with brush bar; no spoiler; rear light guards; electric sunroof and auto-dipping mirror
1991	Range Rover	Black bumpers, gunmetal finish wheels; anti-roll bars; high fuel filler with remote release; heated door locks; improved soundproofing; auto-dipping mirror; tool bag in spare wheel well; 120-watt 7-speaker ICE system with optional CD player; optional electric sunroof with sunblind
	Hunter	Limited production run of 525; no spoiler, ABS or anti-roll bars; no loadspace cover or power-adjusted seats; silver painted alloys; dog guard and luggage net
	County SE	Beluga Black with tan leather and silver five-spoke wheels; aluminium brush bar; removable headlamp guards; anti-roll bars; electric sunroof
1992	Range Rover	Similar to 1991 models
	County	ABS, anti-roll bars and CD autochanger all standard; Beluga Black paint optional
1993	County	3.9-litre V8 now with 181bhp; ABS, ETC and anti-roll bars all standard
	County LWB	4.2-litre V8 and generally as European Vogue LSE; bright bumpers
1994 (to Dec 1994)	County	Air suspension standard; bright TWR five-spoke alloys. Sales ended in approximately March 1994
	County LWB	As contemporary European Vogue LSE; Cyclone alloy wheels with Quicksilver finish
	25th Anniversary	250-strong limited edition introduced in July 1994, based on County LWB. Aspen Silver with Ash Grey leather, TWR five-spoke alloys with sparkle-silver finish; embossed logo on head rests
1995 (from Jan 1995)	County Classic	Similar to European Vogue SE but with chrome bumpers, TWR five-spoke alloy wheels and 160-watt ICE with nine speakers and optional CD player

Camel Trophy Range Rovers

The Camel Trophy adventure challenge was sponsored by Land Rover from 1981 to 1998, and proved a superb showcase for the rugged capabilities of the company's vehicles. Originating in 1980 with sponsorship from RJ Reynolds Tobacco GmbH, the makers of Camel cigarettes, the event was opened to international teams from 1982 and became something of a legend. The vehicles – typically around fifteen to twenty, crewed by teams of two – made their way in convoy through inhospitable terrain, followed by support crews and media representatives. A great deal depended on driving skill, but there were also special tasks, and points were awarded for such things as team spirit.

Exotic locations were an important element in the appeal of the Camel Trophy. This picture was taken on the 1982 event in Papua, New Guinea. Note that the vehicle is a two-door model, even though the four-door had already gone on sale.

Range Rovers were used on three Camel Trophy events. There were 3.5-litre carburettor models for the national teams on the 1981 event in Sumatra and the 1982 event in Papua, New Guinea, and the Range Rover's final Camel Trophy appearance was on the 1987 event in Madagascar, when the latest Turbo D models with the 2.4-litre VM diesel engine were used.

All the vehicles were painted in the Camel Trophy colour of Sandglow, and all were prepared by the Special Projects division at Solihull (which was renamed Special Vehicle Operations in 1985 and later still became Land Rover Special Vehicles). Equipment included a heavy-duty roof rack which carried additional driving lamps, a front-mounted winch for self-recovery, skid plates to protect the underside, a full internal roll cage, and in most cases tyres with an off-road bias.

system when the vehicle was used in rough terrain.

So a huge amount of effort went into developing a dedicated ABS system that would work effectively off-road. Land Rover engineers worked closely with Wabco, who were best known for their truck braking systems, and by 1989 the two companies had come up with a system that used electronics to monitor each wheel's turning speed 250 times a second. If one wheel's turning speed deviated by more than a specified amount from the speeds of the other wheels and the driver used the brakes, the anti-lock system kicked in and prevented the wheel lock-up that causes skids. ABS was introduced on Range Rovers for the 1990 model-year, and although it was initially confined to the top models only, it soon became a popular if expensive extra-cost option.

Defined by Luxury

For the remaining six-and-a-half seasons of the Range Rover's production, the model was defined in most markets by the Vogue and Vogue SE four-doors with their 3.9-litre V8 engines. In North America, their nearest equivalents were badged as County and County SE models. Luxury options such as air conditioning, electric windows, a sunroof, metallic paint and leather upholstery with wood trim became increasingly common as the Range Rover brand became firmly entrenched in the luxury-car sector.

Gradually, the entry point for Range Rover ownership moved higher and higher, and the cheaper models disappeared from most markets, replaced in Land Rover showrooms by the new Discovery model which had made its debut in autumn 1989. Yet there were still

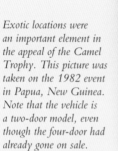

The last Range Rover of all was completed with the specification of the run-out 25th Anniversary edition. It was pictured outside the Heritage Motor Centre at Gaydon, where it forms part of the museum collection.

Specifications for Range Rover First-Generation Models

Layout and chassis

Two-door (1970–1994) or four-door (1981–1996) estate with horizontally split tailgate
Box-section ladder-frame chassis

Engine

3528cc (88.9mm × 71.1mm) OHV 90-degree petrol V8

1970 models:	Two Zenith-Stromberg carburettors
	8.5:1 compression ratio
	135bhp at 4750rpm
	185lb ft at 2500rpm
1971–1977 models:	Two Zenith-Stromberg carburettors
	8.25:1 compression ratio
	130bhp at 5000rpm
	185lb ft at 2500rpm
1978–1981 models:	Two Zenith-Stromberg carburettors
	8.13:1 compression ratio
	132bhp at 5000rpm
	186lb ft at 2500rpm
1982–1986 models:	Two Zenith-Stromberg carburettors
	9.35:1 compression ratio
	125bhp at 4000rpm
	185lb ft at 2500rpm
1987–1989 models:	Two SU carburettors
	9.35:1 compression ratio
	125bhp at 4000rpm
	185lb ft at 2500rpm
	or
	Lucas L-Jetronic electronic fuel injection
	9.35:1 compression ratio (8.13:1 for USA)
	165bhp at 4000rpm (150bhp at 4000rpm for USA)
	206lb ft at 3200rpm (190lb ft at 3200rpm for USA)

3947cc (93.98mm × 71.1mm) OHV 90-degree petrol V8

1989 models (USA only):	Lucas L-Jetronic electronic fuel injection
	8.13:1 compression ratio
	179bhp at 4750rpm
	227lb ft at 3500rpm
1990–1996 models:	Lucas L-Jetronic electronic fuel injection
	9.35:1 compression ratio (8.13:1 for USA)
	188bhp at 4750rpm (178bhp for USA, 1990–1992; 181bhp for USA, 1993–1995)
	235lb ft at 2600rpm (227lb ft at 3500rpm for USA, 1990–1992; 231lb ft at 3100rpm for USA, 1993–1995)

4278cc (93.98mm × 77mm) OHV 90-degree petrol V8

1993–1995 models:	Lucas L-Jetronic electronic fuel injection
	8.94:1 compression ratio
	200bhp at 4850rpm
	250lb ft at 3250rpm

2393cc (92mm × 90mm) VM OHV 4-cylinder indirect-injection diesel with turbocharger and intercooler

1986–1989 models:	22:1 compression ratio
	112bhp at 4200rpm
	183lb ft at 2400rpm

2500cc (92mm × 94mm) VM OHV 4-cylinder indirect-injection diesel with turbocharger and intercooler

1990–1992 models:	22:5:1 compression ratio
	119bhp at 4200rpm
	209lb ft at 1950rpm

2495cc (90.47mm × 97mm) OHV 4-cylinder direct-injection diesel with turbocharger and intercooler ('200Tdi' 1993–1994; '300Tdi' 1994–1996)

1993–1996 models:	19.5:1 compression ratio
	111bhp at 4000rpm
	195lb ft at 1800rpm

Transmission

Permanent four-wheel drive with lockable centre differential (1970–1989) or with centre differential incorporating viscous coupling to give automatic locking (1990–1996). Limited-slip centre differential on early 1970 models.
Final drive ratio: 3.54:1

Primary gearbox

Four-speed LT95 manual with integral transfer gearbox (1970–1983); ratios 4.069:1, 2.448:1, 1.505:1, 1.00:1, reverse 3.664:1
Five-speed LT77 manual (1983–1994); ratios 3.32:1, 2.13:1, 1.39:1, 1.00:1, 0.77:1, reverse 3.42:1
Three-speed Chrysler A727 automatic (1982–1985); ratios 2.45:1, 1.45:1, 1.00:1, reverse 2.20:1
Four-speed ZF 4HP22 automatic (1986–1996); ratios 2.47:1, 1.47:1, 1.00:1, 0.72:1, reverse 2.08:1

Transfer gearbox

Integral two-speed gear-driven type (1970–1982); High ratio 1.174:1 (1970–1976), 1.116:1 (1977–1980), 1.003:1 (1981), or 0.996:1 (1982–1984); Low ratio 3.32:1
Separate LT230R (1982–1985) or LT230T (1986–1988) 2-speed gear-driven type; High ratio 1.19:1 (with LT77 primary gearbox) or 1.003:1 (with A727 automatic); Low ratio 3.32:1
Separate Borg Warner 2-speed chain-driven type with viscous locking centre differential (1989–1996); High ratio 1.19:1; Low ratio 3.32:1

Suspension

Front and rear live axles with coil springs and telescopic dampers; height-adjustable electronic air suspension optional from 1993
Front axle located by radius arms and Panhard rod; anti-roll bar standard from 1991
Rear axle located by radius arms, support rods and central wishbone assembly incorporating a Boge Hydromat self-energizing ride-levelling strut

Steering

Recirculating-ball system; power assistance optional from 1973 and standard from 1979

Brakes

Four-wheel disc brakes with dual hydraulic line and servo assistance; Wabco four-channel ABS available from 1990
Front discs with 11.75in diameter and four-piston callipers; ventilated discs from 1990
Solid rear discs with 11.42in diameter and two-piston callipers
Separate parking brake: internal expanding drum-type operating on transmission output shaft

Vehicle dimensions

Wheelbase:	100in (2540mm); 108in (2743mm) for LSE and County LWB, 1993–1995
Overall length:	176in (4470mm); 183in (4648mm) for LSE and County LWB, 1993–1995
Overall width:	70in (1780mm)
Overall height:	70in (1780mm)
Track:	58.5in (1480mm)

Kerb weight (for typical UK-market models):
  Two-door models 3800lb (1723kg), 1970–1979; 3872lb (1756kg), 1980 and later
  Four-door models 3942lb (1788kg); 4379lb (1986kg) with Vogue SE specification
  Long-wheelbase models 4739lb (2150kg)

Performance

Two-door carburettor V8 models
  Maximum speed: 95mph (153km/h)
  0–60mph: 14secs
Four-door injected 3.5-litre V8 models
  Maximum speed: 102mph (164km/h)
  0–60mph: 12secs
Four-door VM 2.4-litre diesel models
  Maximum speed: 92mph (148km/h)
  0–60mph: 16.5secs
Four-door 3.9-litre V8 with standard wheelbase and 4.2-litre long-wheelbase models
  Maximum speed: 110mph (177km/h)
  0–60mph: 11secs with automatic transmission
Four-door VM 2.5-litre diesel models
  Maximum speed: 95mph (153km/h)
  0–60mph: 15.8secs
Four-door 200Tdi and 300Tdi diesel models
  Maximum speed: 94mph (151km/h)
  0–60mph: 16.8secs with manual transmission

Several Range Rovers were converted to ceremonial review vehicles, the first one being built at Solihull for Her Majesty the Queen in 1974–1975. This example dates from around 1984 and was converted by the Royal Air Force for parade work.

two-door models in some countries, the last one not being made until 1994, and there were still diesel-powered models which allowed the brand to become more firmly established in Europe. For the 1990 season, the original 2.4-litre VM diesel was replaced by a more powerful 2.5-litre derivative; then for 1993 Land Rover's own 200Tdi direct-injection engine took over, to be followed for the 1995 season by the more refined 300Tdi version. There were even Vogue diesels from the 1991 model-year, and later, diesel automatics as well with the 300Tdi engine.

Land Rover was quite clear about where it wanted to position the Range Rover in the luxury-car market after 1988, and at that point the company began serious work on the second-generation model. Meanwhile, the existing production car was gradually upgraded even more, partly to see just how much luxury the buyers would accept. The 1991 models could be fitted with anti-roll bars, which made a big difference to stability at speed in corners; during 1992 a bodykit designed by TWR (Tom Walkinshaw Racing) became available, and for 1993 there was an air suspension system for top models which both softened and quietened the ride.

This brought other benefits, too. It allowed the body's height from the ground to be adjusted to suit circumstances, dropping slightly to improve stability at speed, dropping more when stationary to allow easier passenger access, and increasing markedly to prevent bellying-out in rough terrain off the road. It was standard on another new model – badged as Vogue LSE or County LSE according to market – which arrived for 1993. This had an extra 8in (21cm) in the wheelbase and lengthened rear doors to provide limousine-like room for rear-seat passengers. It also had the task of preparing customers for the extra size of the planned second-generation Range Rover, which would share its 108-inch wheelbase almost exactly.

With the long-wheelbase models came a further-enlarged V8 engine, this time a long-stroke version of the 3.9-litre with a 4.2-litre swept volume. Its main purpose was to ensure that the heavier flagship LSE models were no slower than the 3.9-litre types on the standard wheelbase and, though capable of being tuned for higher outputs, it was restricted to 200bhp in production. Generally speaking, the 4.2-litre was associated with the LSE, but some markets (Switzerland and Australia among them) had 3.9-litre LSEs to avoid expensive and time-consuming homologation procedures for the larger engine. The 4.2-litre was also used in standard-wheelbase models for the Gulf States, and in a limited 'Autobiography' edition of the standard-wheelbase model for the UK in 1994.

Range Rover Prices in the UK, 1970–1996

These figures are showroom prices for Range Rover models without extras. Before April 1973, the list price was subject to purchase tax (PT); from April 1973 it was subject to car tax and value added tax (VAT).

Date		Model	List price (£)	Car tax	PT or VAT	Retail (£)
1970	June		1,528 12s 7d	N/A	469 7s 5d	1,998.00
1970	July		1,528 12s 7d	N/A	469 7s 5d	1,998.00
1970	September		1,528 12s 7d	N/A	469 7s 5d	1,998.00
1971	January		1,706 0s 0d	N/A	523 11s 5d	2,229 11s 5d
1971	May		1,706.00	N/A	523.57	2,229.57
1971	July		1,706.00	N/A	428.37	2,134.37
1971	October		1,706.00	N/A	428.37	2,134.37
1972	January		1,792.00	N/A	449.87	2,241.87
1972	April		1,881.00	N/A	393.44	2,274.44
1972	August		1,984.00	N/A	414.90	2,398.90
1972	October		1,984.00	N/A	414.90	2,398.90
1973	January		2,024.71	N/A	423.38	2,448.09
1973	April		2,024.71	168.73	219.34	2,412.78
1973	August		2,205.00	183.75	238.88	2,627.63
1973	October		2,251.00	187.58	243.86	2,682.44
1974	February		2,493.00	207.75	270.08	2,970.83
1974	June		2,842.00	236.83	307.88	3,386.71
1974	July		2,842.00	236.83	246.31	3,325.14
1974	September		3,055.00	254.58	264.77	3,574.35
1974	December		3,354.00	279.50	290.68	3,924.18
1975	March		3,689.00	307.42	319.71	4,316.13
1975	April		3,689.00	307.42	319.71	4,316.13
1975	June		3,947.00	328.92	342.07	4,617.99
1976	January		4,417.00	368.08	382.81	5,167.89
1976	April		4,638.00	386.50	401.96	5,426.46
1976	July		4,863.00	405.25	421.46	5,689.71
1976	November		5,359.00	446.58	464.45	6,270.03
1977	February		5,895.00	491.25	510.90	6,897.15
1977	May		6,396.00	533.00	554.32	7,483.32
1977	August		6,844.00	570.33	593.15	8,007.48
1978	January		7,289.00	607.42	631.71	8,528.13
1978	April		7,289.00	607.42	631.71	8,528.13
1978	July		7,821.00	651.75	677.82	9,150.57
1978	December		8,389.00	699.08	727.05	9,815.13
1979	May		8,976.00	748.00	777.92	10,501.92
1979	June		8,976.00	748.00	1,458.60	11,182.60
1979	August		9,483.61	790.30	1,541.09	11,815.00
1979	October		9,950.00	829.16	1,616.87	12,396.03
1980	June	Two-door	10,425.00	868.75	1,694.06	12,987.81
		Fleetline	9,775.00	814.58	1,588.44	12,178.02

Range Rover Prices in the UK, 1970–1996 *continued*

Date		Model	List price (£)	Car tax	PT or VAT	Retail (£)
1981	February	In Vogue				13,787.64
1981	April	Two-door	10,840.00	903.33	1,761.50	13,504.83
		Fleetline	10,170.00	847.50	1,652.63	12,670.13
1981	September	Two-door	10,840.00	903.33	1,761.50	13,504.83
		Fleetline	10,170.00	847.50	1,652.63	12,670.13
		Four-door	11,557.00	963.08	1,878.01	14,398.09
1982	February	Two-door	11,290.00	940.83	1,834.62	14,065.45
		Fleetline	10,595.00	882.92	1,721.69	13,199.61
		Four-door	12,037.00	1,003.08	1,956.01	14,996.09
		Monteverdi	13,642.00	1,136.83	2,216.82	16,995.65
1982	August	Two-door	11,290.00	940.83	1,834.62	14,065.45
		Fleetline	10,595.00	882.92	1,721.69	13,199.61
		Four-door	12,037.00	1,003.08	1,956.01	14,996.09
		Monteverdi	13,642.00	1,136.83	2,216.82	16,995.65
1983	May	Two-door	11,625.00	968.75	1,889.06	14,482.81
		Fleetline	10,860.00	905.00	1,764.75	13,529.75
		Four-door	12,340.00	1,028.33	2,005.25	15,373.58
1984	January	Two-door	12,080.00	1,006.67	1,963.00	15,049.67
		Fleetline	10,860.00	905.00	1,764.75	13,529.75
		Four-door	12,820.00	1,068.33	2,083.25	15,971.58
1984	June	Two-door	12,080.00	1,006.67	1,963.00	15,049.67
		Fleetline	10,860.00	905.00	1,764.75	13,529.75
		Four-door	12,820.00	1068.33	2,083.25	15,971.58
		Vogue	14,030.00	1169.17	2,279.88	17,479.05
1985	January	Two-door	12,172.00	1014.33	1,977.95	15,164.28
		Fleetline	10,942.00	911.83	1,778.07	13,631.90
		Four-door	12,948.00	1,079.00	2,104.05	16,131.05
		Vogue	14,381.00	1,198.42	2,336.91	17,916.33
1986	January	Two-door	12,647.00	1,053.92	2,055.14	15,756.06
		Four-door	13,554.00	1,129.50	2,202.53	16,886.03
		Vogue	15,593.00	1,299.42	2,533.86	19,426.28
1986	April	Two-door	12,647.00	1,053.92	2,055.14	15,756.06
		Four-door	13,554.00	1,129.50	2,202.53	16,886.03
		Four-door Turbo D	14,536.00	1,211.33	2,362.10	18,109.43
		Vogue	15,593.00	1,299.42	2,533.86	19,426.28
1986	November	Four-door	14,651.00	1,220.92	2,380.79	18,252.71
		Four-door Turbo D	15,110.00	1,259.17	2,455.38	18,824.55
		Vogue	16,200.00	1,350.00	2,632.00	20,182.50
1987	September	Four-door	15,384.00	1,282.00	2,499.90	19,165.90
		Four-door Turbo D	15,866.00	1,322.17	2,578.23	19,766.40
		Vogue	17,010.00	1,417.50	2,764.13	21,191.63
		Vogue Turbo D	17,492.00	1,457.67	2,842.45	21,792.12

Range Rover Prices in the UK, 1970–1996 *continued*

Date		Model	List price (£)	Car tax	PT or VAT	Retail (£)
1988	April	Four-door	15,846.00	1,320.50	2,574.98	19,741.48
		Four-door Turbo D	16,342.00	1,361.83	2,655.57	20,359.40
		Vogue	17,521.00	1,460.08	2,847.16	21,828.24
		Vogue Turbo D	18,017.00	1,501.42	2,927.76	22,446.18
		Vogue SE	21,953.00	1,829.42	3,567.36	27,349.78
1988	October	Four-door Turbo D	17,524.00	1,460.33	2,847.65	21,831.98
		Vogue	18,485.00	1,540.42	3,003.81	23,029.23
		Vogue Turbo D	19,008.00	1,584.00	3,088.80	23,680.80
		Vogue SE	23,161.00	1,930.08	3,763.66	28,854.74
1989	June	Four-door Turbo D	18,050.00	1,504.17	2,933.13	22,487.30
		Vogue	19,040.00	1,586.67	3,094.00	23,720.67
		Vogue Turbo D	19,579.00	1,631.58	3,181.59	24,392.17
		Vogue SE	23,856.00	1,988.00	3,876.60	29,720.60
1990 MY		Four-door Turbo D	19,091.00	1,590.92	3,102.29	23,784.21
		Vogue	20,473.00	1,706.08	3,326.86	25,505.94
		Vogue Turbo D	20,793.00	1,732.75	3,378.86	25,904.61
		Vogue SE	25,645.00	2,137.08	4,167.31	31,949.39
1990	September	Four-door Turbo D	20,050.84	1,670.90	3,258.26	24,980.00
		Vogue	21,347.16	1,778.93	3,468.91	26,595.00
		Vogue Turbo D	21,660.20	1,805.02	3,519.78	26,985.00
		Vogue SE	27,066.22	2,255.52	4,398.26	33,720.00
		CSK (manual)				28,995.00
		CSK (automatic)				30,319.32
1991	September	Four-door Turbo D	20,692.63	1,724.39	3,922.98	26,340.00
		Vogue	22,039.94	1,836.66	4,178.40	28,055.00
		Vogue Turbo D	22,358.10	1,863.18	4,238.72	28,460.00
		Vogue SE	28,210.80	2,350.90	5,348.30	35,910.00
1992 MY		Vogue manual (V8 or Tdi)	22,794.08	949.75	4,155.17	27,899.00
		Vogue automatic (V8)	23,692.80	987.20	4,319.00	28,999.00
		Vogue SE	30,144.00	1,256.00	5,495.00	36,895.00
		Vogue LSE	32,676.77	1,361.53	5,956.70	39,995.00
1992	November	Vogue manual (V8 or Tdi)	22,794.04	N/A	3,988.96	26,783.00
		Vogue automatic (V8)	23,692.77	N/A	4,146.23	27,839.00
		Vogue SE	30.143.83	N/A	5,275.17	35,419.00
		Vogue LSE	32,674.89	N/A	5,718.11	38,393.00
1995	June	Tdi manual				29,475.00
		Vogue SE				37,230.00
1995	October	Classic 25th Anniversary				40,000

The Autobiography custom-building service had been announced in the autumn of 1993. Operated by Land Rover Special Vehicles, it allowed customers to have their vehicles custom-finished by Land Rover's own dedicated specialists. Mainly, it offered a selection of special paint finishes and interior trims – although very little was impossible, if the customer insisted and was prepared to pay. Major variations in the mechanical specification – such as fitting a 4.2-litre engine and manual gearbox combination – were not on the options list because they would have required expensive development work.

Autobiography vehicles were essentially one-offs, although small-run limited editions such as the 4.2-litre on the standard wheelbase for the UK were also in the plan. Autobiography vehicles normally carried a discreet identifying decal on the lower tailgate, and the scheme of course allowed Land Rover to discover more about customer tastes and preferences in a very direct fashion. This aspect of the service would be exploited to a much greater extent when the second-generation Range Rover came onstream, and small-run limited editions tested the market for planned new mainstream features.

The final major change to the Range Rover came for the 1995 model-year, which had an early start in March 1994, partly to suit US market demands and partly to avoid a clash with the arrival of the second-generation models later that year. This time, the change was driven by new and anticipated legislation in various countries, and the 1995-

model Range Rovers had a completely redesigned dashboard which incorporated driver's and passenger's airbags as standard. The front of the chassis was modified at the same time to incorporate 'crush cans', progressively deformable ends to the chassis rails which would simplify and reduce the cost of accident repairs. At the same time, LSEs were fitted with a new bodykit which helped to distinguish them more readily from the standard-wheelbase models.

Arrival of the 'Classic'

It was only a few months after that, in September 1994, when the second-generation Range Rover was announced. However, Land Rover was well aware of how deeply affection for the long-established first-generation model ran within its customer base, and recognized that the new model would probably take some time to gain acceptance. So the plan was to keep the first-generation Range Rover in small-volume production for as long as was necessary, as an alternative to the new model.

To distinguish one from the other, the first-generation model was rebranded as the Range Rover Classic in October 1994, and carried a special version of the Land Rover green oval badge on its tailgate, with the word 'Classic' underneath. As is the way with these things, the name caught on, and in some parts of the trade and the enthusiast movement all first-generation Range Rovers have subsequently become known as 'Classics' even though they were never known as that when they were new.

Land Rover was undoubtedly right to play for safety and to keep the first-generation model in production for a time until the second-generation Range Rover had gained customer acceptance. However, that acceptance was not long in coming, and by the end of 1995 it was clear that there was no real need for the original model any more.

Yet, after twenty-six years in production (if the date is calculated from the time when the first pilot-production models were built), the Range Rover could not be allowed simply to fade away. Again capitalizing on great public affection for the original model, which had genuinely become an automotive icon, Land Rover decided to make some publicity capital out of the end of production.

The celebrations began in autumn 1995 with a limited-edition '25th Anniversary' model for the UK, based on the standard-wheelbase Vogue SE with several special features. (Some other markets had their own 25th Anniversary editions, notably the USA which had a 25th Anniversary County LSE.) The final example of this, a 26th vehicle after the promised 25 had been built for sale, was put back onto the assembly line after passing through LRSV for its special fit, and became the official last first-generation Range Rover. It was driven off the lines in a special ceremony by TV personality and Range Rover owner Noel Edmonds, and was given to the Heritage Motor Centre at Gaydon for its museum collection. The real last-of-line vehicle, however, a red four-door diesel destined for Portugal, was sold to a customer in the normal way without ceremony.

CHAPTER FOUR

Building the Original Range Rover

The first-generation Range Rover was assembled in three different locations at Solihull over the years. In the beginning, the assembly line was installed in the South Block (since renamed Block 1), which was part of the wartime factory and had become the main assembly hall immediately after the war in 1945. The Range Rover line was fitted in alongside the two Land Rover assembly lines, which were moved over slightly to make room.

This arrangement of course placed a limit on the quantity of Range Rovers that could be built, especially on the single-shift system that was then normal practice at Solihull. So when Land Rover Ltd was established in 1978 and was promised a large investment from the British government, moving Range Rover assembly to somewhere with more room was a top priority. The obvious choice was the North Works, originally built in the early 1960s for the assembly of Rover P6 saloon cars but empty since their production had ended in 1976.

The North Works was refurbished and extended for its new role between 1979 and 1981 at a cost of £85 million. The work was carried out under Stage 2 of the government funding (which also financed the introduction of the first coil-sprung Land Rovers). The most obvious effect, as far as customers were concerned, was the introduction of the four-door model; the old assembly lines could not have coped with building two-door and four-door models at the same time.

When the second-generation Range Rover was ready for production, the plan was to scale down assembly of the old model progressively. So to allow the new assembly lines to go into the North Block, an assembly line for the old model was installed in a new 'Infill' building next to the South Works. First-generation Range Rovers were built here in gradually reducing quantities between summer 1994 and February 1996, when the last example was completed.

The Assembly Process

The original Range Rover assembly line was laid down at the end of 1969 in the South Block, and both the final prototype and all the pilot-production vehicles were built on it.

Many components reached the assembly lines from outside companies; for example, John Thompson Pressings in Wolverhampton delivered complete chassis frames into the factory, already dip primed and painted, and these would be placed into storage until needed. Other items were delivered to Solihull from the Land Rover 'satellite' factories; V8 engines, for example, were assembled at Acocks Green and were delivered into the Solihull plant by road. Before reaching Solihull, they had been bench tested.

On site, assembly of each Range Rover began as its chassis frame entered the assembly hall. As each frame was brought forward to the line, it passed through a jig, where the body mountings were drilled and

This was the Range Rover chassis assembly line in 1981, shortly after the move to the North Block. Axles, suspension and propshafts have already been fitted, and here the engine and transmission assembly is being lowered into place.

Body frame assembly was a labour-intensive process in the early days. This picture was taken in 1981; the four-door frames have already been primed in black.

The Comsteel programme introduced all-welded body frames and more automation in 1985. Here, the tailgate frame is added as the main frame moves along an assembly line.

Another shot of the automated body framing line, showing completed four-door frames.

spot-faced. The frame then passed on to the moving line, where it was gradually built up with axles, fuel tank, self-levelling strut, an engine, transmission components and wiring harness. The engine and gearbox assembly was lowered into place as a single unit, having already been adjusted, tuned and partially run-in on a test bed within the plant.

Meanwhile, the body began life in another part of the factory as the elements of its steel framework were electro-coated with primer and then painted in a hard acrylic black finish. The painted sections then passed into the main assembly hall, where they were hand-assembled into complete

body frames in a designated area alongside the moving assembly line, each section being bolted to the next. There were eight sections in all: left and right body sides, a tailgate frame, a front bulkhead, two front inner wings, a front panel, and a floor pan with gearbox tunnel.

The completed body frames then met up with their outer panels, brought in as single vehicle sets on trucks (known as 'skids'). The skids had been loaded with panels from a storage area before moving into the paint shop along tracks let into the floor. The Paint Shop, located in the old West Works, then put them through several stages of paint

and hand preparation before applying their acrylic top coats. All exterior panels were initially treated with Alochrome (to enhance corrosion resistance and assist paint adhesion), and their inner surfaces and those of the wheelarches were sprayed with a corrosion-resistant wax to protect the metal and reduce drumming. Still on their original skids, the panels then arrived in the main assembly hall, to be removed from the skids and bolted to the body frames.

The completed bodyshells were then ready to be taken to the final trim line. Here, most of the internal trim, wiring, instruments and glass were added as each bodyshell

Meanwhile, in a separate part of the factory, the body panels would be made up into 'sets'. In this shot from the North Block era, note the line-side stillages and the tracks in the floor along which the trollies run.

In this picture, note how Land Rover bodies are being assembled in the same area, with their line-side stores on the other side. Also visible in the background are completed body frames on their way to the Paint Shop.

Panels sets were checked visually, degreased, and if necessary flatted down before progressing to the Paint Shop.

Each set of unpainted panels was then carried by trolley into the Paint Shop.

As a first stage, all panels were sprayed with a mist-coat primer. Note that the grille and headlamp panels, later to be painted black, were also primed at this stage.

After the introduction of welded body frames, the frames were also mist-coated in the Paint Shop.

Newly-painted panel 'sets' emerge from the Paint Shop. A run of silver bodies was being painted when this picture was taken. Note how the headlamp and grille panels have been masked before application of the top coats.

The headlamp and grille panels, sprayed black before being masked as the panels passed through the top-coat paint process, have been uncovered here. The paint finish is being checked for imperfections under powerful line-side lights.

Painted panels and body-frames now begin to meet up as the roof panels are fitted. After the switch to the North Block, rear wing panels followed this stage; on earlier models, they were fitted after the 'marriage' of body and chassis.

Further down the assembly line, the body-and-chassis assemblies have now received seats and some interior trim; additional interior trim is now being fitted. Note that the doors have not yet been added.

The Body Drop: the partially-assembled bodies, with glass but no doors, are swung up and across the factory floor to end up above the chassis line. Here, they are lowered onto the chassis and bolted into position. These are carburettor two-doors being assembled on the original South Works lines in the later 1970s.

BELOW: *The end of the line, some time in the mid-1980s. With wheels now added, the vehicles touch the floor for the first time. Clear here once again is how batches of vehicles in a single colour were assembled.*

progressed down the line. The next stage was the Body Drop, where the completed shells were lifted up above the adjacent chassis line and were carefully lowered onto the chassis, to be bolted to it. The last of the interior trim was then added, along with the last of the pre-painted exterior panels.

At the end of the assembly line, each vehicle was inspected, the cooling system was filled, and a quantity of petrol was put into the tank. It then passed onto a rolling road where initial checks were done, and was then driven out of the assembly hall and to the 2.5-mile (4km) test track in the factory grounds, where it would be given a final shakedown run and inspection. If all was well (and there was a Line Rectification system if something was amiss), it would be passed from the Production Department to the Despatch Department, whose job was to deliver it to a UK dealer or overseas sales company as appropriate.

Later Changes

This system remained largely unchanged when the lines were transferred to the North Block in 1981. However, from the beginning of four-door assembly there, a change was made to the assembly sequence: the 'sets' of body panels passed through the paint shop on their trolleys and were mounted to the

ABOVE: *With fuel and water added, vehicles came off the assembly lines and into a test booth. This LHD two-door from the mid-1980s is going through its rolling-road test routine.*

CENTRE: *The sequence was slightly different in the early days, but the principles were the same. Here, two-doors are receiving final inspection during the 1970s. Note the exhaust extensions to carry fumes away through a roof-level extractor, and that the floor mats have yet to be fitted.*

BELOW: *... and on their way. These vehicles, with a County LWB in the foreground, were pictured at Southampton Docks in November 1992 on their way to the USA. They had been delivered by road from Solihull to Southampton, as the Solihull factory had no rail link.*

body frames afterwards. As a result, the exposed parts of the body frames – the door pillars and the front of the rear wheelarch panel – remained matt black instead of taking on the body colour. Two-door bodies were put through the same process after September 1982.

The next set of changes occurred in 1985, towards the end of the 1985 model-year in the spring. All-welded body frames were introduced under the programme known to Land Rover as Comsteel. The frames were now assembled in jigs to give a greater degree of dimensional accuracy. These bodies were painted in the same way as before, with sets of painted panels being mounted to a black body frame so that elements of black were visible on the body pillars.

A further set of changes arrived in 1989. From the summer of that year, panels were assembled to the body frames before passing through the paint shop, and the whole body was then painted together. One very obvious result of this new process was that, on the finished vehicle, the matt black paint applied to the body frame was no longer visible on the lower sections of the A- and B/C-pillars and the forward edges of the rear wheelarches. Instead, these were now finished in the body colour; the black window pillars above the waistline were achieved by masking them off during the body spraying process.

There were no fundamental changes to this process when the Range Rover line moved into its final home alongside the South Block in 1994. However, this line was designed for much lower production volumes. By August 1995, it was turning out only 69 vehicles a week, and the ceremony for the last-of-line Range Rover was held on 15 February 1996.

Building Range Rovers Overseas

Some countries place high import taxes on vehicles brought in from

Range Rover assembly was transferred from the old South Block to the new North Works in 1981. This picture shows the new assembly building under construction in September 1979.

For the final phase of Range Rover assembly, the lines were moved again, this time to what had once been a transmission store alongside the old South Works. The much smaller building and reduced build volumes called for many changes, one of which was the introduction of 'buffer' stores like this one for painted body shells.

This was the end of the line in August 1995, a few months before production ended.

Very different processes were used in the overseas assembly plants, which were of course much smaller. Note the use of red oxide primer, sprayed by hand, in this picture from the Australian assembly operation in Enfield, New South Wales.

Enfield again – and note how the roof was assembled to the body frame here before the whole structure was sprayed with top coat.

Venezuela

The first Range Rover to be assembled from CKD in Venezuela came off the lines in 1972 and was painted Bahama Gold. Like all the early Range Rovers built in Venezuela, it was initially registered as a Land Rover 110 Forward Control (a model also built from CKD in Venezuela) because the appropriate paperwork had been delayed! Venezuelan vehicles were built with a local content defined as 40 per cent by weight.

overseas, but encourage in-territory assembly of vehicles because this provides work for the local labour force. In many cases, items such as tyres, glass, paint and batteries are sourced locally. To make the most of this, Land Rovers (and, to a lesser extent, Rover cars) had been shipped to several overseas territories in CKD form (the initials stand for Completely Knocked Down) for local assembly. So the Range Rover was drawn up with CKD assembly in mind.

An absence of records makes it difficult to pin down the date of the first CKD Range Rovers, but they probably left Solihull some time in 1972. The final kits were shipped during 1985, and overseas assembly of Range Rovers then ceased. One reason was the switch to all-welded bodyshells: some territories did not have the welding facilities to build them up, and they could not be shipped economically as complete assemblies. Another reason was that Land Rover's policy was to develop the Range Rover as a luxury vehicle, and this would eventually become incompatible with an assembly operation that was not centralized.

Normal practice seems to have been for the vehicles to be shipped in groups of six, probably because that number of vehicle kits could be comfortably fitted into a standard shipping

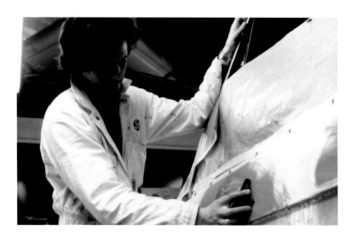

Hand-flatting of paint on the panels after the spray process: this is the front door of a Tuscan Blue Range Rover being built at the Australian plant.

The different Australian assembly sequence is clear from this picture of four-door Range Rover bodies, some painted and some not. The Australian plant also assembled Peugeot 505 cars, and used some of the Peugeot paints to give a range of colours that was different from the contemporary UK range.

A two-door Range Rover on the Australian assembly lines at Enfield.

Another sight that would never have been possible at Solihull: in this picture, a two-door Range Rover is followed down the final assembly line by a Land Rover 109, painted in the unique-to-Australia colour of Palomino Gold.

Range Rover CKD Assembly Plants		
Australia	from 1979	(Pressed Steel Corporation, Enfield, NSW)
Kenya	from 1973	(KVM Ltd, Nairobi)
Nigeria	from 1975	(probably Bewac Ltd, Lagos)
South Africa	from 1979	(Leykor, Blackheath, The Cape)
Venezuela	from 1972	(Mack de Venezuela, Caracas)
Zaire	from 1972	(probably Inzal, Kinshasa)
Zambia	from 1972	(Central African Motors Ltd, Ndola)
Zimbabwe	from 1981	(probably Quest Motors, Mutari)

Range Rover CKD Figures

These individual year figures were provided by the Land Rover Press Office in the late 1990s to George Mitchell for his Open University thesis about Land Rover CKD operations.

Model-year	Numbers
1973	225
1974	1,356
1975	984
1976	1,404
1977	600
1978	1,404
1979	2,328
1980	1,464
1981	1,356
1982	1,476
1983	588
1984	390
1985	144
Total	13,719

container. A KD manual prepared at Solihull shows that there were two types of kit, the KD II type allowing a greater degree of local assembly than the KD I type. In a KD I kit, the elements of a Range Rover were delivered as large sub-assemblies (so, for example, the chassis frame was shipped as a single unit) while in a KD II kit they were delivered as smaller components (so the chassis was shipped as a kit of side-members, cross-members and other items for welding at its destination).

Fortunately, quite detailed information is available about the Australian CKD operation at Enfield, near Sydney. The Enfield plant was owned by the Pressed Steel Corporation, and had been building a variety of British cars from CKD kits since the 1950s.

Assembly of Range Rovers began there during 1979 and, as this was a sophisticated and well-established operation, the kits were the KD II type which allowed greater scope for local assembly.

Many items were of course locally sourced, but the Australians also developed and produced their own variations on the basic vehicle. So, for example, a locally made AMC air conditioning system (Solihull then favoured the ARA type) was on the options list, and when this was fitted the small auxiliary instruments were mounted above its air outlets in holes drilled into the top of the facia. A 'factory-approved' automatic transmission conversion was also made available some two years before Solihull produced its own.

CHAPTER FIVE

Developing the 38A

Land Rover started thinking about a replacement for the original Range Rover in 1985. By then, the model had been on sale for fifteen years, and could reasonably be expected to have another five years or so of sales potential. In fact, its production life had to be extended by another six years after that, and the fact that it remained highly regarded until the very end was an indication of how difficult an act it was to follow.

From the start, the company appears to have had some quite ambitious plans for the replacement model. But these were difficult times for Land Rover. The company was still reeling from the collapse of its African sales in the early 1980s, and a recovery plan was still being prepared. So the initial plans for a new Range Rover reflected the climate of the times.

The thinking in 1985 was that Land Rover should develop replacements for the Land Rover and the Range Rover off a common platform and body structure. This would save considerably on engineering devel-

opment costs. The idea had come from Alan Edis, the Product Planning Director, and the twin future models were known as Project Inca (the Range Rover) and Project Ibex (the Land Rover). Although the Inca-and-Ibex product strategy gained ground quite quickly at Solihull, the projects only ever existed on paper.

As Managing Director Tony Gilroy's product strategy review of 1985 neared completion, so it became clear that Land Rover could and should develop a third model to compete against the Japanese family 4 × 4 estates that had become so popular since the start of the decade. During 1986, development of this third model – code-named Project Jay and brought to market in 1989 as the Discovery – became the top priority, and as a result the Inca-and-Ibex plan lost some momentum.

It had in fact already run into some difficulties. Ideas under consideration included using a body of welded construction rather than one that was bolted together in traditional Land Rover fashion, and this tended

to force the Land Rover and Range Rover apart in design terms rather than bringing them together. Peter Chalmers was working on schemes for extruded aluminium sections in his advanced design area, but eventually it became clear that this was not going to work.

Nevertheless, some important initial work had been done. It was already clear that the new Range Rover would have to become a fully credible competitor in the luxury-car class while retaining its essential Land Rover characteristic of superb off-road capability. It was this latter aspect of the vehicle – even though it would probably never be used by many owners – which gave the Range Rover its unique selling point. To meet the luxury-market requirement, it would have to be bigger than the existing model, in particular to provide more legroom in the rear. This new size ruled out the possibility of building the vehicle as a monocoque, so it would have to have a separate chassis and body.

It might have happened! Early ideas for the second-generation Range Rover included this MPV-like 'monospace' rendering.

No fewer than ten full-size two-dimensional renderings were lined up for appraisal in Land Rover's Drayton Road premises during the Inca and Ibex phase of the project in the mid-1980s.

Three themes were selected for the next stage of the process. This was Theme A, produced by the Italian styling consultants Bertone and requested by Managing Director Tony Gilroy as a 'sanity check' to compare with the in-house Land Rover work.

Theme B was an in-house design and was the one eventually selected for production, although there were several subsequent modifications to the version seen here.

The stepped waistline of Theme C was favoured for a time, but in the end MD Tony Gilroy decided against it. Theme C also had a very American-looking front lamp arrangement.

Some very basic work had also been done on the body shape as well. One early proposal even looked at an MPV-like single-box design, but it soon became clear that the new Range Rover would need to be a two-box estate car along the lines of the existing vehicle. It would also have to incorporate some design cues from the original Range Rover in order to appeal to the same target group of buyers, who tended by nature to be rather conservative. So as the Inca-and-Ibex planning ground to a stop in 1987, the outline shape and size of the eventual new Range Rover were already becoming clear.

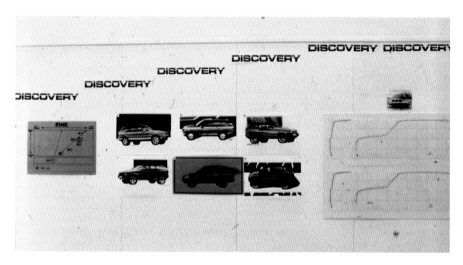

During the Project Discovery phase in 1988–1989, the key themes were still being explored and developed. This was a wall in the design studios; one version of the stepped-waistline theme is still in evidence.

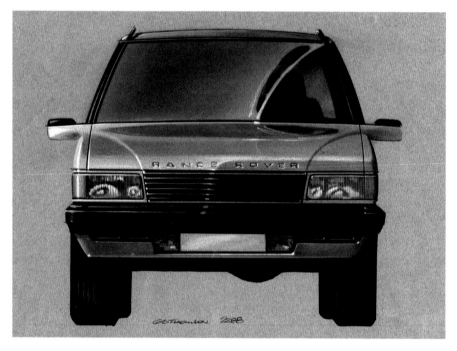

This was a 1988 proposal for the front end put forward by designer George Thomson.

Second Stage

With Project Jay now well under way and integrated into Land Rover's forward engineering schedules, the company was able to take a fresh look at ideas for a new Range Rover during 1988. Inca and Ibex were formally abandoned, and the work that had already been done on Inca was fed into a new project called Discovery.

At this stage, the person with overall responsibility for Land Rover design and engineering was Bill Morris. Under him, John Hall was Group Chief Engineer covering the Styling Department (as Design was then called) and Forward Engineering, and Bob Allsopp was in charge of the small team working on Project Discovery. Although the new project name indicated that there was some work going ahead on a new Range Rover, not much changed during 1988 because Project Jay still had priority in the Engineering Department.

However, John Hall did review the scope of the project, and one of the things that his review made clear was that Land Rover did not have a diesel engine that was refined enough to suit the pretensions of the new Range Rover. The new 4-cylinder direct-injection engine being developed for Project Jay was certainly a ground-breaking engine when it was announced as the 200Tdi in 1989, but it was not an engine that would find acceptance in the luxury market.

So John Bilton, who was the powertrain planner working for Alan Edis's Product Planning department, set about locating a suitable engine to buy in. It was clear it would have to be a 6-cylinder to get the necessary refinement. Engines from various European manufacturers were evaluated at Solihull – 6-cylinders from Steyr, Mercedes-Benz, VM and BMW, and even a 5-cylinder from Audi – and the BMW ended up a clear winner. It was a further development of the company's existing production 2.4-litre engine, which had been widely acclaimed as the world's most refined passenger car diesel, and was due for introduction in the company's own cars in autumn 1991.

BMW was taken aback when Land Rover said the engine would need further development for its Range Rover application: as a saloon car engine, it had not been waterproofed to the standards Land Rover needed and its oil system had not been designed to work on side-slopes. However, once BMW understood what was needed, it was happy to go ahead. A development contract was signed in late 1989, and the production contract the following year.

Meanwhile, work had been going ahead in the Styling Department to find an acceptable appearance for the new model. To satisfy himself that the stylists were on the right track, Managing Director Tony Gilroy

There was unhappiness about the rectangular headlamps, and several different proposals for round lamps which would create more of a link with the first-generation model were tried out. These are two of them; the rendering shows a rather attractive twin-lamp proposal from 1989.

also commissioned the Italian styling house of Bertone to come up with a proposal. Then, still under the aegis of Product Inca, a major styling review was held in the department's premises at Drayton Road in Solihull – a great barn of a place which lent itself well to the job. Full-size two-dimensional renderings of ten different proposals were lined up for review, and three were selected for further work. These three were turned into quarter-scale models, and in October 1988 they were shown to the Rover Board.

Getting Serious

It was 1989 that became the critical year in the development of the new Range Rover. It was the year when the Rover Board made its decision about which of the three body styles to go for, and it was the year when the hardware for the programme began to come together. It was also the year when John Hall was appointed as Programme Director to oversee what was going to be a complicated and costly programme.

The project gained another new name, too. In the first few months of 1989, the name Discovery was chosen as the marketing name for the new third Land Rover model, developed as Project Jay. So the Range Rover, known up to that point as Project Discovery, now became Project Pegasus. The development team was gradually assembled, under Mike Pendry as Chief Engineer. Working to him were Bob Allsopp as Chief Engineer, Vehicle Development, and Frank Bolderstone as Chief Engineer, Vehicle Layout. There were then eight 'component' teams, each under a team leader who reported to Mike Pendry. These teams covered Chassis, Body In White, Body Hard-

ware, Lower Trim, Upper Trim, Electrical (two teams) and Powertrain Systems (with sub-teams for Engine, Transmission and Engine Management Systems).

Project Jay had pioneered a new method of working called simultaneous engineering, in which engineers from several disciplines worked together on aspects of the vehicle; this prevented the conflicts which arose with the traditional way of working, when a project was passed sequentially from one specialist area to the next. So Land Rover adopted

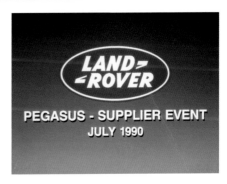

When the new Land Rover Discovery took the Range Rover's original project name, the name Pegasus was adopted. This slide was used in a presentation during 1990 and bears witness to the name – which quickly leaked out into the media.

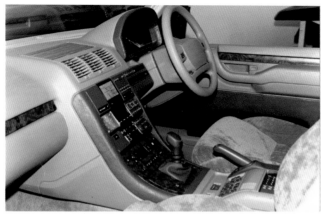

FEBRUARY '89

THEME SELECTED FACIA.
INC. REFINEMENTS FROM THEME 2.

It was during 1989 that an interior theme was chosen, after several quite radical ideas had been rejected. These pictures show full-size models dating from February and May of that year.

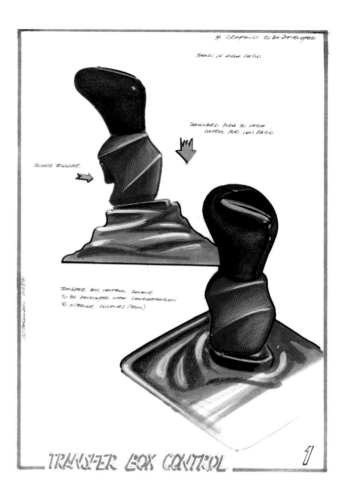

TRANSFER BOX CONTROL

Every detail was studied carefully. This is a proposal for the design of the transfer box lever, done by George Thomson in 1991.

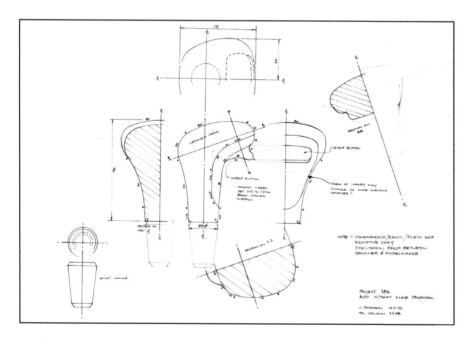

PROJECT 38A
AUTO G/SHIFT KNOB PROPOSAL

Another proposal by George Thomson, this time for the hand grip on the automatic shift lever. It was dated April 1993 and is clearly marked as intended for 'Project 38A' – the correct development name by this stage.

the same system for Project Pegasus. Over the next few years, a total of some 250 engineers and designers would make their contribution to the new Range Rover – a very large number for a single project and only possible, in John Hall's view, because his team were able to 'borrow' people from the Rover Cars side of the business who had recent experience of bringing new designs to market.

The powertrain strategy now called for two petrol engines in addition to the diesel, the aim being to offer a more sporty model alongside the mainstream petrol derivative. The engines team were already making evolutionary changes to the 3.9-litre V8, and this would offer enough power to become the core engine. Some paper design work was done on a high-performance deriva-

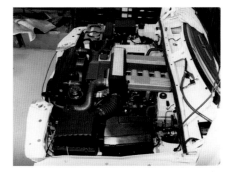

The engine strategy was clear by about 1991, and these pictures show the three proposed engines being tried out in engine bay mock-ups where the underbonnet layout was being developed in mid-1992. All three engines show differences from the eventual production types: the 4.0-litre has '3.9' on its plenum chamber, the 4.6-litre carries a '4.5' badge, and the BMW M52 diesel has a mocked-up label on its air intake ducting.

tive that would use 4-valve cylinder heads and twin camshafts on the existing block, but no metal was cut. Instead, attention turned to using a supercharger – advanced thinking for the time – on the 2-valve engine.

Prototypes of this were built, using a supercharger made by Eaton. Graham Silvers, an engineer on the Pegasus team, remembered this as a 'lovely, refined engine' and that it was tested in various 'mule' prototypes based on the existing production Range Rover. However, it was probably the cost that ruled it out in the end, and the team decided to play for safety by lengthening the stroke of the 4.0-litre engine to give a capacity of around 4.5 litres for the high-performance engine. Later, some eighteen months before the new vehicle was announced, a decision was made to call this engine a 4.6-litre: the name made it sound bigger

than the 4.5-litre engines offered in some competitive vehicles!

As for transmissions, the existing ZF 4-speed automatic was wholly satisfactory, and Land Rover needed only an upgraded version to cope with the extra torque of the high-performance engine. Manual gearboxes were another story, though. A new 5-speed gearbox called the R380 was under development but would not be strong enough to take the torque of the high-performance engine. So the Pegasus team decided to go for a new manual gearbox proposed by Borg Warner. Prototypes were tried in vehicles, and one prototype fitted with the 4.6-litre engine and manual gearbox achieved 140mph (224km/h) downhill on a German autobahn. However, costs were tight: Land Rover decided not to go ahead with the new gearbox, or with an intelligent locking centre differential from

the same company, and as a result the 4.6-litre engine was made available only with an automatic transmission.

Production Range Rovers were already using a Borg Warner chain-driven transfer box with a viscous-coupled centre differential, and there was no reason to change that. However, there were concerns at an early stage over 'beaming' – a torsional flexing between engine and transmission – and some thought went into mounting the transfer box remotely to avoid this. Even though the remote transfer box was rejected quite quickly, the mounting of the transfer box did present another problem.

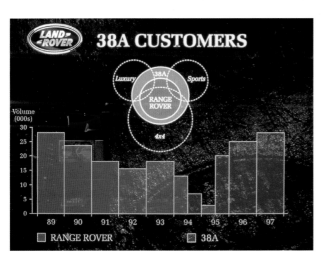

LEFT: *These are sales projections for the new model, which was by this stage known within Land Rover as '38A'.*

RIGHT: *Like its predecessor, the 38A Range Rover rode on a separate chassis, with beam axles and the height-adjustable air suspension introduced in 1992. This close-up is of a cutaway model used for display purposes in Australia.*

Early prototypes were painted in dull colours and given registration numbers that made them look a few years old; the idea was to deflect public and media interest if they were seen in daylight.

This problem was associated with front footwell room, which had been an issue on the first-generation models. The best solution that the Pegasus team could find was to mount the transfer box on the other side of the primary gearbox. This meant that the propshafts would be on the left-hand side of the vehicle instead of the right-hand side as was traditional to Land Rover; it also meant that the axle differentials would be on the left rather than the right. In later years, that caused two different problems. One was that drivers going off-road had to get used to allowing for the reduced ground clearance under the differentials on the opposite side to the one they were used to; the other was that the Range Rover axles could not be used on any other Land Rover product.

Chassis design went ahead under John Kellett, and was based on a traditional ladder-style frame with some box-section and some tubular sections for strength. Much more of a headache was the suspension system.

Land Rover knew that its traditional reliance on beam axles for off-road ability went against the luxury market expectations of ride comfort and refinement. However, all experiments with independent suspension on Land Rovers had so far proved abortive because such systems compromised off-road ability so badly; the latest 4 × 4s from Mitsubishi and Isuzu simply reinforced the point.

So as a first step, Solihull's engineers looked for ways to reduce the weight of axles and suspension components, which would minimize the negative effect of the beam axles on ride quality. They then hit on the idea of de-coupling the axles from the vehicle's structure by using air suspension: instead of noise from the wheels and axles being transmitted directly into the structure through steel springs, air suspension would allow the vehicle to ride on four columns of air, which would minimize the transmission of that noise.

Air suspension was therefore built into a series of eight chassis proto-

types that were built in late 1990 and early 1991. These ran under the stretched bodies of first-generation Range Rovers and were fitted with 4.2-litre V8 engines because the new 4.6-litre was not yet ready. The air suspension was still at an early stage, without the electronic control system that had not yet been developed, and the air springs had to be pumped up to the required ride height manually, while the engineers used a measuring stick to make sure that the ride height was equal at all four corners! As a last-ditch attempt, two prototypes were built with independent front suspension and air springs all round, but they proved once again that IFS was unsatisfactory for off-road use.

The basic idea of air suspension soon led on to other things. It became obvious that the vehicle's ride height could be varied by altering the amount of air in the springs, and this had several potential benefits. The vehicle could be lowered right down to make access easier; it could be lowered just a little to reduce

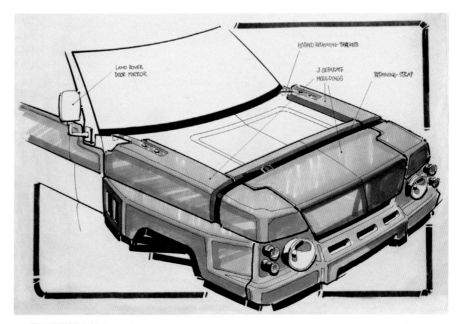

When the first production-style prototypes went out on the roads, they were disguised by a series of add-on panels. These had been drawn up by Land Rover's own stylists, as these pictures demonstrate.

wind resistance and reduce cornering roll at speed; it could also be raised above the normal ride height to reduce grounding risks off-road. So work began on a sophisticated electronic control system and, as Chapter 3 explains, this was also earmarked for early introduction on the existing production Range Rover.

Curiosity

Until this point, Land Rover had managed to keep secret most of the work it was doing towards a new Range Rover. However, customer clinics, in which groups of potential buyers were shown pictures or mock-ups of the new vehicle without being told what it was, had begun to raise the project's public profile. The name of Pegasus had also leaked out to the media. Nobody is sure how, but there was a briefing for component suppliers in July 1990 and shortly after that, the first hints were made to UK police forces about the new vehicle.

As John Hall remembered,

> Pegasus was really a great name for motivating the team and, you know, getting excitement, but unfortunately… people outside the business – either through talking to people within Rover or talking to our supplier base – also found it a very interesting and exciting name, and we started getting a lot of pressure from journalists.
>
> So we decided to change the name of the project to the name of the building that we worked at up at Solihull. That was tremendous because, you know, 'Project 38A' sort of goes … whoof, very boring!

Block 38A at Solihull was the studio and design headquarters for the Range Rover project, while Block 38 next door was the workshop. It is interesting, though, that UK police forces would always refer to the second-generation Range Rover as Pegasus, the name by which it was introduced to them. They never did take to the 38A name, which has given trouble ever since. Many people at Land Rover subsequently referred to the project as P38A, and in the aftermarket and among enthusiasts that has sometimes been corrupted even further to P38.

As this pressure was gradually building, the final design was coming together. The exterior design, developed by a team under George Thomson, was signed off in spring 1990. Among the last features to be settled were the headlamps. Some people felt quite strongly that the new model should have round headlamps like its predecessor, and the styling team tried several alternative designs, including paired round lamps. In the end, though, the rectangular lamps already in the design were chosen for production.

The interior design, meanwhile, had come together fairly easily. Its deliberately car-like ambience was

Barely disguised is this late prototype, which has white paint to help it blend into its snowy surroundings and black-painted wheels to disguise the three-spoke production style.

Most testing was in any case done at night, when the vehicles were less likely to be spotted, but Rover Group maintained a very strict security regime throughout the test phase of the 38A project. A key reason for this was that a leak about the forthcoming Rover 100 (a redeveloped and re-skinned Metro) had led to buyers holding back to wait for the new models, with the result that the Metro became nearly unsaleable in its run-out period. There were some well-known overnight test routes in the UK, particularly in the Cotswolds, in the Derbyshire Peak District, and in Staffordshire, but Land Rover were lucky.

Less fortunate was their attempt to use a military ordnance base in Aylesbury as a test centre. Rover Cars had run the R17 (hatchback 800) out of it successfully, but word leaked out about the Land Rover plans, and scoop photographers were waiting for the vehicles on the first day. So they moved to another military base at Malvern, and managed to keep security unbroken for about fifteen

complemented by a new H-gate automatic transmission selector which removed the need for a separate transfer box control (although manual-transmission models had a push-button on the dash which switched the transmission from high to low range through a servo motor). It also incorporated a sophisticated new heating, ventilation and air conditioning unit and an electronic message centre ahead of the driver. Chief Engineer Mike Pendry had wanted another screen as well, which would show the driver which way the front wheels were pointing when the vehicle was being used off-road, but this had been ruled out on the grounds of cost and complication.

The project was now approaching a critical stage when the first full prototypes with the production body

shape would go out on the roads for testing. With press interest growing, it was imperative to provide these vehicles with some kind of disguise, and in fact the Styling Department got the job of drawing up a kit of panels which could be strapped to the vehicle to make it look like a small military truck from a distance.

The first of five hand-built prototypes went on test in October 1991. These were known as the 'DO1' vehicles (*see* sidebar). Sure enough, scoop photographer Hans Lehmann spotted one, and in Britain *Car* magazine published it in a special supplement with its November 1991 issue. Fortunately for Land Rover, the vehicle was wearing disguise panels, so the picture revealed only that the new model bore some resemblance to the existing Range Rover and was very big!

The test drivers did not like those disguise panels, because they added to noise levels at speed. They also attracted unwelcome attention. On one occasion, when some disguised prototypes were being used for squeak and rattle tests in Galway, a remote and sparsely populated area in the west of Ireland, the unusual-looking vehicles attracted the attention of a local IRA terrorist unit. One day the team found themselves stopped by an IRA roadblock. Not long after that, Land Rover abandoned testing in Ireland.

Programme Director John Hall, pictured in his office during 1995 under one of the 38A design renderings.

**Launching the
New Range Rover**

The new Range Rover was introduced to the media in September 1994 at a ride-and-drive event based on Cliveden, the stately home in Buckinghamshire that had once been the residence of Lord and Lady Astor. The press had the opportunity to drive examples of the new 4.6 HSE and 2.5 DT and 2.5 SE diesels on the road, with a group of 4.0-litre models reserved for the brief off-road element of the exercise.

Second-generation Range Rover Prototypes

Between 1988 and 1991, elements of the proposed new design were tested in modified first-generation Range Rovers. These 'mules' could safely be used on the roads without attracting attention.

The full prototype programme began in October 1991 with the construction of the DO1 vehicles. The programme followed Honda's build methodology (one of the few areas where the Rover Cars alliance with Honda filtered across to Land Rover Ltd), and this is how Graham Silvers remembers the prototype sequence.

DO1 phase (5 vehicles)
These were hand-built vehicles made from prototype tooling and intended as concept proving prototypes. All looked like the finished article but there were short cuts; for example, the facias were made of GRP. One was crash-tested, and the build of the fifth vehicle was delayed so that it could be turned into a DO2.

DO2 phase (about 30 vehicles)
This was the main development programme, and the vehicles were built from 'soft' tools (that is, made from cheaper materials and with a limited useful life). There were two build phases, DO2/1 and DO2/2, the idea being to catch in the second phase any problems that the first-phase vehicles had already shown up.

D1 phase (over 30 vehicles)
These were the engineering proving vehicles. Again, they were built in two phases, called D1/1 and D1/2.

QP phase (about 40 vehicles)
The letters QP stood for Quality Proving, and these prototypes were used for such things as reliability mileage tests. The final 'QP2' vehicles were built in December 1993 and January 1994, at the start of what the project team knew as the 'five-month rollercoaster' leading up to production.

M Build (about 60 vehicles)
These were the Methods Build vehicles, built from production tooling and intended to test out such things as assembly line procedures. In most respects, they were to production standard. They were built between February and April 1994, and included the media and dealer launch vehicles. Volume production then began in May 1995.

---

months. After that, tests were based at a farm near Malvern.

Meanwhile, hot-weather testing was done out of Borrego Springs in the USA, an isolated area well away from the known vehicle test circuits. Some testing had to be done in Death Valley, which is where all vehicle manufacturers regularly take their prototypes. However, Land Rover managed to do a deal with the local

Rangers. They gave them a first-generation Range Rover free for a year (and Land Rover North America made great capital out of the fact), and in return the Rangers allowed them to use gated roads that were not open to the public. So the test team was able to carry out the vital heat-sink tests – where an undisguised prototype has to be left all day facing the baking sun – without fear of detection.

Once it was clear that the basic design of the vehicle was sound, the focus of development switched to crash testing, reliability testing, and refinement. This period lasted from approximately the end of 1992 into early 1994, when the first of the M Build (*see* sidebar) vehicles that would include the media launch fleet were assembled.

... And Finally

The first production-specification vehicles were assembled on a dummy production line that had been set up in Solihull's Block 7. These tested assembly methods and were in fact used as the launch fleet when the new Range Rover was announced in September 1994. They had registration numbers in two main sequences: Lxx LGL (all dark blue vehicles that were lent to VIP customers and media organizations in advance of the launch) and Mxxx CVC (which had the full spectrum of production colours and became the press launch batch).

However, launching the new Range Rover was still a gamble. Its target market was notoriously conservative, and Land Rover was genuinely worried that buyer acceptance might be a long time in coming. As a result, and as explained in Chapter 3, plans were made to keep the first-generation model in limited production for as long as necessary. Rebadged as the Range Rover Classic, it ran alongside the new model – somewhat unhelpfully called the New Range Rover in publicity material at the time – for just under a year-and-a-half before Land Rover was confident that the new model really had taken over.

CHAPTER SIX

The Life and Times of the Second-generation Range Rover

The lines of the second-generation Range Rover were a little bland, but arguably also timeless. This is a 2.5 DT model, which was the entry-level variant. The three-spoke alloy wheels were probably intended as a deliberate echo of the three-spoke alloys on the first-generation model, but did nothing for the new Range Rover's looks.

A more attractive wheel design on the top-model 4.6 HSE helped the vehicle's looks. This bright gold colour was called Roman Bronze and was available only for the first year.

The production story of the second-generation Range Rover was very different from that of its predecessor. While the original Range Rover grew into its luxury-vehicle role over a number of years, the 38A entered the market as a fully-formed luxury car.

The attempt to provide a realistic alternative to the Mercedes-Benz S Class, BMW 7 Series and Lexus LS saloons in the luxury market was an ambitious one for Land Rover. The company had never attempted anything like it before, and despite all the careful preparation that had gone into the 38A, the model's first four years on the market embraced a steep learning curve for Land Rover.

Customers who were paying for what was presented to them as an expensive luxury car did not expect it to suffer from the niggling electrical and build-quality faults that plagued the early models. Production standards which had been good enough for Land Rover in the past were no longer adequate, and new owner BMW was swift to recognize the fact.

So at an early stage, the company rolled out a programme called Project Achilles to rectify common build faults at dealerships. This was typical of the BMW approach, and it had done and would continue to do the same for its own cars when problems arose. Many quite major faults were rectified when vehicles came in for routine servicing, without their owners ever being made aware of a potential problem. Tales of poor quality control were rigorously suppressed, too, and Land Rover quickly

The interior looked best with light-coloured upholstery. This is the SE trim level, with leather as standard. The H-gate transmission selector, which did away with the need for a separate transfer box lever, was simple but effective.

In the early days, only the HSE came with wood trim on the doors. The light-coloured leather trim again worked much better than the alternative dark grey, but the plastic cubby-box lid let the ambience down a little.

improved assembly line procedures to ensure that early problems would not recur. Even so, quality did not really live up to customer expectations with any degree of consistency until around 1998. It was no accident that this was the year when Land Rover extended their new vehicle warranty to 60,000 miles.

Unfortunately, word of the 38A's faults did circulate, and although it probably did little to deter buyers of new vehicles, it certainly did affect the second-hand market. The models needed more skilled maintenance than Land Rover products traditionally had, and this also led independent servicing specialists to mistrust

them. All this had the cumulative effect of reducing the 38A's appeal to the enthusiast market – where, of course, DIY maintenance plays a large role. Nevertheless, a well-maintained 38A Range Rover, and particularly one built in the last two years of production, can be a superb vehicle in the best Land Rover tradition.

The First Three Years

Land Rover obviously recognized that it was taking a giant leap into the unknown with the 38A, and made sure that it had several months' experience of the vehicle on sale in the

UK before releasing it elsewhere. Europe, the Far East and South America began to receive examples towards the end of 1994, but the model was not launched in the vitally important North American market until the spring of 1995. This gave Solihull the maximum possible time to sort out early teething troubles.

Those first twelve months of production revealed two things: first, that quality control was not yet adequate; but second, that customers absolutely loved the vehicle. Sales got off to an exceptional start. The original plan had been to build up to the maximum production capacity of 620 vehicles a week over thirty

The 38A was as practical as its predecessors had been, with a huge rear loadspace available when the rear seats were folded forwards. The 40-60 split seat allowed maximum flexibility.

The avenue of trees stretching evocatively away into the distance was chosen as the launch image for what Land Rover called the New Range Rover.

months, but that figure was actually achieved after just fourteen months (in November 1995) because of demand. For Land Rover, it was a vindication of the way they had positioned the 38A in the market, and it also allowed them to bring production of the old model, by then called the Range Rover Classic, to an end in February 1996.

Changes were introduced gradually. Paint options changed after a year, and two new interior colours were added – both lighter than existing options and reflecting customer feedback. For the 1996 model-year came the diesel-plus-automatic combination not available earlier, and shortly after that the standard 16-inch wheels were complemented by an 18-inch Mondial alloy wheel option, which was very much dictated by customer demand and current fashion.

For 1997, dual exhaust systems were introduced across the range to meet new European requirements, and Land Rover announced the availability of custom-finished Autobiography models. However, these were not available in practice until the following spring, when a Philips CARiN satellite navigation system and a TV and video system with screens embedded in the backs of the front seat head rests were the headline attractions.

Mid-life Facelift

By this stage, strong sales of the diesel-engined models had more than justified Land Rover's faith in the BMW 6-cylinder. Even though it was already apparent that the engine gave no more than adequate performance, its refinement had struck a chord with Range Rover buyers. For the first-generation Range Rovers, diesels had arrived on the scene late and had never been wholly satisfactory. For the 38A, the diesel appealed perhaps to older buyers who valued the Range Rover for its refinement rather than its speed.

So towards the end of the 1998 model-year, which in other respects was mainly one of consolidation for the 38A, a limited edition 2.5 dHSE was introduced in the UK to test the market for the combination of top trim level and diesel engine. The results were positive, and eleven months later in May 1999, a production 2.5 DHSE (this time with the capital D and a proper tailgate badge) was introduced. Even though there would be no diesel-powered Vogue when that was introduced as the new top specification for the 2001 model-year, it was clear that the diesel Range Rover was no longer the poor relation of the family.

Perhaps the 1998 model-year had been quiet partly to give the

novelties of the 1999 model-year more impact. This year had to deliver the critical make-over which would see the 38A through to the end of its production life, and which many commentators assumed would be the mid-point in its career. In fact, it was well beyond that mid-point. It was also more than a little disappointing for anyone who had been reading the scoops about Range Rover upgrades in the motoring press. They all turned out to be wrong, as the sidebar on page 65 makes clear.

Even so, there were dozens of changes for 1999. Central to them were revised petrol engines – not the new BMW V8s that commentators had been expecting, but instead heavily-revised 'Thor' versions of the long-serving Rover V8s. Both 4.0-litre and 4.6-litre types were given new ECUs made by BMW's favoured partners, Bosch, and these changed their characteristics slightly to give improved high-speed torque. They also took on twin coils, double platinum spark plugs and silicon HT leads for more reliable electrics; and they had a new 'fast throttle' system.

This 'fast throttle' was achieved by electronics. Traditionally, the accelerator travel on all Land Rovers had been very long, in order to give maximum control during slow going over rough terrain. However, the long travel also led to slower response

The diesel engine was so much better than anything available in the previous Range Rover. It was the BMW 6-cylinder that was widely acknowledged as the best passenger-car diesel in the world at that time.

The good old Rover V8 design provided the two petrol engines. This is the 4.6-litre under the bonnet of a 4.6 HSE; the 4.0-litre had '4.0' cast into its plenum chamber cover.

The 1999 Model-year That Wasn't

BMW bought the Rover Group in early 1994, and wisely did not interfere with plans for the launch of the second-generation Range Rover later that year. However, by late 1995, when work began on the mid-life facelift planned for the 1999 model-year, BMW was beginning to assert more control.

The German company's engineering supremo, Wolfgang Reitzle, had been seconded to the Rover Group to oversee its operations, and he was highly critical of the original 38A interior. So for 1999, some significant interior upgrades were on the cards. It was also clear that the elderly Rover V8 could be very effectively replaced by much more modern BMW engines, and the plan was for the 1999 model-year vehicles to have these. In the beginning, the 235bhp 3.5-litre V8 was considered, but this was dropped from the schedule early on. The 286bhp 4.4-litre V8 remained in the plan, and the plan was broadened to include a new top model that would feature the 326bhp BMW V12 engine.

BMW built two engineering 'mules' of the V12 model in Germany, and these were used for a time by Reitzle and BMW's Chairman, Bernd Pischetsrieder. The extra length of the V12 engine demanded a longer engine bay and greater overhang ahead of the front wheels. Mike Sampson was given the job of restyling the front end to disguise this, and the plan reached the full-size mock-up stage. It is probable that all the 1999 models would have had the lengthened nose if the plan to use BMW engines had gone ahead.

However, it quickly became clear that this ambitious facelift plan was going to be very expensive. BMW decided to spend the money on developing an all-new third-generation Range Rover instead, and in early 1996 the planned 1999 model-year changes were cancelled. Instead, a much more limited programme of upgrades was put in place for the 38A's mid-life facelift.

BMW wanted the 1999 models to have its own engines and some prototypes were built. This is the 4.4-litre V8 under the bonnet of a 38A; the engine later appeared in the third-generation Range Rover.

BMW also wanted a flagship Range Rover with its 5.3-litre V12 engine. This is the engine in one of the prototypes. It was a very tight fit!

The V12 installation demanded extra length, and Land Rover's designers had to restyle the front end to disguise the extra inches ahead of the front axle. The new design would probably have been used with all variants. This is a full-size mock-up of a 1999-model proposal; there is an alternative proposal on the other side of the mock-up.

times at speed. So the new system used a potentiometer to provide a fast throttle response in High range and a slower response in Low range. It was an ingenious solution.

Still on the mechanical side, the manual-gearbox 4.0-litre V8s disappeared because there was such a small demand for them. All models now took on the 255-section tyres originally unique to the 4.6 HSE, and all models also took on '4ETC' (four-wheel electronic traction control). This was ready in time for the 1994 launch, but had been held over deliberately so that it could be offered later in the model's life as a new feature.

On the cosmetic front, there were new alloy wheels, all still with a 16-inch diameter, but the popular Mondial 18-inch option was supplemented by a second 18-inch style called Hurricane. The electric sunroof now became optional on all derivatives, which of course meant it was no longer standard on the top-model 4.6 HSE.

There were also major changes to the interior. Most obvious was a new leather stitch pattern; all seat adjustment was now electrically powered, all electric seats came with a two-position memory, and height adjustment for the driver's seat was standardized across the range. There were chrome interior door handles, an upholstered lid for the centre cubby box, and side airbags (actually concealed in the front seats) along with load-limiters and pre-tensioners on the seat belts. Unbranded Alpine ICE head units also replaced the Clarion types, except on the 4.6 HSE which now gained a superior harmon/kardon system.

Reaching the Pinnacle

Despite these changes, it was really not until a year later that the Range Rover fulfilled its original potential as a top-class luxury vehicle. Quality control issues had finally been banished; the bottom end of the range had largely disappeared from most markets (although there were still manual diesels with cloth seats

A Range of Specifications

The second-generation Range Rover was launched with a range of three trim levels, and these varied only slightly from one market to the next. As time went on, a fourth trim level was introduced. Within Land Rover (although not to the public), these were known as Trim Levels 1 to 4, the entry-level specification being Trim Level 1. Trim Level 4 was not introduced until the 2000 model-year.

All models had air suspension, ABS, side impact beams in the doors and remote central locking with an anti-theft system. Most models had airbags for the driver and front passenger, but in some markets neither was fitted. Many features standard on a higher trim level could be fitted to a lower-specification model as extra-cost options.

- Trim Level 1 was the entry-level specification. In the UK, this initially meant the 4.0 and 2.5 DT models.
- Trim Level 2 was the mid-range specification. In the UK, this initially meant the SE and DSE models.
- Trim Level 3 was the original top specification. In the UK, this meant the HSE models.
- Trim Level 4 was the later top level specification. In the UK, the only model to have it was the 4.6 Vogue, from mid-1999.

The second-generation Range Rover was an excellent off-road vehicle as well as a luxury car, although few first owners used their vehicles' abilities to the full.

The arrival of 18-inch wheels was eagerly awaited, and the Mondial five-spoke style that arrived first made a big difference to the 38A's appearance. This is a US model dating from 1997: note the body-coloured apron spoiler.

for those who asked); and overall specifications had finally attained the levels that the model's pretensions deserved.

But the 2000 model-year changes were an important part of a longer-term plan. Land Rover needed to move the Range Rover up a notch in the luxury class in order to prepare the way for the third-generation model which would be announced just two years later. So with the 2000 model-year came a new top trim level, known to Land Rover as Trim Level 4 and badged as Vogue. In the UK and in several other markets, this specification was available only with the 4.6-litre V8 engine.

Most of the components of Trim Level 4 – and indeed, many of the new items introduced on other 2000 model-year derivatives – had been previewed in a series of limited editions during the 1999 model-year. These had tested the water for upgrades then in the planning stages, and had helped Land Rover get a better understanding of the specifications that Range Rover customers now wanted.

The flow of limited editions continued through the 2000 model-year as well, this time taking the Range Rover into a very rarefied territory by offering a model priced at £100,000. The Linley was an all-black special edition developed with input from designer Viscount Linley, a nephew of the Queen. Land Rover

The North American Models

Sales on the North American continent accounted for some 25 per cent of all 38A models built. The lion's share obviously went to the USA, although the model was also available in Canada. The Canadian model strategy followed the same pattern as that in the USA, but Canadian models were distinguished by the addition of daytime running lights and an engine block heater.

Model-year	Designation	Characteristics
1995	4.0 SE	Automatic with Stratos (HSE style) wheels and 255/65 tyres; electric sunroof; leather upholstery with powered driver's seat; two-position memory for driver's seat and mirrors; Clarion 120-watt ICE with CD player
1996	4.0 SE	As 1995 with minor changes
	4.6 HSE	Mondial 18-inch alloy wheels; Homelink system; Ash Black leather
1997	4.0 SE	As 1996 with minor changes including darker glass tint
	4.6 HSE	Darker glass tint; body-coloured front apron; leather gearshift gaiter; Lightstone leather now alternative to Ash Black
	Kensington	750-strong limited edition based on 4.0 SE; Lightstone leather, extra wood trim and harmon/kardon ICE system
	Vitesse	Limited edition, possibly of 356, based on 4.6 HSE; Monza Red or AA Yellow; harmon/kardon ICE system
1998	4.0 SE	Spyder 16-inch alloy wheels; leather gearshift gaiter and harmon/kardon ICE system
	4.6 HSE	New seat stitching; leather gearshift gaiter and harmon/kardon ICE system
	50th Anniversary	50-strong limited edition based on 4.0 SE; Woodcote Green with Proline 18-inch alloy wheels, Lightstone leather and Walnut wood trim
	TreK	Vehicles prepared for the TreK dealer challenge event; yellow paint with special decals; roof rack; three-spoke alloy wheels; later sold on to the public but not marketed as a limited edition
1999	4.0	As 1998 4.0 SE, with GEMS engine ECU; sold early in the model-year
	4.0 S	As 1998 4.0 SE, with GEMS engine ECU; 18-inch alloy wheels; sold early in the model-year
	4.0 SE	Now with Thor engine and Typhoon alloy wheels; twin-pipe exhaust system; 4ETC; sold later in the model-year
	4.6 HSE	Thor engine and Hurricane 18-inch alloy wheels; twin-pipe exhaust system; 4ETC
	Callaway	220-strong limited edition based on 4.6 HSE, with performance modifications by Callaway Cars; uprated GEMS-type engine (240bhp at 5000rpm, 285lb ft at 3500rpm), lowered transfer box gearing and four-pin front differential; 0–60mph in 8.6 seconds; Proline 18-inch alloy wheels
2000	County	As 1999 MY 4.0 SE and sold early in the model-year; Lightning 16-inch alloy wheels; Lightstone leather
	4.0	As 1999 MY 4.0 SE and sold early in the model-year; with brush bar, roof rack and lamp guards
	4.6 HSK	As 1999 MY 4.6 HSE and sold early in the model-year; additional wood trim; hands-free cellphone kit
	4.0 SE	Incorporating smoked glass lenses and other 2000 MY upgrades; Lightning 16-inch alloy wheels; sold later in the model-year
	4.6 HSE	Incorporating smoked glass lenses and other 2000 MY upgrades; Hurricane 18-inch alloy wheels; sold later in the model-year
	Vitesse	250-strong limited edition based on 4.6 HSE; Java Black with body-colour grille; additional wood trim; satellite navigation system
	Linley	As UK limited edition of the same name; only one example sold
	Holland & Holland	As UK limited edition of the same name
2001	4.6 SE	Lightning 18-inch alloy wheels
	4.6 HSE	Hurricane 18-inch alloy wheels; satellite navigation system; interior upgrades
	Rhino	125-strong limited edition based on 4.6 HSE; 'rhino-skin' effect leather, JAMES satellite navigation system; Hurricane 18-inch alloy wheels
	30th Anniversary	As UK 2000 MY limited edition of the same name
2002	4.6 HSE	18-inch wheels; dark privacy glass behind B-pillars; heated driver's and front passenger's seats; 460-watt harmon/kardon ICE system
	Borrego	100-strong limited edition based on 4.6 HSE; Borrego Yellow paint with Ash Black leather and Kryton alloy wheels
	Westminster	250-strong limited edition based on 4.6 HSE; all-black finish with Proline 18-inch alloy wheels
	Rhino	100-strong 'final' edition with Proline 18-inch alloy wheels

The 1998 Vogue 50 limited edition brought many Autobiography features into the wider marketplace. It was far and away the most expensive Range Rover yet, but at long last the 38A model was beginning to fulfil its luxury potential.

Wheel styles and sizes made a huge difference to the way the Range Rover looked, and for 1999 the options were at last worthy of the model. These are the Mondial 18-inch wheels, which were optional across the model line-up.

The Hurricane wheels were another extremely attractive design. On some special models, they had sections painted to match the bodywork.

The Lightning wheels belonged to entry-level models, but were still a huge improvement over the wheels available on the first 38As.

Specifications for Range Rover 38A Models

Layout and chassis

Four-door estate with horizontally split tailgate
Box-section ladder-frame chassis

Engine

2497cc (80mm × 82.8mm) BMW M51 OHC diesel in-line 6-cylinder with indirect injection, turbocharger and intercooler

1995–1996 models:	22:1 compression ratio
	134bhp at 4400rpm
	199lb ft at 2300rpm
1997 and later models:	22:1 compression ratio
	136bhp at 4400rpm
	197lb ft at 2000rpm

3947cc (93.98mm × 71.1mm) OHV petrol V8

1995–1998 models:	GEMS electronic engine management system
	9.34:1 compression ratio
	190bhp at 4750rpm
	236lb ft at 3000rpm
1999 and later models:	Bosch Motronic 5.2.1 electronic engine management system
	9.38:1 compression ratio
	185bhp at 4750rpm
	250lb ft at 2600rpm

4554cc (93.98mm × 82mm) OHV petrol V8

1995–1998 models:	GEMS electronic engine management system
	9.34:1 compression ratio
	225bhp at 4750rpm
	277lb ft at 3000rpm
1999 and later models:	Bosch Motronic 5.2.1 electronic engine management system
	9.37:1 compression ratio
	218bhp at 4750rpm
	294lb ft at 2600rpm

Transmission

Permanent four-wheel drive with centre differential incorporating viscous coupling to give automatic locking

Final drive ratio:	3.54:1

Primary gearbox

Five-speed R380 manual available with 2.5-litre diesel and (1995–1998 models only) 4.0-litre petrol engines; ratios (diesel) 3.69:1, 2.13:1, 1.40:1, 1.00:1, 0.73:1, reverse 3.53:1; ratios (petrol) 3.32:1, 2.13:1, 1.40:1, 1.00:1, 0.73:1, reverse 3.53:1
Four-speed ZF 4 HP 22 automatic (diesel and 4.0-litre petrol); ratios 2.48:1, 1.48:1, 1.00:1, 0.73:1, reverse 2.09:1
Four-speed ZF 4 HP 24 automatic (4.6-litre petrol); ratios 2.48:1, 1.48:1, 1.00:1, 0.73:1, reverse 2.09:1

Transfer gearbox

Separate 2-speed Borg Warner chain-driven type; High ratio 1.22:1, Low ratio 3.27:1

Suspension

Front and rear live axles with height-adjustable electronic air suspension and telescopic dampers
Front axle located by cranked radius arms and Panhard rod; anti-roll bar
Rear axle located by composite trailing links and Panhard rod

Steering

Power-assisted recirculating-ball

Brakes

Four-wheel disc brakes with dual hydraulic line, servo assistance and four-channel ABS
Ventilated front discs with 11.7in diameter and four-piston calipers
Solid rear discs with 12in diameter and two-piston calipers
Separate parking brake: internal expanding drum-type operating on transmission output shaft

Specifications for Range Rover 38A Models *continued*

Vehicle dimensions

Wheelbase: 108.1in (2745mm)
Overall length: 185.6in (4713mm)
Overall width: 74.4in (1889mm)
Overall height: 71.6in (1817mm) at standard ride height
Track (front):   60.6in (1540mm)
      (rear):   60.2in (1530mm)

Kerb weight (for typical UK-market models):
2.5-litre diesel models:
    4662lb (2115kg) with manual gearbox
    4695lb (2130kg) with automatic gearbox
4.0-litre V8 models:
    4607lb (2090kg) with manual gearbox
    4630lb (2100kg) with automatic gearbox
4.6-litre V8 models:
    4894lb (2220kg)

Performance

2.5-litre diesel models
Maximum speed: 105mph (170km/h) with manual gearbox
                        101mph (162km/h) with automatic gearbox
0–60mph: 13.3secs with manual gearbox
                        14.7secs with automatic gearbox
4.0-litre V8 models
Maximum speed: 118mph (190km/h) with manual gearbox
                        116mph (187km/h) with automatic gearbox
0–60mph: 9.9secs with manual gearbox
                        10.4secs with automatic gearbox (1995–1998 models)
                        11.4secs with automatic gearbox (1999 and later models)
4.6-litre V8 models
Maximum speed: 125mph (200km/h), 1995–1998 models
                        122mph (196km/h), 1999–2002 and later models
0–60mph: 9.3secs, 1995–1998 models
                        9.6secs, 1999 and later models

Once the radical overhaul that BMW wanted had been cancelled, the 1999 model-year Range Rovers nevertheless ended up with new engines – the Thor V8s that were designed among other things to meet new emissions regulations. The curvaceous inlet manifold is clearly visible on this 4.6-litre variant.

The County SE was a limited edition created by adding some tasty extras to the mid-range models for 1999.

Limited Editions

The first Autobiography custom-built versions of the 38A Range Rover were announced in October 1996, but in practice deliveries did not begin until spring 1997.

Note that there was at least one 'batch' of Autobiography models which was in effect a limited edition. This was built in summer 1998 at the start of the 1999 model-year. The vehicles were based on 4.6-litre models in Rioja Red, and were fitted with the latest satellite navigation system.

All Autobiography models, and most of the special and limited editions, were hand-finished by Land Rover Special Vehicles.

Model-year	Designation	Characteristics
1997 (July 1997)	HSE+	100 examples, based on 4.6 HSE. Often known simply as 'the Limited Edition'. British Racing Green metallic paint extended to bumpers, front apron, sills and mirror bodies; cream coachline; 18-inch Mondial wheels; Lightstone leather with dark green piping
1997 (July 1997)	CARiN	30 examples, based on 4.6 HSE. British Racing Green metallic paint extended to bumpers, front apron, sills, mirror bodies and bib spoiler; cream coachline; Autobiography tailgate badge; 18-inch Triple Sport wheels; Parchment leather with Lincoln Green piping and over-rugs; extra burr walnut trim; CARiN satnav system
1998 (November 1997)	DSE+	400 examples, based on 2.5 DSE automatic. Epsom Green, Rioja Red, Oxford Blue or White Gold paint extended to bumpers, front apron, sills and mirror bodies; cream coachline except with White Gold when coachline was grey; no tailgate badge; 16-inch Spyder wheels; harmon/kardon 11-speaker ICE system; electric sunroof and front seats; Lightstone leather with piping to match exterior paint (green piping with White Gold)
1998 (April 1998)	Vogue 50	100 examples, based on 4.6 HSE. Atlantis Blue paint extended to bumpers, front apron, sills and mirror bodies; White Gold coachline; Vogue 50 tailgate badge; darkened privacy glass; 18-inch Proline wheels; numbered limited edition plate on B posts; Parchment full leather seats with blue piping; blue door pulls, gearshift and handbrake gaiters; chromed interior door handles; deluxe walnut trim and picnic tables; video player with twin screens; three-piece branded luggage set
1998 (June 1998)	dHSE	600 examples, based on 2.5 SE automatic, with HSE trim level but no mudflaps or fog lamps. Cobar Blue, Epsom Green, Niagara Grey, Oxford Blue, Rioja Red or White Gold paint extended to bumpers, front apron, sills and mirror bodies; cream coachline except with White Gold when coachline was grey; 16-inch Stratos wheels with 255-section tyres; Lightstone leather with piping to match exterior paint (red piping with Niagara Grey and green piping with White Gold)
1998 (August 1998)	County	240 examples, based on 4.0-litre automatic. Epsom Green, Niagara Grey, Oxford Blue or White Gold paint extended to front apron and mirror bodies; no tailgate badge; Lightstone leather; duotone steering wheel; chrome interior door handles; Ash Grey (with Niagara Blue and Oxford Blue) or Saddle (Epsom Green and White Gold) interior highlights
1998 (August 1998)	Vogue SE	220 examples, based on 4.6 HSE. Epsom Green, Oxford Blue, Rioja Red or White Gold paint extended to bumpers, front apron, sills and mirror bodies; twin coachlines in gold (dark green with White Gold); no tailgate badge; 18-inch Proline wheels; Lightstone leather with piping and other trim to match paint (green with White Gold); additional wood trim
1999 (December 1998)	County SE	250 examples, based on 2.5 diesel automatic or 4.0-litre automatic. Blenheim Silver, Oxford Blue, Rioja Red or Woodcote Green paint extended to front apron and mirror bodies; silver coachline (black with Blenheim Silver); no tailgate badge; standard interior colours with trim details to match seat piping; duotone steering wheel
1999 (December 1998)	Vogue SE	100 examples, based on 4.6 HSE. Epsom Green, Java Black, Oxford Blue or Rioja Red paint extended to bumpers, front apron, sills and mirror bodies; twin silver coachlines; 18-inch Pro-Sport wheels; Walnut leather with Lightstone contrasts; Ash Grey steering wheel; additional wood trim
1999 (August 1999)	Vogue SE	150 examples, based on 4.6 HSE. Epsom Green, Java Black, Oxford Blue or Rioja Red paint extended to bumpers, front apron, sills and mirror bodies; twin silver coachlines; 18-inch Hurricane wheels; Walnut leather with Lightstone contrasts; Ash Grey steering wheel; additional wood trim
2000 (October 1999)	Linley	6 examples (5 for the UK, 1 for USA), based on 4.6 HSE. Black paint extended to bumpers, front apron, sills and mirror bodies; shadowchrome 18-inch Hurricane wheels with black highlights; Linley plate-badge on tailgate; all-black interior including headlining and parcels shelf; black wood trim with stainless steel 'starburst' inlay; picnic tables and twin-screen TV-video system

2000 (October 1999; deliveries from March 2000)	Holland & Holland	400 examples (100 for UK, 300 for USA), based on 4.6 HSE. Tintern Green paint extended to bodykit and grille; 18-inch Hurricane wheels with Tintern Green highlights; Bridle leather, gunstock-grain wood trim; 20 UK examples with twin-screen TV-video system
2001 (March 2000; deliveries from June)	30th Anniversary	100 examples (plus unspecified numbers for overseas markets), based on 4.6 HSE. Wimbledon Green paint extended to bumpers, front apron, sills and mirror bodies; '30th Anniversary' tailgate badge; 18-inch Hurricane wheels with bright finish; green leather with Lightstone piping and trim highlights; duo-tone steering wheel; chromed door lock escutcheons; burr maple wood trim with 'amber' stain; second UK batch of 50 with twin-screen TV-DVD system, rear privacy glass, picnic tables and additional wood trim
2001 (February 2001; deliveries from August)	Westminster	200 examples, based on 2.5 DSE (50) or 4.0 SE (150). Blenheim Silver, Bonatti Grey or Java Black paint extended to bumpers and sills; 18-inch Hurricane wheels with gunmetal finish; Westminster plate-badge on tailgate; Ash Grey leather with Charcoal piping, Ash Grey carpets and grey Poplar Anthracite wood trim; TrafficMaster satellite navigation, 17-speaker ICE
2001 (April 2001)	Cairngorm	Available in Scotland only; unknown quantity, based on 4-litre. Micatallic paint; 18-inch Triple Sport wheels; Cairngorm decal badges on front wings; roof rails and cross-bars; front and rear lamp guards; front fog lamps; privacy glass; wood-rim steering wheel and top-level ICE system
2001 (June 2001)	Bordeaux	200 examples, based on 2.5-diesel or 4-litre petrol County. Alveston Red paint extended to bumpers, front apron, sills and mirror bodies; 18-inch Pro-Sport wheels with Alveston Red highlights; Lightstone leather with red piping and red carpets
2002 (September 2001)	Vogue SE	300 examples, based on 4.6 Vogue. Alveston Red, Epsom Green, Java Black or Oslo Blue paint extended to bumpers, front apron, sills and mirror bodies; 18-inch Comet wheels; Vogue SE tailgate badge; Lightstone leather with piping to match exterior paint; carpets to match exterior paint (Lightstone with Java Black); Ash Grey steering wheel; burr walnut wood trim with highlights to match exterior paint; TrafficMaster satellite navigation system; 17-speaker ICE; 50 examples with twin-screen TV-DVD system and rear privacy glass
2002 (November 2001)	Braemar	Available in Scotland only; 25 examples, with 2.5-litre diesel (15) or 4-litre petrol (10) engine. Blenheim Silver paint. Ash Grey leather, picnic tables, privacy glass and PlayStations for rear passengers

The Autobiography custom-finishing scheme was a very important one for the 38A's story. Although some of the striking interiors seen in these pictures probably remained one-offs, other items pioneered through the Autobiography service later became available on the line-built models.

promised to sell no more than ten and in fact made six (of which one was stolen from a dealership and never recovered). The price also had to be dropped to £96,000 in line with price cuts made across the range in late 2000, but the Linley was above all a statement of intent, and another step in moving customer perception of the Range Rover brand a little higher.

All the 2000 model-year 38As were distinguished by body-coloured bumpers and mirror heads, by the smoked indicator lenses which were the latest fashion in the motor industry, and by what Land Rover called headlamp masks. These were in fact smoked sections in the headlamp units around the lamp bowls, which gave the impression of twin lamps mounted within a rectangular housing rather than a single rectangular unit.

Elliptical foglamp lenses were a new feature, and the wheel options

There was a further minor facelift for the 2000 model-year. The headlamps had been criticized from the beginning as bland, so shading was introduced into the light units to give the appearance of twin round lamps.

The 38A in Police Use

The rising cost of the Range Rover towards the end of 1980s had persuaded many UK police forces to look for alternatives, and it was only the timely arrival of the Discovery in 1989 that saved Land Rover from losing the motorway patrol vehicle market altogether. Acutely conscious that the second-generation Range Rover would – eventually, at least – become much more expensive than its predecessor, Land Rover therefore sought police input during the design stages of the new model.

The precise date is not clear, but at some point in 1989 or 1990, Land Rover discussed the project as it then was to representatives of the West Midlands Police. At that stage, the project was known as Pegasus, and the name stuck: all British police forces knew the second-generation as the Pegasus throughout its service life.

The aim of these discussions was to ensure that any features which would debar the new model from consideration by police forces were eliminated. Solihull also put considerable effort into developing a police specification for the 38A, and examples were offered at suitably attractive prices. Land Rover was well aware that every Range Rover patrol car was an invaluable advertisement for the brand because the general public knew police forces would not choose an unreliable vehicle for the hard life of a motorway patrol car.

The police market had been an important one for the first-generation Range Rover, and Land Rover wanted to repeat its success with the new model. This was an early police demonstrator, pictured while on loan to a Scottish police force.

At least six police-specification demonstrators were ready as early as October 1994, all based on the 4.0-litre model and all finished in 'part-Battenburg' livery without the silver reflective panels employed by many forces. These all had SE-style five-spoke alloy wheels.

The first Police 38As entered service during 1996, by which time the entry-level three-spoke alloy wheels had been standardized, and a second demonstrator fleet had replaced the first. Although the 38A was never as common in UK police service as its predecessor had been, it was well liked by those forces which bought it and proved generally reliable – a clear indication of the importance of regular and thorough maintenance on these vehicles.

Range Rover 38A Prices in the UK, 1994–2002

These figures are showroom prices for Range Rover models without extras. All figures are inclusive of value added tax (VAT). From October 1996, Land Rover quoted an On The Road (OTR) price which included VAT, number plates, twelve months' road tax and a first service charge.

Date	Model	Price (£)	Remarks
1995 June	4.0	32,850	
	2.5 DT	32,850	
	4.0 SE	37,200	
	2.5 DSE	37,200	Manual gearbox only
	4.6 HSE	44,850	
1995 Oct	2.5 DSE Auto	38,650	
1996 Oct	Autobiography	61,190.43	Example price only
1997 July	HSE+	53,000	
	CARiN edition	63,000	
1998 June	dHSE	47,075	
	Vogue 50	68,000	
	Vogue 50 CARiN	71,000	
1998 Sep	2.5 DT	39,640	
	4.0	40,995	Automatic only
	2.5 DSE	42,700	
	4.0 SE	44,055	
	4.6 HSE	51,165	
1998 Dec	County SE	42,595	Diesel or 4.0
	Vogue SE	54,495	4.6
1999 Mar	2.5 DT	39,645	
	4.0	41,000	Automatic only
	2.5 DSE	42,705	
	4.0 SE	44,060	Automatic only
	2.5 DHSE	48,705	
	4.6 HSE	51,170	
1999 Sep	County	40,000	Diesel or 4.0
	2.5 DSE manual	42,000	Special order only
	2.5 DHSE	46,000	
	4.0 HSE	46,000	
	4.6 Vogue	53,000	
	Holland & Holland	65,000	Estimated price
	Linley	100,000	
2000 July	County	40,000	Formerly £41,375
	4.6 Vogue	53,000	Formerly £53,995
2000 Oct	County	40,000	Diesel or 4.0
	HSE	46,000	Diesel or 4.0
	Vogue	53,000	4.6 only
	30th Anniversary	57,500	Plus £6000 for DVD
	Holland & Holland	64,495	Plus £5000 for TV & video
	Linley	100,000	
2001 Feb	County	36,995	Diesel or 4.0
	HSE	42,995	Diesel or 4.0
	Vogue	49,995	4.6 only
2001 Sep	Bordeaux	38,995	Diesel or 4.0
	Westminster	46,495	Diesel or 4.0
	Vogue SE	53,995	4.6 only; plus £4000 DVD

changed on top models. Both Trim Level 3 and the new Trim Level 4 derivatives had 18-inch Hurricane wheels as standard, and from early 2000 there was another new wheel option called Comet. Automatic dimming mirrors with blue-tinted glass became standard, along with a chromed button for the tailgate release.

Interior upgrades made a big difference, too, with green instead of white instrument graphics, a leather handbrake gaiter and chrome on the handbrake release button and on the gearshift surround and détente button of automatics. All models now had the reversible 'cupholder' lid for the centre cubby box, and from Trim Level 2 upwards there were pop-out cupholders in the rear armrest as well from shortly after the start of the model-year. The options list now included both ruched Oxford leather upholstery and the latest satellite navigation system, and there was even a new fourth cloth upholstery option.

The Final Years

Despite the teething troubles of its early days, the 38A had attracted a loyal customer base, as conservative in its own way as the customer base of the original Range Rover had been. As the launch of the new model drew closer, Land Rover began to worry whether the transition would go smoothly, and a plan was hatched to develop a 'classic' derivative of the 38A which could go on sale alongside the first of the third-generation models. The idea was to sell a stripped-out version of the 38A, and in order to keep its price below that of the new model (but still above that of the top Discovery) the product planners intended to market it with steel coil springs in place of air springs. In practice, though, that plan was abandoned.

Not much changed for the 2001 model-year, although the top Vogue models did get satellite navigation as a standard fit. As the model-year went on, various items disappeared

The Autobiography scheme was still pioneering new finishes and new equipment. This was a 2001 model-year creation; note how the wood trim had spread across the centre console to the cubby box lid as well.

Limited editions continued to showcase Autobiography features, but the Holland & Holland was a very special model created with the respected gun manufacturers. It was, if nothing else, discreet in its combination of colours.

The Hurricane alloy wheels made this 2001-model 4.6-litre Vogue look the part. By now, the electrical teething troubles that had plagued the 38A were mostly in the past, too.

Most 38A models carried a model designation on the tailgate. The 2.5 DSE was an early mid-range diesel; the 2.5 DHSE was a later top-model diesel; and the Holland & Holland was an expensive limited edition.

from the specification, supposedly as a result of supplier shortages rather than the result of a policy decision, but there can be little doubt that Land Rover would have tried harder to find alternative suppliers if the 38A had not been so close to the end of its production life. The items affected were the Ash Grey cloth option, the automatic dimming mirror glass, and the rear door lamps.

There were just six months of the 2002 model-year. The third-generation Range Rover was announced towards the end of 2001 with the promise of showroom sales early in 2002, and this strategy had the effect of reducing demand for the 38A. The range was cut back, too: manual-transmission models were now available only to special order, and in the UK at least only the Trim Level 3

The Bordeaux was a mid-range special edition for 2001 with the 4.0-litre V8, but it was every inch a luxury car.

The last 38A was an American-specification model and was driven off the assembly lines by John Hall, who had overseen the original development programme. Sitting next to him was Spen King, father of the original Range Rover.

(HSE and DHSE) and Trim Level 4 (Vogue) derivatives were available.

Production came to an end on 13 December 2001, when 38A Programme Director John Hall drove the final vehicle off the assembly lines in a special ceremony. The vehicle was a North American specification 4.6 HSE, chosen deliberately because of the importance to the model's success of the US market, and in February 2002 it was handed over to the keeping of the Heritage Motor Museum at Gaydon along with the first production example of the new third-generation model. However, when the museum was obliged to thin out its collection just over a

year later, the vehicle was sold off at auction.

That last-of-line example was the 167,401st 38A to be made, and it is easy to misinterpret that figure, which is barely more than half the 317,615 total claimed for the original Range Rover. The reality lies not in the overall totals, however, but in the yearly production averages. The first Range Rover reached that total over a period of twenty-five-and-a-half years, which gives an average annual production of 12,455 vehicles. The 38A was in production for seven-and-a-half years, which gives an average annual production of 22,320. Clearly, Land Rover had got something right.

Annual Production Figures	
Figures relate to calendar year, not to model-year	
1994	5,861
1995	25,427
1996	29,442
1997	30,066
1998	26,556
1999	18,202
2000	18,253
2001	13,452
Total	167,259

CHAPTER SEVEN

Building the 38A Range Rover

The structure of the first-generation Range Rover had been deliberately designed to suit assembly from kits of parts, because the vehicle's creators had seen it as an extension of the Land Rover range – and Land Rovers had been built from kits of parts overseas for very many years. However, CKD assembly of the first-generation Range Rover had ceased in 1985, and

there was never any intention that the second-generation model should be assembled anywhere other than at Solihull. This, of course, gave the designers greater latitude in designing its structure.

However, re-jigging the Solihull works to assemble the new Range Rover was a massive and expensive undertaking. Even though the main

assembly hall was to be in the same North Works that had assembled first-generation Range Rovers since the start of the 1980s, that building complex had to be completely refitted. The Paint Shop also had to be upgraded, and there were knock-on effects on other areas of Land Rover's manufacturing operations as well.

By the time the second-generation Range Rover came onstream, the Solihull factory consisted of three major blocks of buildings – the North Works, the South Works, and the East Works. Within each of these major units, individual departments had their own areas, which were identified by numbers. So, for example, the old administrative offices were Block 1, located on the north side of the South Works, while Block 38A (where the Range Rover design team had been located) was on the south side of the same South Works.

As far as the Range Rover was concerned, the most important areas were in the North Works. This was divided into two main sections, one which was given over to engine assembly and one which was the main assembly hall for the vehicle.

In the South Works, the areas relevant to the Range Rover were those where gearboxes and axles were assembled. The other main activity in the South Works was assembly of Defender and Discovery models.

The East Works was sub-divided into three areas, all of them relevant to the Range Rover. At the eastern end was the Transmissions plant; next to that and in the middle of the building was the Body In White plant (where bodies were put together from individual panels); and at the western end of the building was the Paint Shop, where the newly-assembled bodies

In this sub-assembly zone in the BIW plant, body side pressings are being fitted with inner sections for reinforcement; each panel, for example, had to have the upper B/C pillar reinforced to take the upper seat belt mounting.

In another area of the BIW plant, front bulkheads are being assembled and welded by robot machines.

were painted before being transported to the final assembly lines in the North Block.

However, many of the components that made up a 38A Range Rover were not manufactured at Solihull but were brought to the site by road from the factories where they were made. Of the major elements, the chassis frames were delivered as complete assemblies from John Thompson Pressings in Wolverhampton. The BMW diesel engines and ZF automatic gearboxes reached Solihull from their own assembly plants in Austria (Steyr) and Germany (Freidrichshafen) respectively. Body panels, of which there were 260 in every Range Rover, came from the Rover Body and Pressings plant at Swindon. Castings for the engines, manual gearboxes, transfer boxes, differentials and axles came from several outside suppliers, as did the smaller items such as electrical components, glass, tyres and so on.

Building the Bodies

The start of the build process for the 38A Range Rover was in the Body In White (BIW) plant that was located within the East Works. This plant could turn out a minimum of sixteen bodyshells per hour.

The body panels arrived at the Solihull BIW plant from the Rover plant at Swindon, many of them with

A body side panel with its inner reinforcements in place, ready for the next stage of bodyshell assembly.

Completed bodyshells pass out of the BIW plant into the Paint Shop on a conveyor line.

Robot welders played a major part in the assembly of the 38A's bodyshell, and seem to swarm all over the shell as it passes down the body framing line.

At the start of the chassis assembly line, sets of axles were placed in the assembly cradles.

A V8 engine with its transmission is lowered into a chassis.

The sub-assemblies were then fed onto the main framing line, which was fully automated. Here, they passed through nine stations to emerge as recognizable Range Rover bodies – though at this stage still without doors and tailgate. Each bodyshell consisted of an inner steel frame to which were fitted aluminium alloy outer panels – although the finished result was more of a monocoque than the body of the original Range Rover, which had used a similar 'skeleton-frame' construction. Bodies were automatically jigged using pins and clamps, and each one received sixty welds. The cycle time for this part of the assembly process was 3.3 minutes per body.

Each body then moved on to the robot weld station where two robots applied another 264 welds. These two robots automatically changed their welding heads three times during the process cycle, thus in effect doing the job of six robots. The bodies then passed to a manual finish weld stage, where those welds not accessible to the robots were completed by assembly line staff.

Meanwhile, the doors and tailgate frames were assembled separately. Their build process involved thirty-one jigs and twenty-three welding guns, followed by six power clinches which fixed their aluminium skins to the frame assemblies. Doors, tailgates, bonnets and wings all then met up with the completed body frame assemblies on a final line, where they were fitted and set to the correct clearances.

Finally, a team of inspectors carried out a cosmetic inspection under high-intensity lighting, and the completed bodies passed on to a lift which took them out of the BIW plant into the adjacent paint shop.

Painting the Bodies

The Paint Shop was situated on three floors of a self-contained building which was linked to the assembly areas by conveyors. Range Rover bodies arriving from the BIW plant entered

weld nuts already fitted to facilitate the later stages of assembly. All were delivered as individual panels except for the bonnet, which came as a complete assembly.

Range Rover bodies began to take shape in fourteen sub-assembly zones within the framing plant. Here, the incoming panels were jigged and welded manually to create the six main constituents of the body frame – the front end, the main floor, the rear floor, the two body sides and the roof. There were, of course, two alternative roof panels, one with an aperture for a sunroof and one without. A total of 120 jigs and more than 140 welding guns were used at this stage of manufacture.

the Paint Shop on the ground floor. By this time, every body had been allocated to an order – which might have been a specific customer order that had come in from a dealer or in some cases was an order 'for stock'. So the Paint Shop's first task was to 'sequence' the bodies – order them into batches so that those destined to be a particular colour would go through the spray booths together. This reduced the number of times the process had to be stopped while spray heads were changed and equipment cleaned to take a different colour paint.

However, the colour painting process was still some time away at this stage. The 'sequenced' bodies were held in buffer zones on the ground floor until it was time for their batch to be taken by conveyor up to the first floor, where the body coating process began.

The first stage in this process was corrosion protection. The bodyshells were coated with zinc phosphate in an eight-stage spray process. This zinc coating had two main purposes. One was to act as a protective barrier against penetrating stone damage; if the zinc coating itself became damaged, it would oxidize to form a protective layer in a process known as 'sacrificial protection'. The coating's second main purpose was to prevent the electrolytic corrosion which can take place when two different metals are bonded together – such as the steel and aluminium alloy used in the Range Rover bodyshell.

Further corrosion protection was then provided by PVC seam sealing and underbody coating. Each body also received additional stone chip treatment to vulnerable areas such as the leading edge of the bonnet, the roof, and the front and rear wheelarches. Only then did the actual paint process begin, as a high-build primer-surfacer paint was applied by remotely controlled high-voltage electrostatic equipment.

The primed bodies then passed through a drying area, and on to the final paint area. Here, they received

Further down the chassis assembly line, the chassis frames have been lowered on top of the axle sets. Propshafts, exhaust and brake lines have already gone in.

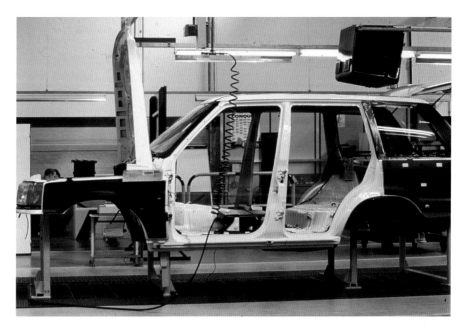

Fresh from the Paint Shop, a bodyshell is equipped with rubber protective covers to prevent scratching during the later stages of the assembly process. The bonnet panel is now in place and the doors have been removed.

two coats of the final colour, again from high-voltage electrostatic spray equipment, and these were followed by a coat of tough clear lacquer that was designed to give both a deep shine and high durability. All these coats were applied using an environmentally friendly water-based process. The last stage in each body's progress through the Paint Shop was

then a trip to the top floor by conveyor, where the new paint was dried in stoving ovens.

Engine and Transmission Assembly

While the bodies were being assembled and painted, engines and transmissions were being assembled in

Dash assemblies were pre-assembled before fitting into the vehicles as a complete unit. This is the view that owners never saw – the back of the assembly. Note the purpose-built handling arm.

With dash assembly, carpets and pedals all in place, the bodyshells progress down the line.

other parts of the Solihull factory complex. As explained above, the raw castings for the Range Rover's V8 engines arrived in the North Works engine build plant from outside suppliers, where they were first machined and heat treated as necessary.

From the machine shops, components then passed to the assembly area, where both 4.0-litre and 4.6-litre engines went down the same line. This was not the only line in the building; there were also lines for the 300Tdi diesel engines and, in a dedicated separate area, for the L-series diesel initially used in Rover cars but from 1997 also in the Land Rover Freelander.

Each engine was built on an automatic guided trolley that moved from station to station following magnetic coils embedded in the floor of the building. These trolleys had sensors which automatically brought them to a halt if they hit an obstruction – such as an errant human being. Assembly still depended on line-side workers, but the assembly plant was far more automated than in earlier times, with multi-spindle nut runner and torque units to aid assembly of cylinder

Meanwhile, the doors progress down a separate sub-assembly line, and will join up with their original bodyshells later. There was a mass of equipment to install inside the door shells before the trim casings could be put on.

The Range Rover becomes a recognizable entity as the bodyshell, lifted up by an overhead conveyor, is lowered onto its designated chassis.

This was one reason why the doors were left off: the seats are installed with the aid of special line-side handling equipment.

… and finally, the doors are reunited with their parent bodyshell.

ABOVE RIGHT: *Wheel and tyre sets were made up in advance, and are here seen being installed on a nearly completed Range Rover.*

RIGHT: *The end of the line. Lights are being tested here, but the vehicles still have their protective cladding panels.*

New Processes

Land Rover invested very heavily in new buildings, new plant and new processes to ensure that the Range Rover 38A was built to the very highest standards the company could achieve. This was not simply a matter of corporate pride; it was an essential requirement for a car which was going to compete for sales with top-class luxury saloons from BMW, Lexus and Mercedes-Benz.

A total of £15 million was invested to prepare the 6,600-square metre BIW plant within the East Works for assembling the 38A body shell, which was very different indeed from that used on the first-generation Range Rover. A further £3 million went into the Paint Shop, which as a result had become one of the largest of its kind in the UK.

The improvements to Solihull's existing Paint Shop had included new overhead conveyors, a new colour application machine, a new underseal booth, a new surface distribution system and a new anti-chip application. Other facilities had been uprated or relocated to make better use of the existing building, such as the electrostatic application and the sealer line. The inspection line had also been extended and its lighting had been improved to allow for better quality control.

A great deal of effort had also gone into the control of fumes, contamination and dust within the Paint Shop, in order to achieve the best possible working environment for a top-quality paint finish. To this end, all ancillary equipment and plant not directly involved in the various processes were kept carefully isolated.

In the engine build area of the North Works, new crankshaft and conrod machining lines had been put in as part of the plant upgrades. The transmission assembly area in the South Works had also undergone a major re-fit in late 1993 and early 1994 to cater for the introduction of the new R380 gearbox, which would be shared by all Solihull's models.

However, the biggest investment – over £13 million – had gone into the Trim and Final Assembly area within the North Works. This vast assembly hall covered an area of 35,000 square metres (42,000sq yd) and, when 38A production began in 1994, the North Works assembly line represented state-of-the-art technology for hand-building motor vehicles.

Although assembly techniques had become far more sophisticated since the early days of the original Range Rover, there was still plenty of human involvement in the assembly process. Other manufacturers were increasingly relying on robots to deliver consistent quality on their assembly lines, but there was in fact only one robot in the North Works, and that was in the glazing cell. Nevertheless, the human involvement in building a 38A Range Rover was very different from that traditionally associated with car manufacture.

Right from the start, the new assembly lines had been designed to eliminate the need for excessive stretching and bending – the activities which most commonly resulted in strain and other injuries to assembly line workers. Land Rover had also drawn on the experience which the Rover Group had gained when ergonomics consultants advised on the design of the Rover 600 assembly plant at Cowley.

Among the key features of the new lines was the large quantity of 'helpers' and power-assisted machinery which made it easier to lift and locate heavy items such as doors, wheels, sunroofs, seating and facias. These assisters had been specially developed to take the weight of components while manoeuvring them into place.

In addition, lessons learned during the pilot-build phase of production had been incorporated into the full-production phase. So, for example, the team who had assembled the pilot-production vehicles advised the plant engineers to ensure that the vehicles on the final assembly line travelled at the optimum height. Advice from the same team resulted in the bins and racks containing parts for fitting being placed where they could most easily be reached alongside the assembly line. All this in turn reduced the physical stresses of the assembly process to a large degree, and allowed the assembly line workers to concentrate on building a quality vehicle.

---

heads, conrod joints, main bearing caps and sump pans.

At the end of the build process, engines were sent for testing before being bolted to their gearbox. This testing involved a 20-minute 'cold cycle' test, when the engine was connected to an electric motor. This allowed it to 'run' without the need to introduce volatile petrol into the working environment. Once signed off as satisfactory, complete engines were then moved into another area of the North Works to be mated up with their gearboxes and transfer boxes.

Most 38A Range Rovers had automatic gearboxes, which of course were shipped into the assembly area

from outside. However, the manual gearboxes were simply transported across the factory from their assembly area on the south side of the South Works, behind the Discovery and Defender assembly lines. Completed gearboxes were tested before leaving the South Works, and were mated to their transfer boxes in an assembly area within the North Works.

The North Works was also fed with axle and differential assemblies from the South Works. The raw castings of course came into Solihull from outside and were machined and heat-treated as necessary on-site before joining the assembly line. Each axle then took about an hour to travel along the assembly line before

being checked and sent to the chassis assembly area in the North Works.

Trim and Final Assembly

Everything finally came together in the North Works, home of the Trim and Final Assembly area. This consisted of a Chassis Build Line and a Body Line which eventually converged as the Final Line, and several line-side sub-assembly build and test areas.

The Chassis Build Line was where the engine, transmission, axles, brakes, steering, suspension and fuel tank were assembled to the chassis frame. While this process was being carried out, painted bodies were

As each Range Rover came off the assembly lines, so it passed through a series of test booths. These pictures appear to show a trial run through the booths (note the number plates showing that the Range Rovers belong to Vehicle Operations). In the first case, the air conditioning system is being tested; in the second, the bodywork is being examined for flaws under very bright lights.

being prepared for the final line after their arrival from the Paint Shop.

Two important processes were carried out as bodies entered the North Works. First, they were loaded onto the moving conveyors in strict order so that they would meet the correct trim and engine on the assembly line. In addition, each body was fitted with protective panels to safeguard against accidental damage to the paint finish during the assembly process.

As each body entered the Body Line, its doors were removed and placed onto their own 'cradle'. This cradle then travelled round its own assembly line within the North Works, and glass, winder motors, speakers and trim were fitted before the doors rejoined their original body towards the end of the assembly sequence.

Meanwhile, the doorless bodies were going through stations for underbody assembly work, electrical wiring, sunroof panels (where needed), glazing, and facia installation. The partially-completed bodies were then carried by overhead conveyor to the Mount Line at the end of the Chassis Build Line, where bodies were lowered onto chassis assemblies and the two were bolted together.

The body-and-chassis assemblies now passed down the Final Line. Here, each one had seating fitted,

engine coolant and brake fluids were added and the bumpers, doors and wheels were fitted. Right at the end of the process, fuel was put into the tank and the vehicle was driven off the end of the line.

The final stage was a series of tests and calibrations. The brakes were tested on a rolling road, there were

tests for water sealing and for the electrical systems, the air suspension would be calibrated and the steering would be set up. Once each vehicle had been 'bought off' – passed its inspection – it was then driven to a despatch area within the factory grounds for onward shipment to a Land Rover dealer.

CHAPTER EIGHT

Developing the
Third-generation Range Rover

The story of the third-generation Range Rover goes right back to the mid-1990s, when work on the planned 1999 model-year derivatives of the 38A was being planned. David Sneath had been appointed as Chief Engineer for the 1999 model-year Range Rover, but he had barely settled into the job when the whole of the original plan was turned on its head.

Land Rover had been bought by BMW in 1994, and the German company had appointed its Research and Development chief, Wolfgang Reitzle, to oversee both Land Rover and the Rover Cars division. Reitzle was an extremely enthusiastic owner of a first-generation Range Rover, which he used regularly to take him from Munich to the ski resort of Kitzbühel in the Austrian Tyrol. He considered it the only vehicle available that fulfilled all his needs, and it was this passion for the Range Rover which had been behind his initiation of BMW's E53 project – the vehicle which would be launched in 1999 as the X5.

However, Reitzle was no fan of the 38A. Clearly anxious to improve the vehicle according to his own vision as soon as he could, he decided that the 1999 model-year variants should have a radical overhaul. They should have new BMW engines, improved suspension and major interior and exterior changes. So the Land Rover team under David Sneath put together a revised 1999 model-year package which matched Reitzle's vision. But when it came to the engineering sign-off, Reitzle was not happy. He could see that the revisions were going to be very expensive, and he

believed that the result was still not going to meet his expectations. So he scrapped the 1999 model-year plans and told the Land Rover engineers that he wanted to spend the money on an all-new Range Rover instead. The 1999 model-year Range Rover was therefore developed with a much more limited brief, as Chapter 6 explains.

Reitzle's first idea was to develop the new Range Rover on the platform that BMW had already developed for its E53 project. So in early 1996, Land Rover scrambled a team of four people to Munich to look at the feasibility of doing this. David Sneath was sent as the engineer, Don Wyatt as the designer (the job that was once known as stylist), Alastair Patrick was the manufacturing representative, and Paul Ferraiolo was the marketing head.

At this stage, the E53 project had been mothballed; after buying Land Rover, BMW was in two minds about the need to have an SUV-type product in its range. Some of the early prototypes were brought out for the Land Rover team to look at, including one which did have real off-road ability, but it soon became apparent that the E53 platform was simply not up to the job. Sneath discovered that the driveshafts, differentials and aluminium suspension arms were nowhere near strong enough for the punishment a Range Rover would be expected to take off-road.

There was a certain amount of scepticism at BMW about this result, so as a next stage the four Land Rover people had to prove their point by writing a very detailed paper about what was necessary in a Range

David Sneath was the Engineering Manager for the third-generation Range Rover, and is seen here with a pilot-production example.

Rover. 'It was the whole DNA of the vehicle,' David Sneath remembered later; 'the customer expectations as well as the engineering.'

Once BMW had seen that, the Land Rover team was asked to prepare a full Programme Investigation paper. There was some BMW input to this, and the Land Rover team found themselves having to justify all kinds of assumptions which they had always taken for granted. Sometimes, they discovered that their assumptions did not hold up; sometimes, BMW had to give ground. In the end, the paper was approved. Land Rover had made its case for a stand-alone Range Rover project.

This was now the middle of 1996, and BMW had owned the Rover Group for just over two years. In the beginning, the two companies had been run separately, but BMW had now decided that more integration was necessary. This meant that the

The original Phil Simmons sketch was inspired by high-end power boats. Although its spirit was retained for production, many details changed – not least those stand-off bumpers, which would have been impractical to manufacture. Note the V12 badge behind the power vents: the proposed flagship model was very much in the designers' minds.

A later version of the Simmons design, now featuring the overlapping lamp units adopted for production but still retaining the sculpted feature on the rear wings that would later be dropped. Although the sketch is in some ways still a caricature, its intent is quite clear.

early stages of new projects would be carried out in Munich, with British engineers working in Germany alongside German engineers.

BMW allocated the project code of L30 to the new Range Rover. Not long afterwards, work also began in Munich on a new medium-sized

Rover saloon known as R30. The coincidence of the number 30 was probably no more than that, although the choice of that number has never been explained. The L prefix stood for Land Rover, of course, and the R prefix for Rover.

BMW also put in its own Programme Director for L30. This was Wolfgang Berger, who had been Reitzle's right-hand man in the Rover Group and had come to understand the British way of working. All four members of the original team that Land Rover had sent out remained on the project, and David Sneath found himself having to pick the engineers he wanted from the UK. There were eventually eighty British staff on the team, each one shadowed by a German opposite number, and in the end there were 300 people working on project L30. Their project office was set up in a disused BMW powertrain building in Munich; some members of the team chose to move to Germany while others, like Sneath

himself, commuted home to the UK at weekends.

One of the earliest tasks that Sneath identified was that of educating the BMW engineers in what Land Rover was all about. Off-road driving is illegal in Germany, 'and they just didn't have the experience of it,' he explained later. So he found a forested estate on the Czech border and rented it for a three-week period. BMW engineers were invited along for a series of off-road demonstrations with existing Land Rover products to show just what a Land Rover – and by extension a Range Rover – was expected to do, and why BMW's own E53 platform would not fit the bill. 'Then they understood!' said Sneath with a smile.

It must have been at about this time that BMW shipped an E53 prototype across to the UK with the intention of putting it through some off-road testing at Land Rover's Eastnor Castle test ground. Land Rover Experience Manager Roger

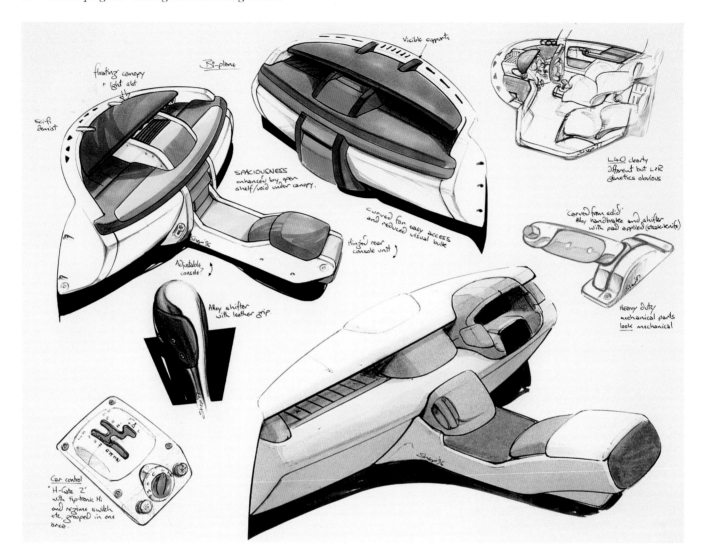

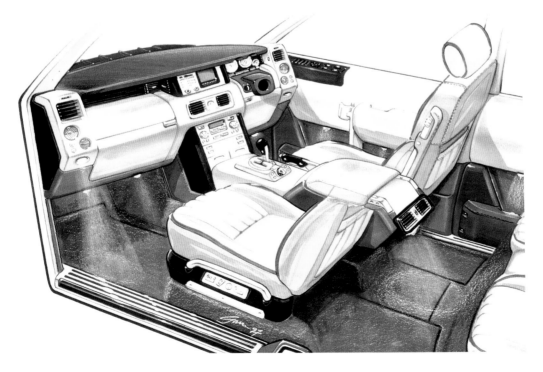

ABOVE: *Alan Sheppard was one of the interior designers, and these 1996 renderings show the strong horizontal and vertical emphasis that was present in interior proposals from the start.*

LEFT: *However, it was Gavin Hartley's interior design that was chosen for production. This is an early version of it, dating from 1997.*

Mike Sampson's 1997 exterior proposal did not make the final cut, but did feature a particularly successful front-end treatment.

Crathorne was allocated to help out, and he remembers the E53 arriving in a covered truck. With it was the E53 project leader, Gerhard Boeschel, and Crathorne decided to take him round the test sites first in one of Solihull's products. When they had finished, Boeschel turned to Crathorne and said that he was not even going to bother to get the E53 out of the truck, because it was not engineered to do the kind of thing he had just seen!

Nevertheless, the Land Rover engineers who worked on L30 were unanimous in their praise of the skill and determination of the BMW engineers. Once they had understood what was required in a Range Rover, they got on with the job and came up with some top-class solutions which were better than those the

Land Rover people had proposed. There were, of course, difficulties on the project from time to time. Even though the project language was English and the Land Rover engineers did their best to learn German as well, there were cultural differences in the working environment that had to be overcome. Many of the Land Rover team were not very impressed to hear that BMW wanted to build the new Range Rover at its new US plant in Spartanburg, North Carolina, and Alastair Patrick spent a lot of time shuttling back and forth to discuss the feasibility of this scheme.

The Design Takes Shape

From the very earliest days of the L30 programme, it had been understood that BMW would take the lead

in most areas – such as engines, body, suspension and packaging. Land Rover took the lead in just two, which were Commercial and Marketing, and Design.

Also clearly understood from the beginning was that the actual development would take place in Munich. So Don Wyatt as L30 Chief Designer and his team of designers moved into the FIZ – the BMW advanced engineering centre – and into the design area then headed by Chris Bangle. Bangle was exceptionally busy at the time, 'and he needed Range Rover like the proverbial hole in the head,' remembered Don Wyatt later. Nevertheless, the Land Rover designers soon established a good working relationship with their BMW colleagues. It turned into 'an experience from which both design groups

Toned down somewhat but still recognizable, this is the Phil Simmons design as translated into a scale model in March 1997. Those stand-off bumpers were still present, as was the sculpted line on the rear wing.

benefited,' as confirmed by designer Mike Sampson many years later.

Work on the Range Rover's appearance began with a project meeting held in autumn 1996. Don Wyatt remembered that one of the young designers, Gavin Hartley, set the tone of the proceedings by bringing in a beautifully manufactured yacht pulley. It was carefully engineered, expensively manufactured, and functioned beautifully – all characteristics which seemed to define what was needed in the next Range Rover.

However, Wolfgang Reitzle was not content just to let the Land Rover design studio get on with the job. 'He was one of those people who needed to know he had explored every possibility,' remembered Don Wyatt afterwards. So Reitzle set up what was in effect a design competition: Chris Bangle's BMW designers were invited to submit ideas, and so was the company's California design studio, Designworks.

Remarkably, there was already quite a strong consensus on the basics of the design, probably thanks to that paper which had set out the Range Rover's DNA that the Land Rover team had so recently prepared. The overall package size had already been established, which ensured a dimensional similarity among the competing designs, and part of the brief was that the new vehicle had to look like a Range Rover. That, to most of those involved, probably meant that it had to look like the first-generation Range Rover which had only gone out of production a few months earlier. The 38A, which was the current model, was probably considered off-limits for inspiration because Reitzle did not like it; Land Rover's Don Wyatt also felt that it lacked the personality that the original had embodied, and that this characteristic had to be recaptured for the new model.

Fundamental to the design process at this stage were the precepts of what was called the Land Rover Design Bible, a document drawn up as long ago as 1988 by designers George Thomson and Alan Mobberly. In this document, key characteristics of the Range Rover were identified as

Some other models now incorporated the 'power vents' seen on the Simmons model. These are three of the contenders from March 1997. The first is by Paul Hanstock, the second by Mike Sampson, and the third by Oliver LeGrice.

the clamshell bonnet, chunky grille bars, and strong horizontal and vertical lines on both the exterior and the interior. However, the 'bible' was not inflexible; it allowed for evolution, and in fact during the design period of the L30 it was modified to incorporate pocketed light units with overlapping circular elements, thick horizontal grille bars, and 'power vents' in the front wings – all elements which first appeared early in the L30 design process.

The key Range Rover elements were present in the sketches produced as the first stage of the design process, but in addition the first ideas incorporated body 'shoulders', which Don Wyatt felt added the character that had been missing from the 38A design. Most striking at this stage was a sketch by Land Rover's Phil Simmons, which was inspired by the Italian-made Riva power boat – a hugely expensive but elegantly styled millionaires' plaything. It focused all the character of the

The next stage was for the favoured exterior designs to be translated into full-size clay models. The notched door pulls suggest that this is the Phil Simmons design under construction.

vehicle at the front, tapering rearwards and featuring a cabin almost perched at the rear like the superstructure of the boat.

At Land Rover, eight scale designs were produced, seven from the in-house team and the eighth from Design Research, the external studio

Four full-size models line up at Gaydon for the final design selection in August 1997. With them, for comparison, are the last-of-line first-generation Range Rover and a current-production 38A. The model on the left has a front end and one side by Mike Sampson, while the other is by Paul Hanstock. Next to it is the BMW Munich proposal (note the M for Munich and the ED – the designation for the BMW Design Studio – on the number-plate). Third from left is the latest iteration of the Phil Simmons design, which would win the day. The fourth design was by BMW's Designworks studio in California.

Reitzle was not happy with the rear treatment of the Phil Simmons model, and a lot more work went into it to achieve the production design. The sculpted rear wing design, the chromed twin exhausts and the edge-pull door handles that recalled the original two-door Range Rover of 1970 were all casualties of the refinement process. Note, once again, the V12 badge on the tailgate!

Yet another V12 badge! This is the rear of the Mike Sampson/Paul Hanstock full-size model. The tail lights are in many respects closer to the production design than those on the Simmons model.

set up by former Rover Group Design Director Roy Axe. 'After an internal presentation,' according to Don Wyatt, 'we narrowed these down to three proposals which were then produced as full-size models. The initial final design selection, at Gaydon, involved only two full-size models from Land Rover, one full-size model from Designworks in California, and a full-sized model from BMW Design in Munich. Those were narrowed down to two proposals.' The two were Phil Simmons' Riva-inspired model and the proposal from Chris Bangle's team at BMW in Munich.

'The Land Rover Board had preferred the Land Rover model,' remembered Wyatt, 'but Reitzle was uncomfortable and wanted to see more work on both. To be honest, the Land Rover model was somewhat eccentric and questionably feasible in

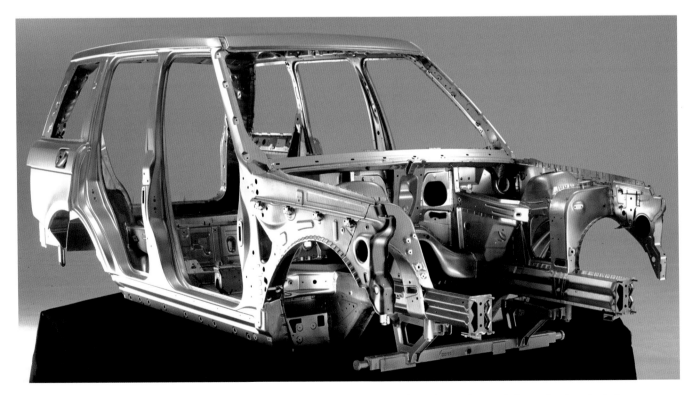

While the designers designed, the engineers were working on the monocoque structure. This is the production design, which was thought to be the largest monocoque in production anywhere in the world when it was announced in 2001.

Both front and rear wheels were carried on sub-frames, and there was height-adjustable independent air suspension all round. A third sub-frame just forward of the middle of the vehicle supported the transmission.

some areas (mainly the bumpers). In the ensuing two months, we put in a concentrated effort solidifying the design. This really was when New Range Rover was designed. For the final design selection in Munich, due to limited resources, Chris only gave a two-dimensional presentation of improvements to the BMW design. Dr Reitzle agreed to the major changes on the Land Rover model, and gave the go-ahead.'

This was in late 1997.

Immediately, the Land Rover model, the designers, and the interior bucks were all shipped to an outside contract studio near Munich, who supplied the clay modellers. BMW's Chief Designer, Ian Cameron, came on board at this time and brought with him three outstanding studio engineers... I was responsible for the Range Rover design for Land Rover, Ian was charged with conducting the integration of the Range Rover design into the BMW system – an impossible undertaking for Land Rover with no knowledge of that system... Fortunately, Ian and I rapidly established a close, amiable working relationship... Ian left the programme in the spring of 1999 to head up the new Rolls-Royce design programme,

which left me to complete the production design within the BMW organisation.

Just as for exterior design, there were some pre-existing guidelines for interior design in the Land Rover Design Bible. Interior design had also been the subject of a major review during 1996, and the generic ideas carried forward from this emphasized strong vertical and horizontal elements for the dashboard. The L30 interior design team also drew inspiration from the work of leading British architect Nicholas Grimshaw.

However, Reitzle hated the first interior designs he saw in March 1997. New proposals went down rather better at a second review that June, and the final selection was made in November. Although the Land Rover Board preferred a proposal by Alan Sheppard, Reitzle immediately latched on to the alternative proposal from Gavin Hartley, and it was this which was taken forward.

Hartley's theme was once again inspired by ocean-going yachts. His proposals envisaged an air of spaciousness within the interior and were influenced by the design of Bang and Olufsen hi-fi equipment.

It was Hartley and Sheppard who developed the chosen theme to production readiness, overseen by Don Wyatt. Part of their task was also to deliver better rear seat accommodation than had been incorporated into the 38A Range Rover. There, the backrest angle was wrong, so the team took inspiration for its angle and for the seat foaming from the BMW E39 7 Series. The underfloor packaging dictated that the rear seat should be set a little higher than the front seats, which brought the advantage that rear-seat passengers could comfortably see forwards out of the vehicle. This 'stadium' seating would later become another Land Rover design trademark, noticeable particularly in the Discovery 3 model.

Structure, Suspension and Steering

Right from the start, L30 had been drawn up with a different balance of characteristics from the two previous Range Rovers. They had been primarily off-road vehicles, which had been extensively refined to turn them into credible luxury car competitors. However, luxury car design had not remained static, and the latest BMW

Testing Times

This was how Land Rover explained the L322 test programme in a press release when the vehicle was launched.

For more than three years, pre-production Range Rovers have been 'world tested' in more than 25 countries from Australia to Zambia. The programme took in North and South America, Europe from Scandinavia to the tip of Italy, the Middle and Far East, Africa and Australasia.

The vehicle has undergone testing extremes from the high speeds of the German Autobahnen and the famous Nürburgring race track to the stop-start of the Tokyo rush hour.

It has survived the frozen wastes of the Arctic Circle and the searing heat of the Sahara – undergoing temperature changes from minus 40 deg to plus 55 deg – and has been tested in sand, through rivers and mud and over rocks. It has been driven up almost vertical boulder-strewn tracks and over the roughest terrain. It has been tested at high altitude and in high humidity.

It even covered more than 15,000 high-speed kilometres (9,320 miles) towing a 3.5-tonne trailer in northern Greece. Such was the fierce pace of this test, the trailer had to be rebuilt at the end of each day. The Range Rover emerged from the ordeal unscathed.

In all, more than 2.4 million kilometres (1.5 million miles) were covered in testing. In addition, thousands of hours of component and assembly testing were undertaken in laboratories in the UK and Germany.

Among the highly specific off-road tests undertaken by the new Range Rover was the climbing of an infamous boulder-strewn hill, deep in the Ardèche region of France. The site is one of the trickiest of France's off-road tracks and often used in 4 × 4 competition. It combines gradients – in places up to 45 deg steep – with slippery loose surfaces and deep gullies and is a test that regularly defeats the experts. The new Range Rover took the climb in its stride, adding exceptional levels of comfort to its sheer ability.

In common with its Land Rover predecessors, the new Range Rover was also tested at Eastnor Castle in England. One test saw the vehicle being driven continuously for 400 kilometres (25 miles) through thick sticky mud. Durability testing was also completed at military proving grounds in the UK including a 1,600 kilometre (1,000 mile) test over sharp flint stones to verify the under floor protection and the strength of the monocoque itself.

In Scotland, the Blair Atholl estate was used to test the vehicle's river wading capabilities while a quarry in southern England was used to check water ingress – the vehicle was driven through deep water that came over the top of the wheels.

Tests which involved the vehicle being driven over extremely rough surfaces confirmed the durability of the air suspension system and also the airbag safety systems … further off-road testing took place in Alaska and in the high altitude of Mexico, in the forests of Bavaria and on the plains of the Sierra Nevada in Spain.

On-road testing reflected the sporting ability of the new Range Rover and included a number of sessions at the Nürburgring in Germany where the handling was fine tuned. The twisting circuit in the Eifel mountains offers a unique challenge to any vehicle and it is regularly used by the motor industry for the testing of performance cars.

High speed testing was also undertaken on speed restriction-free stretches of German Autobahnen. Petrol and diesel versions of the Range Rover were subjected to dedicated 'V-max' high speed testing on the motorways, covering 64,000 kilometres (40,000 miles) at a time. In addition, the Range Rover went through a tough 40,000 kilometre (25,000 mile) high-speed programme in Italy.

At the other end of the scale, camouflaged examples of the new vehicle were driven extensively in Galway in southern Ireland, an area infamous for its poor road surfaces – perfect for highlighting, and thus eliminating, squeaks and rattles.

The new Range Rover was also subjected to many days stuck in Tokyo's rush hour traffic jams where the ability of the air conditioning to cope with the high humidity levels was under scrutiny.

All these real world tests were backed up by a programme of stringent laboratory testing, including 'accelerated corrosion' and 'whole life' tests.

---

7 Series, Mercedes S Class and Lexus LS saloons were remarkably refined vehicles. If L30 was to compete for sales with these cars, its design had to be approached differently. Instead of being a 4 × 4 that was also a luxury car, it had to be a luxury car that was also a 4 × 4 – and yet it could not lose any of the traditional Land Rover ruggedness or off-road capability in the process.

So L30 could not have a separate body and chassis like the two previous generations of Range Rover. It needed the refinement that could only be delivered by a monocoque body. When Land Rover had considered a monocoque design in the early days of the second-generation Range Rover, the company simply did not have access to the engineering expertise to deliver one as big as would be needed. However, since those days, two things had happened. First, the company had learned a great deal about monocoques for off-road vehicles during the design of the Freelander (which was announced at the end of 1997) and, second, Land Rover could call on BMW's experience with large monocoque structures – although even the Germans had never designed one quite this large before.

It certainly was big. L30 was drawn up with a wheelbase of 113.4 inches (2880mm), which was 5.3 inches (135mm) longer than the 38A's wheelbase. It also ended up standing 1.8 inches (45mm) taller. Overall length went up by 9.3 inches (237mm) and body width

The key components of the final package are seen in this demonstration assembly showing the vehicle's underpinnings. The third sub-frame in the centre is clearly visible. The engine in this case is a BMW V8.

The transmission assembly was very long. This cutaway demonstration model shows the torque converter, the automatic gearbox and the chain-driven 2-speed transfer box.

by 2.6 inches (67mm). These additional dimensions were not simply to pander to the US market, where giant SUVs like the Cadillac Escalade and Lincoln Navigator were appearing – although there can be no doubt that the introduction of such large vehicles made the Range Rover's new size more readily acceptable. They were dictated by the plan that L30 should be able to accommodate occupants of all sizes, up to and including a '100th percentile' male – the typical US basketball player – and still feel spacious.

The structural strength of this monocoque was of course a prime consideration. Not only did it have to be strong enough to carry the anticipated load of passengers and luggage on top of all the powertrain and interior elements that would be bolted to it, it also had to meet existing and foreseen crash safety regulations, to tow a trailer weighing 3500kg (7700lb), and to withstand Land Rover's hugely demanding off-road criteria. These included the snatch recovery of a bogged-down vehicle, where a shock loading of up to 5.5 tons might be put into a recovery eye welded to the monocoque. In the end, the monocoque was bolted to no fewer than three sub-frames. One carried the engine and front suspension, one carried the

rear suspension, and the third one in the middle carried the gearbox, transfer box and rear engine mount.

Nevertheless, all this strength did not inevitably add weight. Even though the Range Rover did weigh more than its predecessor when it entered production, the use of aluminium in its construction had reduced that weight considerably. David Sneath singled out the all-aluminium doors as an example. These were based on technology that BMW had developed for its Z8 sports car, and the total weight saving from that alone was around 40kg (88lb).

There was never any doubt that the suspension would be a height-adjustable type with air springs. The system had worked well in production since its introduction on the first-generation Range Rover in 1992, and since then Land Rover's engineers had developed and refined it further. Most important was that it could now be adapted to provide all-round independent suspension that did not suffer from the grounding problems which had made Land Rover reject independent suspension for so long. This was a huge step forward, because the beam axles of the 38A Range Rover did compromise its ride and handling, and handicapped it by comparison with more conventional luxury saloons.

The critical design breakthrough was achieved by cross-linking suspension units. It was off-road where independent suspension was weakest, so selecting Low range in the transfer box also engaged an electronic control system that made the wheels behave as if they were mounted on Land Rover's traditional beam axles. In other words, as one wheel hit a bump and moved up into the wheelarch, so the opposite wheel moved down to prevent the body making contact with the ground. On the road, when High range was selected, the electronic control system also allowed the vehicle to smooth out side-to-side movements of the vehicle such as could be provoked on some types of rough surface.

The suspension was drawn up with MacPherson struts and double lower wishbones at the front, and with a double-wishbone system at the rear. The differentials, meanwhile, were mounted high up on the sub-frames under the body and did not hang down below the wheel centre-lines as they had on the beam-axled Range Rovers. This meant that L30

Land Rover Australia had a full-size cutaway to demonstrate the construction and layout of the L322. Note the huge bracing members under the floor which gave the monocoque its rigidity in the absence of a separate chassis.

would have better underbody clearance than its predecessors, and that its air suspension no longer needed the Extended height function that the earlier cars had had: it simply did not ground out in the same way and did

The first prototypes of the new model were 'mules' with the running-gear of the new model concealed under appropriately modified bodies from existing production vehicles. Seen here on test in Lansdale Forest is one of the first full L30 prototypes to be built; note the Munich registration number and the tape over the front light units.

Testing of an early UK-assembled prototype in the immersion tank at the British military test ground at Longcross in Surrey.

not therefore need to be lifted off an obstruction.

Land Rover had always used recirculating-ball steering, because this absorbed some of the shocks encountered in off-road use before transmitting them to the driver through the steering wheel. However, it could also be rather vague in on-road use, and that ruled it out for L30, which had to deliver the same crisp and satisfying handling as the latest luxury saloons. So Land Rover chose a ZF rack-and-pinion system with the speed-variable power assistance system that BMW knew as Servotronic. By careful installation, they managed to get it to damp out as many off-road shocks as earlier systems had done.

To add to the steering's sharpness on the road, they also arranged for the front sub-frame to be bolted directly to the bodyshell instead of cushioned on rubber bushes. This removed yet another area of imprecision from the steering response. However, they did not attempt to go for the sporting feel of the BMW X5's steering; that, they believed, was unnecessary for their vehicle.

Further handling precision was imparted by BMW's insistence on fitting a saddle-type fuel tank. The

Land Rover engineers had wanted a minimum fuel capacity of 100 litres, which translated to a large weight of fuel that could move from one side of the vehicle to the other quite quickly under hard cornering and so upset the handling. However, the saddle tank reduced the amount of fuel that would move and also the distance it was likely to move, so minimizing the impact of weight transference on the vehicle's handling.

Powertrain Development

Engines, as was only to be expected, were to be BMW units, and in fact when work re-started on the E53 project, the two vehicles were developed in parallel with the same two engines. These were the M62 4.4-litre petrol V8 and the M57 3.0-litre 6-cylinder diesel. Both, in BMW's terms, were 1999 model-year engines, although the V8 had been available in an earlier version since 1996. What made it new for 1999 was the addition of VANOS variable camshaft timing on the two inlet camshafts.

VANOS stood for VAriable NOckenwelle Steuerung (which translates as variable camshaft control), and had

An early pre-production model, this time painted in a real production colour, on test at Land Rover's Gaydon test centre in Warwickshire. The lights are disguised with tape, the side vents are masked and there are of course no identifying badges.

originated as a product of BMW's M Division, its bespoke motor sport arm. First introduced in September 1992 on 6-cylinder engines, it was operated electronically by the engine's management system, and could vary the valve timing by hydraulically moving the camshaft forwards or backwards in its housing, so bringing different cam profiles into play. Its main benefit was that valve timing could be optimized at all engine speeds, so giving both good bottom-end torque and good top-end power without compromise to either.

As for the 6-cylinder diesel, it was a further development of the M51 2.5-litre engine that was already being used in the Range Rover 38A. Aside from the larger swept volume, its key differences lay in the fuelling system and the cylinder head. Fuel delivery

More testing, this time off-road at Land Rover's Eastnor Castle proving ground. The vehicle is again unbadged, and has tape and limited disguise panels. Yet even with that 1996 registration number to make it look old, there could have been no mistaking it as anything but a Range Rover.

was now achieved by a common-rail direct-injection system rather than the less fuel-efficient indirect injection of the earlier engine, which had a conventional diesel pump operating at lower pressures. The M57 design also incorporated four valves per cylinder rather than the two valves of the 2.5-litre engine. It was closely related to the M47 2-litre 4-cylinder diesel which Land Rover would later use in its Freelander model. For marketing purposes, Land Rover called

the new 6-cylinder diesel a Td6; the 4-cylinder M47 became a Td4; and the Td5 name was allocated to Land Rover's own 5-cylinder diesel used in the Discovery and Defender models from 1998.

The plan was to announce the L30 Range Rover in 2001 with these two engines and then to follow up at a later stage with two more BMW engines. So the L30 design was 'package-protected' to allow for later installation of the BMW 6.0-litre V12 petrol

Not all testing was conducted on location. Here, an early production example goes through a test routine in the laboratory cold chamber.

Land Rover had of course carried out its own crash testing on prototype vehicles, but independent tests – such as this one carried out by the Road Research Laboratory at Crowthorne in Berkshire – confirmed that it protected its occupants extremely well in a collision.

engine and the twin-turbo 3.9-litre V8 diesel that were both then under development. In practice, neither would ever go into a Range Rover.

All these engines, of course, had to be (or would have had to be) further developed for Range Rover use. Their oil systems had to be modified to prevent oil starvation at the angles often adopted by Range Rovers off-road, and they had to be better sealed against water ingress while their ancillary drives had to be better protected against mud likely to be thrown up in the off-road environment.

BMW also had its say on gearboxes, although there was never any question that the new Range Rover would need only automatic transmissions. The German company already had a good relationship with ZF, who supplied its gearboxes and were of course the makers of the automatic gearboxes used in existing production Range Rovers. So the designated gearbox for the V8 petrol Range Rovers became a 5-speed ZF type, while the contract for the 5-speed automatic in the diesel models went to GM in Strasbourg, probably because of production volume constraints at ZF. Both were to have selectable Sport and Drive modes, with the manual over-ride function that BMW knew as Steptronic.

The transfer box was also new, and again BMW's choice. It was developed in conjunction with Magna Steyr in Austria, who also built it, and was a chain-driven 2-speed type featuring an electronically lockable Torsen centre differential. The ratio change was achieved by electric servo motors operated from a dash-mounted button control, and the change mechanism allowed a shift-on-the-fly function which was new to Land Rover. Quiet, refined and robust, this transfer box was also manufactured in slightly different versions for the later Porsche Cayenne and Volkswagen Touareg 4 × 4s.

The management stands proudly next to its new flagship. On the right is Wolfgang Reitzle, who had championed the new Range Rover from the beginning. By this stage, he was running Ford's Premier Automotive Group and had bought Land Rover for the PAG from BMW. On the left is Bob Dover, once Land Rover's Manufacturing Director but appointed by Ford as Chairman and Chief Executive of Jaguar and Land Rover.

Critical Dates in L322 Design

1996, September–October

BMW and Land Rover engineers meet for the first time to discuss L30

1996, November

First meeting of designers

1997, March

Wolfgang Reitzle carries out the first review of interior design proposals. Land Rover makes its internal selection from the exterior scale model proposals

1997, June

Second interior interim design review Interim exterior full-size review

1997, August

Reitzle and the Land Rover Board make initial exterior design selections

1997, November

Reitzle and the Land Rover Board make final interior design selection at Gaydon
Reitzle and some members of the Land Rover Board make the final exterior design selection in Munich
On 25 November, all design is transferred to Munich. The Land Rover design team is joined by BMW modellers

1998, January

Colour and Trim show; final choices made

1998, March

Final viewing; the model is digitized for an engineering model

1998, April

Milled and hand-finished model of the exterior

1998, May–June

Design work is frozen; the model is taken away for fibreglass casts to be made; work begins on future updates

Back to the UK

The first proper L30 prototypes were built in Munich. They had all the planned Range Rover hardware bolted underneath E53 bodies; as the X5 had by this stage been announced, the BMW SUV proved an ideal disguise.

The next stage was full prototypes with the production body design. A small number were built by hand at the FIZ (BMW's advanced engineering department in Munich), and these were all left-hand drive examples that were painted black and registered on German plates. Some of these came across to the UK for testing, and all those that went out during daylight hours were mildly disguised with tape to cover the distinctive shapes of their front lamp units and wing vents. Others were tested on the European continent, and it was not long before photographers captured them on camera and pictures appeared in the motoring press and on the internet. Even so, the pictures revealed little except that the vehicle was clearly a Range Rover and was big.

More kits of body parts were produced in Munich, and these were shipped across to Land Rover at Gaydon, where they were assembled into complete prototypes. These were used for various kinds of testing, and were again painted black, this time with older UK registrations that could not be traced to Land Rover if the vehicles were spotted. Exactly how many prototype vehicles were constructed is not clear, although at the time of the new model's introduction Land Rover claimed that there had been around forty-five.

Meanwhile, the transfer of project L30 from Munich to Solihull had begun towards the end of 1998. However, it was a protracted process: although most of the designers, modellers and engineers were back in the UK by early 1999, many remained in Munich. Don Wyatt was among them, and he remembered that all the BMW designers had now been assigned to other work, leaving the Land Rover designers with full authority to operate within BMW as if they were the company's own design team. Wolfgang Berger, who had been the BMW Project Director for L30, left the project at the end of March 1999, and was replaced by Dick Elsey, who had led the original Freelander project. Dick then moved

Geoff Upex became overall head of the Land Rover design studio in 1998, and kept an eye on the L30 design as it evolved under Don Wyatt. Upex had joined the Rover Group in the early 1980s, and carried forward many of the design solutions from the new Range Rover to create a recognizable Land Rover 'family' in the early 2000s.

to Jaguar at the end of September 1999, and was replaced by Bernt Gebler, who saw out the project for BMW.

Those who did return to the UK moved into Block 38A at Solihull, where the previous Range Rover project had been based, and which had subsequently played host to the Freelander project team. In fact, some of the Freelander people were still there, but the building was refurbished for the L30 team. For the next year or so, testing and refinement of the prototypes was their primary activity, but some key issues remained to be agreed. Among them was where the new Range Rover was to be built. BMW still favoured Spartanburg in North Carolina; the Land Rover team were set on Solihull, although they realized that they would not make the final decision; and there was a real chance that it could have been built in both places, with the Spartanburg factory supplying the American market.

Back in Munich, trouble was brewing within BMW. There had for a long time been two factions within the company, one supporting Chairman Bernd Pischetsrieder's belief in the Rover Group, and the other supporting Wolfgang Reitzle's view that the Rover Cars side of the business was beyond saving and should be sold off or closed down.

The battle was finally resolved at a Board meeting on 5 February 1999 in Munich, when first Pischetsrieder and then Reitzle resigned their posts. Joachim Milberg was elected the new BMW Chairman that same day; Reitzle quickly found himself a job with Ford under Jac Nasser as head of the new Premier Automotive Group, and Pischetsrieder would later take on the top job at Volkswagen.

However, that left the future of the Rover Group uncertain. Milberg's policy was initially to integrate Rover Cars and Land Rover more fully within the BMW Group. But declining sales of Rover cars and a strong pound soon made clear that BMW had to dispose of the Rover Group as soon as possible. The L30 team, still relatively newly established in Solihull, were as much in the dark about the future as everyone else at Land Rover. 'We were worried that BMW would keep the Range Rover and sell everything else off,' remembered David Sneath.

In the event, a deal was done. In March 2000, Land Rover went lock, stock and barrel to Ford in order to pay for the financial support BMW undertook to give to Rover Cars, which went to the Phoenix Consortium and emerged as MG Rover. At Ford, where Land Rover was immediately welcomed into the Premier Automotive Group alongside British colleagues Jaguar, it once again reported to Wolfgang Reitzle – who had of course been instrumental in acquiring the company whose products he so admired.

The Range Rover was now just over a year from its public launch and was going through its final refinement stages, and as part of the deal with Ford, BMW undertook to complete work on it and to supply components as necessary during the production phase. There was an unspoken understanding that Ford would replace major components such as engines with engines from its own stable as soon as the vehicle could be re-engineered appropriately.

Ford Takes Over

Those who were working on the L30 project remember that there was a noticeable change of attitude by their colleagues at BMW. The company had agreed to complete work on the new Range Rover, but there had clearly been some kind of management directive that they were to do as much as was necessary and no more. One result, according to an engineer involved, was that the Range Rover team suddenly found they were to get the lower-powered version of the 3.0-litre diesel engine and not the higher-powered variant that was going into production for the BMW X5. When they queried this, they were told that it had always been BMW's intention for the Range Rover to have the lower-powered engine. That had not been the Land Rover team's understanding of the position.

David Sneath admitted many years later that it was a difficult period. Relationships with the BMW engineers became tense, and some of the refinements Sneath had wanted, such as air jacks for wheel-changing and a locking rear differential, were lost in the process. Nevertheless, the BMW engineers did keep to at least the letter of the agreement.

Meanwhile, Ford was busy putting in its own management. Steve Ross became Land Rover Engineering Director, fresh from running the Ford Explorer SUV project, and Jim Holland was put in as Programme Director for the Range Rover. Under the Ford scheme of things, project L30 became project L322. The Land Rover team found themselves having to explain once again the thinking that had gone into their new vehicle, this time not only justifying their own input but also explaining the BMW thinking where that had taken precedence. One particular difficulty in the early days was explaining to the extremely cost-conscious Ford people why a Range Rover had to be designed to be more luxurious than the top-of-the-range Ford Explorer.

Yet despite this enormously difficult last phase of its development, the new Range Rover was delivered on time. Now that production in North Carolina was off the agenda, the Land Rover people were less than secretly relieved that the new model would be built at Solihull. Ford lost no time in investing in new plant for that production to take place, and in May 2001 the first production-standard L322 Range Rovers rolled off the assembly lines. Volume production began later the same month.

The first pictures and outline information were sent to the media in September 2001; further details followed in December; and a ride-and-drive exercise for the media was held in Scotland early in the New Year, based on Skibo Castle. Meanwhile, Land Rover dealers and company personnel were introduced to the new model at a special event based on Lake Garda in Italy, and in January the model made its public debut at the Detroit International Motor Show. Sales began a month later, the UK on-sale date being 15 February. A bare few weeks after that, the Ford engineers were already planning the next phase of the model's existence, which would see the end of BMW's involvement with the vehicle it had helped to develop.

CHAPTER NINE

The Life and Times of the Third-generation Range Rover

The first customers for the third-generation Range Rover in February 2002 were faced with a positively bewildering range of choices. Once they had decided whether to go for a Td6 diesel or a V8 petrol model, they then needed to choose an exterior colour. There were twelve of these, all of them except Adriatic Blue and Giverny Green carried over from the previous models. The wheel choice rested between 18-inch and 19-inch alloys. There were then three interior trim finishes, three seat fabrics and six two-tone background colour options, plus a huge range of equipment and accessory options. All these options could be based around three trim and pricing levels, known as SE, HSE and Vogue.

As a result, no two new Range Rovers ever needed to be exactly alike, and in fact the company quoted 1.8 million possible combinations. This was a deliberate policy: from the outset Land Rover had wanted to give Range Rover buyers unprecedented choice in tailoring their vehicles to their personal tastes: this idea was promoted as the 'Made for Me' concept. And if that was not enough, then the Autobiography custom-building programme was waiting in the wings, and would become available in September 2002.

Just one of the advertised options was withdrawn from the catalogue before most customers saw it. This was a tyre pressure monitoring system, which depended on radio transmissions from special tyre valves to a receiver inside the vehicle. Early examples tended to transmit their messages to any Range Rover within

range, with sometimes amusing results!

There was a lot for customers to take in about the new Range Rover. Although the interior still retained a traditional British wood-and-leather combination, the variety of options was quite staggering. Blenheim leather was standard, but cloth seat facings were also available. The Contour option (its name taken from BMW practice) brought high-grade Oxford leather with electric adjustment and heating for both seats and a memory feature for the driver's side. The rear seat normally had the familiar 60-40 split-fold layout, but the Contour option added seat heating and electric adjustment of the top half of the backrest.

Land Rover claimed that the instruments and controls had been

simplified as much as possible – a BMW preoccupation for some years – and talked of a minimalist approach. In particular, the controls needed off-road certainly had been reduced in number to make them idiot-proof, although it still took some time to learn the functions of the array of dials, knobs and switches on the centre stack.

Among these controls were temperature dials for the latest version of Land Rover's heating and ventilating system, with separate passenger's and driver's side controls. Rear passengers had their own temperature control, too, and the system compensated for solar heating load and monitored pollution, switching automatically to recirculated air if the external air being drawn in fell below a certain quality level.

Silver was a favourite colour on L322 models. This early example shows all the characteristics of the 2002 cars, with the straight front bumper and black mirror bodies.

The dashboard had strong vertical and horizontal features. The handbrake was always on the same side of the console as the steering wheel, the vacant location being occupied by a complicated folding cup-holder.

The L322 retained the traditional horizontally split Range Rover tailgate among many other design cues. The doors opened wide, as they needed to in a luxury car.

Showing a very different aspect of the colour palette is this interior, with Navy seats and the silver Foundry finish where wood veneer otherwise went.

Within the wide variety of ICE options, speaker packages ranged from the standard six to the top-specification eleven, with the option of speed-sensitive volume control. The wide monitor screen in the centre of the dash had multiple functions, acting as a vehicle monitor, trip computer and control panel for the radio. At extra cost, it could also be configured to act as a TV monitor and GPS navigational display. With the optional voice-recognition system activated from a switch on the steering wheel, the driver could have hands-free control over the navigation system, optional integrated telephone system, and CD player.

The controls for most of these systems were on the multi-function steering wheel, itself on an electrically adjustable steering column that lifted out of the way automatically when the ignition key was removed, to make access easier. That wheel could be ordered with a heated rim, and for cold climates there was also an optional fuel-burning heater to warm the passenger cabin while the vehicle was parked. This system could be pre-programmed or remotely operated.

Park Distance Control front and rear gave an audible warning when the vehicle was close to an obstacle. Deadlocks and an ultrasonic alarm were also standard, and 'waterfall' ambient illumination provided a warm glow on the dashboard and allowed easy identification of switches and controls at night. Further options included a sunroof, 'climate control' windscreen (with reflective layers in the glass to reduce heat), and darkened privacy glass behind the B-pillars. There was of course also a variety of towing equipment, and the Hill Descent Control pioneered on the Freelander was standard.

It was a massively comprehensive specification, and very little needed to be changed over the next three-and-a-half years. Yet even before the new model had gone on sale, teams

The blank side panels of the tail-lights on the first L322s looked rather odd. This example has the 19-inch six-spoke alloy wheels.

at Land Rover had started work on a package of upgrades for the 2006 models that were scheduled for autumn 2005 introduction (and even earlier public announcement). Most important of these upgrades would be new engines that would not only replace the BMW units but would also expand the range with a new high-performance flagship.

Meanwhile, the new model was a huge success, both with media commentators and with the public. A few items did deserve criticism, such as the rather bluff front end, the curious blank panels where the tail-lights wrapped around, and the rather unimaginative selection of alloy wheels available. But on the whole, Land Rover had most definitely come up with a winner. It was a formidable off-road performer, too, upholding the best traditions of the brand. With approach and departure angles set at the same 35 and 29 degrees as the 38A's had been, it actually had a better breakover angle of 30 degrees (despite its longer wheelbase) because of the suspension's ability to lift the body higher.

Sales were gradually rolled out across the full range of Land Rover export territories, and by September 2003 the vehicle was on sale in over 120 countries. More important from Land Rover's point of view was that it had met or exceeded its sales targets in every market, while in the UK it was outselling all rival luxury saloons.

By this stage, aftermarket specialists were also getting in on the act. Renowned Range Rover improvers Overfinch announced their 5-litre 580S model during 2003, and in October 2004 Range7 made their rearward-facing bench seat available through 18 nominated UK dealers. It was all beginning to sound very familiar.

The 2006 Models: New Jaguar Engines

The re-engined Range Rovers were actually introduced in two stages,

There was little to see except for a plastic cover under the bonnet, but the BMW V8 engine looked like this…

… and the Td6 diesel looked like this.

Land Rover ensured that the third-generation Range Rover was still best in its class off-road, and in fact it was a more capable off-road vehicle than either of its predecessors.

Armoured Range Rovers

Armoured versions of the new Range Rover were developed early enough to be announced at the same time as the new vehicle. The 'armour' – steel and Kevlar panels as well as bullet-proof glass – was available with different levels of ballistic protection available to suit different requirements, but the typical cost of the 'Security' Range Rover was around £150,000.

The extra weight of the 'armour' was between 800kg and 1000kg (1800–2200lb), and Land Rover Special Vehicles worked with Prodrive to ensure that there was no unacceptable loss of ride quality or of handling ability. The armoured Range Rover therefore had modifications to the springs, dampers and anti-roll bars.

Armoured versions of the L322 introduced in 2003 had these special Alcon brakes. The ventilated front discs had a diameter of 378mm, a width of 36mm, and six-piston callipers; the rear discs were also ventilated, with the same 378mm diameter but a 35mm width and four-piston callipers.

The armoured Range Rover looked just like any other – until you looked a little more closely. In this picture, note the deeper black-out sections around the windscreen glass.

with new petrol engines for the 2006 models but the new diesel being held over until the 2007 model-year. So for 2006, the diesel option remained the BMW-sourced Td6, still with the 5-speed GM automatic transmission.

However, the 2006 models – including the Td6 – were accompanied by a facelift which made them instantly recognizable. They also boasted a suite of new technologies and an even better-equipped interior. It was unfortunate that the rush to get them into production became all too apparent when early examples developed electrical troubles associated with the integration of the new powertrains.

Their public announcement was at the Detroit International Auto Show in January 2005, although showroom sales did not begin before the late spring. At Detroit, they were somewhat overshadowed by the simultaneous announcement of the all-new L320 Range Rover Sport. However,

by this stage it was already obvious that the new petrol engine would be a variant of the Jaguar 4.4-litre V8 introduced in 2004 for the new

Discovery 3; much more of a surprise was the introduction of a supercharged variant as well. In effect, that replaced the BMW V12 that had

Rising prices of Range Rovers had gradually made them less popular as police patrol vehicles, but Land Rover did try hard with the L322. This early demonstrator was pictured by Andrew Fenton in October 2002 while on loan to the Central Scotland force in Stirling. A number of forces did eventually buy examples.

Autobiography

The Autobiography programme was extended to the L322 Range Rover in September 2002 for the 2003 model-year, although it did not become available in all markets at once. In Germany, for example, it was September 2003 before Autobiography Range Rovers were offered.

As before, the Autobiography service was carried out by Land Rover Special Vehicles. As before, it also tested the market for new options, and those which proved popular later became catalogued items. An example of this was the harmon/kardon Logic 7 ICE system with fourteen speakers and a sub-woofer that was offered initially as an Autobiography option. Special Autobiography badges were normally fitted to vehicles built under the scheme.

As announced in 2002, Autobiography offered an extensive range of unique interior and exterior colours. Over thirty hours of hand painting and polishing went into the typical Autobiography Range Rover. Also on offer was a range of technology features which included a Mobile Theatre system incorporating a multi-play DVD player with twin 8-inch screens in the backs of the front head rests, and surround sound hi-fi.

By September 2003, the scheme was offering twenty-five special colours not in the 'standard' options list. These were described as ranging from Bordeaux Red to Sahara Yellow, but Land Rover admitted that any colour a customer wanted could be made available. A colour-keyed body kit was also available.

Autobiography offered ten interior colourways, with perforated leather for the seat centres and four additional real wood veneers: Grand Black Lacquer, Burr Maple Prussian Blue, Lined Oak Anthracite and Vavona Burl Amber. There were also mix-and-match carpet colours and ten choices of colour for sheepskin rugs. Door trim and steering wheel colours could be chosen to taste, and of course two-tone steering wheel rims were available. Door grab handles could be customized to choice and there were several optional leather seat insert colours.

For those who were worried about car-jacking (which was a major problem in South Africa), a Supaglass hi-tech glass coating was available. This resisted shattering in an attack. Full ballistic protection was also available for owners who believed their lives were under threat.

From September 2002, the Autobiography custom-finishing service began to deliver L322 models with features not available on line-production models.

been planned before the Ford take-over of Land Rover. Both the new engines drove through new 6-speed ZF adaptive automatic gearboxes.

The 4.4-litre V8 had first been seen in Jaguar saloons as the 4.2-litre AJ-V8 engine in 1998. Once Jaguar and Land Rover were united within Ford's Premier Automotive Group, it was a natural choice to replace the BMW petrol V8. Land Rover developed it further to give the larger capacity (mainly, it appears, so that it did not look like a step backwards from the 4.4-litre BMW engine) and

of course to withstand off-road use. With 305bhp in Range Rover form, it was actually more powerful than the outgoing BMW engine. This, however, became the new mid-range option for Range Rovers; above it as the flagship engine came the super-charged V8.

Once again a Jaguar-derived engine, the supercharged V8 shared the 4.2-litre swept volume of the supercharged engine already available in Jaguars. That swept volume was retained partly to save development time and costs: the 4.2-litre engine

gave such rapid acceleration in the heavy Range Rover that there was no point in re-developing the engine with the 4.4-litre capacity used for the unsupercharged V8. With 395bhp and a very satisfying whine from the supercharger under hard accelera-tion, this engine delivered the fastest factory-built Range Rover yet.

Not surprisingly, supercharged models had suspension and braking changes to keep this new-found performance under control. There were large Brembo four-piston front brakes, and modifications to the air

Limited Editions: UK market

All the special and limited editions were hand-finished by Land Rover Special Vehicles.

Model-year	Designation	Characteristics
2004 (Nov 2003)	Autobiography Edition	125 examples, based on Vogue V8. Java Black or Zambezi Silver paint; Jet interior with black wood; Logic 7 ICE system; 20-inch wheels; twin-screen DVD system available
2006 (Sep 2005)	35th Anniversary Edition	35 examples, based on Supercharged Vogue SE. Anniversary Claret metallic paint; Carmen Red interior with two-tone steering wheel in Windsor leather; extended burr walnut trim and claret deep-pile sheepskin foot rugs; colour rear-view camera, front and rear Park Distance Control; park heating with timer and remote control
2009 (March)	Westminster Edition	300 examples, based on TDV8. Santorini Black or Stornoway Grey, or Marina Black metallic at extra cost. 20-inch diamond-turned wheels, exterior design pack, tailgate plate badge, half-wood steering wheel and stainless steel accents on pedals

A new textured backing for the tail lights on 2006 models, a vertical reflector strip and clear indicator lenses improved a weak point in the original design.

suspension to give stiffer and more sporting handling. Yet for all its new-found performance, a supercharged Range Rover was still a Range Rover. The new Range Rover Sport was intended to cater for customers who wanted something more nimble and sporting.

The 2006 facelift left the Range Rover with a less forbidding front end. The Land Rover Design Studio was now headed by Geoff Upex, and

his designers had reduced the apparent height of the nose by stressing horizontal elements: the headlamp units now cut into the grille and were shallower, while a restyled grille with less slab-like bars now cut into the scalloped top of a new bumper. On supercharged models, there were three silver mesh-style bars instead of solid bars, and the Land Rover oval had a distinctive black background instead of the usual green one.

The front wing power vents were given a matching mesh pattern on the supercharged cars, and the tail-light units now had clear lenses for both turn indicator and stop-tail lights, plus a vertical red reflector panel on their wrapped-round sides. A selection of new wheels in both 18-inch and 19-inch sizes was introduced, and the supercharged cars took on a new 20-inch wheel.

The much-acclaimed interior did not change for 2006, although there were two new trim combinations for the supercharged models only. Black lacquer wood was also added to the options list, and all supercharged models had special sporty accelerator and brake pedals made of stainless steel.

The dashboard now had a new easy-to-use touch screen that was standard on all derivatives. The satellite navigation system was still optional in some markets, but was now DVD-based and featured both on-road and off-road guidance. The ICE options were extended by a new harmon/kardon Logic 7 audio system with fourteen speakers and 710 watts of power, and there was an integrated telephone system which

The 2006 model-year brought the first of the new engines and also a facelift which gave more definition to the front end.

There was no mistaking one of the new supercharged models. They had a mesh grille and side vents, black Land Rover badges, 20-inch wheels and of course a special badge on the tailgate.

Limited Editions: US market

From 2004, Land Rover North America struck a chord with its Westminster edition, and from then on produced several limited editions of that name almost annually.

Model-year	Designation	Characteristics
2003	Oxford Edition	530 examples, of which 120 in Java Black. Contour seating with Oxford leather; additional leather trim on dashboard and grab handles
2004 (Sep 2003)	Westminster Edition	298 examples. Java Black or (limited quantities) Bonatti Grey; Luxury Interior Package and Heated Accessories Package both standard
2004	Westminster Edition	Further run of 150 examples
2005	Westminster Edition	255 examples
2006	Westminster Edition	300 examples
2007	20th Anniversary	40 examples, to celebrate 20 years of Range Rovers in the USA
2008 (Dec 2007)	Westminster Edition	501 examples. Java Black with special tailgate badge; four-zone aircon, lined oak wood trim, black leather upholstery with tan centre panels

The 2008 Westminster limited edition majored on a special interior treatment. There were just 501 examples, priced at $105,600 each.

G4 Challenge Range Rovers

For the competitors in the 2003 G4 Challenge adventure sports event, Land Rover prepared eight US-specification Range Rovers. All were painted in the event's Tangiers Orange and had the full Cold Weather package of heated accessories. They had clear glass instead of the standard tinted type to make photography of the competitors easier during the event.

These specially-prepared vehicles had the silver 'Foundry' trim instead of the wood trim standard in US models, plus a fire extinguisher mounted under the driver's seat. A dog guard in the rear prevented items in the back from being thrown forwards. A full-length heavy duty roof rack carried four spot lamps at the front and a worklight at the rear. It was reached by a ladder at the rear. Front and rear light units were protected by the optional metal protectors, and there was an A-frame at the front with two additional driving lights. Some of these vehicles also had a front-mounted winch.

For the 2006 G4 Challenge, several Range Rovers were prepared but these were not used by the competitors. Instead, they were used as support vehicles. All were HSE specification models with the V8 petrol engine.

A 2009 G4 Challenge was planned, but was cancelled because of the economic downturn. There were no plans to use Range Rovers on that event.

was Bluetooth-enabled and could be operated by voice or from the touch screen or steering wheel. With the handset in its cradle, SMA text messaging was possible using an on-screen keyboard.

The 2006 models were also even quieter inside than their predecessors. The new engines were inherently quieter than the BMW V8, and were also better isolated from the cabin. In addition, the front side glass was now laminated to cut out more external sound and the profile of the A-pillar had been modified to reduce wind noise.

A few Range Rovers were specially equipped for the G4 Challenge adventures in 2003 and in 2006. The planned 2009 event was cancelled because of the global recession.

Other toys included a rear camera for reverse parking, which displayed the view directly behind the vehicle on the central dashboard screen. The tyre pressure monitoring system which had been promised earlier now became available, and buyers could have swivelling headlamps to light the vehicle's way round corners in the dark. Also optional was a rear seat entertainment package, with 6.5-inch screens in the seat backs, a six-disc DVD autochanger, infra-red remote control, wireless headphones and sockets for auxiliary media sources such as an MP3 player or games console.

A hugely expensive special edition in September 2005 gave a lift to early sales of the new supercharged model. Called the Range Rover 35th Anniversary edition, it marked three-and-

a-half decades of the name. The base model was a supercharged Vogue SE, but it was distinguished by Anniversary Claret metallic paint and a Carmen Red interior.

The 2007 Models: Adding the TDV8

Few people were prepared for the surprise that Land Rover delivered in May 2006 at the Madrid Motor Show when they announced the engine that would replace the 6-cylinder BMW diesel. The new TDV8, a twin-turbocharged V8 diesel with a 3.6-litre swept volume and four overhead camshafts, took the diesel Range Rover into a completely new class. In fact, it went on to prove so successful that in most European countries it rendered the naturally-aspirated V8 engine an irrelevance. In the UK and elsewhere, that engine disappeared from the sales catalogues in autumn 2007, although of course it remained available in diesel-shy markets like the USA and the Middle East.

The TDV8 engine was closely related to the TDV6 6-cylinder diesel engine already seen in the Discovery 3, and there is a more detailed explanation of its lineage in Chapter 11. Land Rover had originally considered using the TDV6 as a replacement for the BMW-built Td6 in the Range Rover, but the installation would have created difficult engineering problems. So Ford approved a plan to develop the bigger diesel, not least because BMW, Audi and Mercedes-Benz were all known to

There were special interior features for the supercharged models, too, with unique 'sporty' pedals and a specially badged rev counter.

be working on V8 diesel engines that would certainly appear in their large SUV models.

The TDV8 turned out to be as perfect an engine for the L322 Range Rover as the original 3.5-litre ex-Buick petrol V8 had been for the first Range Rover. Featuring the latest common-rail direct injection technology, it boasted 268bhp and a huge 472lb ft of torque, which delivered a top speed of 124mph and a zero-to-60 acceleration time of 8.6 seconds. On top of that, the engine was refined enough to be unrecognizable as a diesel from inside the passenger cabin, and it could deliver fuel economy of 27mpg (10.5ltr/100km) into the bargain. Small wonder, then, that it soon became the core engine in European Range Rovers.

This engine also came with the latest 6-speed automatic gearbox from ZF, and to cope with the high performance it delivered, it was matched by the stiffer suspension that had been fitted only to supercharged models in 2006 and by the supercharged models' Brembo braking system. The new TDV8 models also benefited from an important change made right across the 2007 range, which was the introduction of the Terrain Response system.

Terrain Response had first been seen on the Discovery 3 that was announced as a 2005 model in 2004. Essentially, it linked together the vehicle's traction and braking systems, together with its engine and gearbox ECUs, to deliver an overall package that ensured the vehicle would always function in the most appropriate way for the terrain over which it was driven. The default setting was for road driving, but there were four others – for Grass, Gravel and Snow, for Mud and Ruts, for Sand and for Rock Crawling. In each case, dialling in the appropriate terrain optimized the vehicle's responses for the conditions.

Many long-term off-road drivers believed that these systems removed both the challenges and the need for skill that off-road driving had traditionally demanded. Land Rover's view, favouring the majority who would only rarely use their vehicles' off-road capabilities, was that they had to make things as easy as possible for the driver, not least because that was what he or she was paying for in a Range Rover. One way or another, there was no doubt that Terrain Response added to the Range Rover's already astonishing off-road capabilities.

With the 2007 models also came a range alignment: the entry-level SE types disappeared, and the range was realigned so that the HSE became the entry-level model, with Vogue

The limited-edition 35th Anniversary displayed all the best of Land Rover's custom-finishing expertise, but was formidably expensive.

Central to the 2007 model-year changes was the new TDV8 diesel engine, quite possibly the best real-world engine ever used in a Range Rover.

and new Vogue SE trim levels above them. Early in the 2007 calendar year, the upholstery options were rationalized to match this new range. The 'standard' leather took on the name of Blenheim and became the HSE trim; Oxford leather became the Vogue upholstery; and the Vogue SE came with Windsor leather.

There was no need to change the basic cabin architecture, which remained a big hit with Range Rover buyers, but the 2007 models did bring some interior refreshments. So there was a new upper facia with improved ventilation and air conditioning, and the passenger's side glove-box had

also been redesigned and there were now separate upper and lower glove-boxes, each released electronically by a button on the facia. A cleaner centre console design had new switchgear and audio controls, plus an electronic park brake (already seen on Discovery 3 and Range Rover Sport models) and a rotary control for the Terrain Response system.

In addition, there was an increased number of airbags as standard equipment, plus 'active' front head rests that moved forwards to offer better neck protection in a collision. For even greater comfort in hot weather, the standard heated front seats could now be supplemented by an internal air-conditioning system which actually cooled them through perforations in the leather upholstery.

The 2008 and 2009 Models: Boom, Then Bust

Range Rover customers in most markets had a choice of just two engines for 2008. In Europe, their options were the TDV8 and the supercharged petrol V8; in the USA, the Middle East and some other markets, the choice was between the 4.4-litre petrol V8 and the 4.2-litre supercharged engine. With the reduction in engine choice from three to two came a further raft of interior changes.

Most obviously, there was additional leather trim on the heating and ventilating unit and on the centre console, with additional wood trim at its rear. Some models had a matching wooden gear knob; there was an additional interior colour; and there were new tread plates. The instruments and the touch screen both had new graphics, and the choice of wood veneers was now increased to seven – all of them, Land Rover was careful to insist, from sustainable forests. Inside the revised rear armrest was extra stowage space, which could be used for the remote control associated with the optional rear-seat entertainment system.

Less visibly, the 'climate control' windscreen was now standard, and the same glass was used for the side windows. There was also a new four-zone air conditioning system, which allowed passengers in each of the four main seats (there was still a fifth place on the rear bench) to choose their own individual temperature. Finally, the 2008 models were all equipped with automatic rain and headlight sensors, one adjusting the intermittent sweep of the wipers to suit the conditions and the other turning on the headlights in low-light conditions. Both, of course, could be overridden manually.

The year 2008 was a memorable one for Land Rover for a number

The facia was also modified for the 2007 models, and the centre console was re-arranged with the gear selector offset towards the driver. Behind it was the rotary control for the Terrain Response system, and behind that was the switch for the electronic handbrake.

of reasons. First, it was the marque's 60th anniversary, and there were a number of celebratory events associated with this, although none specifically affected the Range Rover. Second, it was the year when owners Ford decided to dismantle the Premier Automotive Group and concentrate on its core business after making huge losses in the USA. And third, it was the year when a world-wide economic recession hit car makers everywhere hard.

Range Rover sales ran into a brick wall in the spring of 2008. Although the very wealthy, who formed a sizeable percentage of Range Rover buyers, carried on much as before, the less wealthy more or less stopped buying new cars. Land Rover had no major new-model plans for 2009, which was just as well. So the company held its breath as the year progressed, reducing build quantities and shedding staff to cope. Range Rover sales meanwhile dropped alarmingly, and a Westminster limited edition in the UK in March was carefully specified and priced to shore up sales.

The 2010 Models: A Final Facelift

By this stage, however, work on the 2010 facelift was already well advanced. Planned as the final major overhaul of the L322, this had been designed to make the vehicle even more expensive and exclusive, as the range was truncated at its bottom end and a new top-level specification bearing the Autobiography name was introduced.

Its timing could hardly have been worse: Range Rover sales had been hit badly in 2009, and more expensive and exclusive models were unlikely to be well received while there was still a recession. But it was too late to change direction. The 2010 models were announced on target in spring 2009 for a June start to sales, and Land Rover simply had to brazen it out and make the best of a bad job. Fortunately, by September 2009, there were signs that world-

A new front-end treatment characterized the 2010 model-year Range Rovers. Also clear in this picture are the new wheels, the mirror backs with their top halves painted to match the body, and the continuation of the three-element design in the power vents.

wide sales were beginning to pick up again.

Overall design responsibility for the new models had fallen to Gerry McGovern as one of his first tasks after replacing Geoff Upex at the head of Land Rover's Design Studio in late 2006. He characterized the 2010 changes by his definition of the Range Rover brand: 'Range Rover is as much about what it doesn't say as what it does say,' was the way he expressed it. Land Rover acknowledged that Range Rover customers tended to be conservative in their tastes and admired discretion, but that a lot of them were very wealthy indeed.

So the 2010 changes were evolutionary and were largely about perceived quality. They brought a new 'face' with slimmer LED-rimmed headlamps and a slightly deeper three-element grille. That three-element design was carried round through the front indicators to the side air vents and ultimately into the rear light clusters as well. Meanwhile, the interior was upgraded yet again, major improvements coming in the use of materials (such as a hand-stitched leather headlining) and being discernible in the way things felt as much as

in the way they looked. McGovern talked about increased levels of precision in the way the whole vehicle was put together, too.

Land Rover Programmes Director Murray Dietsch defined the Range Rover's appeal as having four key elements: Presence, Effortlessness, Majesty and Class. He said that the thrust of the engineering programme for the 2010 models was to deliver these and to integrate new vehicles systems to make the world's best even better.

Central to the new models were two new petrol V8s, known as LR-V8 types, which were the first

Annual Production Figures of the L322	
Figures relate to calendar year, not to model-year	
2001	421
2002	27,595
2003	31,277
2004	33,732
2005	27,780
2006	28,308
2007	29,377
Total (to 2007)	178,490

Specifications for Range Rover L322 Models

Layout and structure

Four-door estate with horizontally split tailgate
Monocoque with three separate sub-frames

Engine

Td6 diesel (2002–2006 models)
2926cc (84mm × 88mm) BMW M57 dohc 4-valve diesel in-line 6-cylinder with common-rail direct injection, variable-vane turbocharger and intercooler
    Bosch DDE 4.0 engine management system
    18:1 compression ratio
    174bhp at 4000rpm
    288lb ft at 2000rpm

4.4-litre BMW V8 (2002–2005)
4398cc (92mm × 82.7mm) BMW M62 4-valve petrol V8 with four overhead camshafts and VANOS variable inlet camshaft control
    Bosch Motronic 7.2 electronic engine management system
    10:1 compression ratio
    282bhp at 5400rpm
    325lb ft at 3600rpm

4.4-litre Jaguar V8 (2005–2009)
4394cc (88mm × 90.3mm) Jaguar AJ-8 4-valve petrol V8 with four overhead camshafts
    Denso EMS engine management system with sequential multi-port injection
    10.75:1 compression ratio
    306bhp at 5750rpm
    324lb ft at 4000rpm

4.2-litre Supercharged V8 (2005–2009)
4197cc (86mm × 90.3mm) Jaguar AJ-V8 4-valve petrol V8 with four overhead camshafts and Eaton supercharger with intercooler
    Denso EMS engine management system with sequential multi-port injection
    9.1:1 compression ratio
    390bhp at 5750rpm
    410lb ft at 3500rpm

TDV8 diesel (2006 on)
3630cc (81mm × 88mm) Ford–Land Rover 4-valve diesel V8 with four overhead camshafts, twin turbochargers and intercooler
    Common-rail direct injection
    17.3:1 compression ratio
    268bhp at 4000rpm
    472lb ft at 2000rpm

5-litre Jaguar V8 (2009 on)
5000cc (92.5mm × 93mm) Jaguar-Land Rover LR-V8 petrol V8 with four camshafts and four valves per cylinder
    9.5:1 compression ratio
    375bhp at 6000rpm
    375lb ft at 2500rpm

5-litre Supercharged V8 (2009 on)
5000cc (92.5mm × 93mm) Jaguar–Land Rover LR-V8 4-valve petrol V8 with four camshafts and four valves per cylinder plus Eaton twin-vortex supercharger with intercooler
    9.5:1 compression ratio
    510bhp at 6000rpm
    460lb ft at 2500rpm

Transmission

Permanent four-wheel drive with Torsen centre differential
Final drive ratio: 3.54:1 (TDV8 models); 3.73:1 (BMW V8, Jaguar V8 and supercharged models); 4.10:1 (Td6 models)

Primary gearbox

Td6 models (2002–2006 model-years)
Five-speed GM automatic with manual over-ride control system; ratios 3.42:1, 2.21:1, 1.60:1, 1.00:1, 0.75:1, reverse 3.03:1

BMW V8 models (2002–2005 model-years)
Five-speed ZF 5HP24 automatic with manual over-ride control system; ratios 3.57:1, 2.20:1, 1.51:1, 1.00:1, 0.80:1, reverse 4.10:1

AJ-V8 models (2006–2009 model-years) and TDV8 models (2007–2009 model-years)
Six-speed ZF 6HP26 automatic with manual over-ride control system; ratios 4.171:1, 2.340:1, 1.521:1, 1.143:1, 0.867:1, 0.691:1, reverse 3.403:1

LR-V8 models (2010 model-year onwards)
Six-speed ZF 6HP28 automatic with manual over-ride control system; ratios as for 6HP 26 gearbox

Transfer gearbox

Separate 2-speed Magna chain-driven type; High ratio 1.00:1, Low ratio 2.70:1 (2001–2006) or 2.93:1 (2006 on)

Suspension

Front suspension with MacPherson struts and double lower wishbones; rear suspension with double wishbones. Cross-linked electronic air springs all round with automatic height adjustment and manual over-ride system

Steering

Rack-and-pinion with Servotronic speed-variable power assistance

Brakes

Four-wheel disc brakes with dual hydraulic line, servo assistance and Bosch 5.2 ABS. Separate parking brake acting on drums in the rear discs

BMW-engined models (2002–2007 model-years)
Ventilated front discs with 13.54in (344mm) diameter and four-piston callipers
Solid rear discs with 13.93 in (354mm) diameter and two-piston callipers

AJ-V8 and TDV8 models (2006–2009 model-years)
Ventilated front discs with 344mm diameter and sliding callipers (AJ-V8); ventilated front discs with 360mm diameter and four-piston fixed callipers (supercharged V8 and TDV8)
Ventilated rear discs with 354mm diameter and sliding callipers

LR-V8 and TDV8 models (2010 model-year on)
Ventilated front discs with 360mm diameter and twin-piston sliding callipers
Ventilated rear discs with 354mm diameter and single-piston sliding callipers

LR-V8 supercharged models (2010 model-year on)
Ventilated front discs with 380mm diameter and Brembo six-piston fixed monoblock callipers
Ventilated rear discs with 365mm diameter and single-piston sliding callipers

Vehicle dimensions

Wheelbase:	113.4in (2880mm)
Overall length:	194.8in (4950mm)
Overall width:	86.26in (2191mm)
Overall height:	73.35in (1863mm) at standard ride height
Track (front):	64.13in (1629mm)
(rear):	64in (1626mm)
Kerb weight (for typical UK-market models):	
Td6 diesel models:	5368lb (2435kg)
4.4-litre BMW V8 models:	5379lb (2440kg)
4.4-litre Jaguar V8 models:	5729lb (2599kg)
4.2-litre supercharged V8 models:	5923lb (2687kg)
TDV8 diesel models:	5990lb (2717kg); 2010MY: 6049lb (2744kg)

Performance

Td6 diesel models
Maximum speed:	111mph (179km/h)	*0–62mph:*	13.6secs

BMW V8 models
Maximum speed:	130mph (209km/h)	*0–62mph:*	9.2secs

4.4-litre AJ-V8 models
Maximum speed:	124mph (200km/h)	*0–62mph:*	8.7secs

4.2-litre supercharged models
Maximum speed:	130mph (210km/h)	*0–62mph:*	7.5secs

TDV8 diesel models
Maximum speed:	124mph (200km/h)	*0–62mph:*	9.2secs

5.0-litre LR-V8 models
Maximum speed:	130mph (210km/h)	*0–62mph:*	7.6secs

5.0-litre supercharged models
Maximum speed:	140mph (225km/h)	*0–62mph:*	5.9secs

Range Rover L322 Prices in the UK, 2002 on

These figures are showroom prices for Range Rover models without extras. All figures are inclusive of value added tax (VAT).

Date	Model	Price (£)	Remarks
2002 Feb	Td6 SE	42,995	
	Td6 HSE	45,995	
	V8 SE	49,995	
	Td6 Vogue	51,995	
	V8 HSE	52,995	
	V8 Vogue	59,995	
2003	Td6 SE	43,995	
	Td6 HSE	46,995	
	V8 SE	49,995	
	Td6 Vogue	52,995	
	V8 HSE	52,995	
	V8 Vogue	59,995	
2003 Nov	Autobiography Edition	65,995	£69,995 with DVD twin-screen package
2004	Td6 SE	45,995	
	Td6 HSE	48,995	
	V8 SE	50,995	
	V8 HSE	53,995	
	Td6 Vogue	54,995	Now more expensive than V8 HSE
	V8 Vogue	60,995	
2005 Sep	35th Anniversary Edition	85,000	
2005 Oct	Td6 SE	46,000	
	Td6 HSE	49,500	
	V8 SE	51,000	
	V8 HSE	54,500	
	Td6 Vogue	57,000	
	V8 Vogue	62,000	
	Td6 Vogue SE	63,000	
	V8 Vogue SE	68,500	
	Supercharged Vogue SE	73,000	
	35th Anniversary Edition	85,000	
2006 Sep	TDV8 HSE	53,995	
	V8 HSE	55,075	
	TDV8 Vogue	61,825	
	V8 Vogue	62,875	
	TDV8 Vogue SE	68,825	
	V8 Vogue SE	69,875	
	Supercharged Vogue SE	74,795	
2007	TDV8 HSE	55,110	
	Supercharged Vogue SE	74,900	
2008	TDV8 HSE	56,000	
	TDV8 Vogue	63,700	
	TDV8 Vogue SE	68,600	First appearance of this model
	Supercharged	72,700	
2009 Mar	Westminster	62,995	£63,995 with Marina Black metallic paint
2009 Sep	TDV8 Vogue	64,695	
	TDV8 Vogue SE	70,995	
	TDV8 Autobiography	75,695	
	Supercharged Autobiography	79,995	

engines to have been designed from the outset for both Jaguar and Land Rover. Both supercharged and unsupercharged derivatives shared the same 5-litre swept volume, and the design brief had been to deliver more refinement as well as more performance. Development had begun some time around 2003, and the engines shared their basic four-cam, 4-valve architecture and all-alloy construction with the outgoing 4.2-litre and 4.4-litre types.

However, there were important changes. The cylinder block, for example, was now high-pressure die-cast rather than sand cast like earlier Range Rover V8s, and both block and cylinder heads were made from recycled aluminium alloy. A new direct-injection fuel system optimized fuel efficiency, and there was torque-actuated variable camshaft timing on all four camshafts. Land Rover claimed that engine noise was reduced by 3dB, or around half, on the unsupercharged engine and that there were improvements in both CO_2 emissions and fuel economy. This engine also met both EU5 and the US ULEV2 emissions requirements. Intended mainly for the US and Middle Eastern markets, the engine boasted 375bhp and delivered performance that was almost equal to that of the outgoing 4.2-litre supercharged type.

The new supercharged 5-litre engine had an equally new Eaton twin-vortex supercharger. It delivered a much greater punch than the old one at all speeds, and Land Rover claimed that engine noise was reduced by 4dB and that supercharger whine had been completely eliminated – which some sporting drivers found disappointing. Electronic torque limitation protected the transmission, and the huge increase to 460lb ft allowed taller final drive gearing to be used, so reducing both CO_2 emissions and fuel consumption.

Not surprisingly, there was a host of new technology elsewhere in the vehicle. The new Adaptive Dynamics system optimized suspension and powertrain settings and incorporated refinements to the Stability Control, Terrain Response and Hill Descent Control systems. For low-speed manoeuvring in confined spaces there was a Surround Camera system which showed views all round the vehicle on the dashboard screen, and a new Blind Spot Monitoring System that flashed a warning in the mirror if one of the cameras detected a vehicle in the driver's blind spot.

Also new was the Adaptive Cruise Control seen earlier on the Range Rover Sport, while a new Advanced Emergency Brake Assist system linked the cruise control's distance radar to the brakes to prevent the Range Rover crashing into the vehicle in front. Last but not least, Trailer Stability Assist worked through the traction systems to help the driver regain control if a trailer starting snaking, and Towing Assist used the cameras and the monitor screen to make reversing up to a trailer for hitching simpler than it had ever been.

There was further innovation in the instrument pack, where a TFT (Thin Film Technology) screen replaced the traditional collection of dials. Blank when the Range Rover was parked, the screen displayed back-projected dials when the car's passive detection system recognized the ignition fob (there was now no actual key). Between the main dials, another virtual screen delivered important driver information, and in some circumstances (such as off-road), the speedometer moved off to the right to make room for a graphic showing what the wheels were doing.

The 2010 models were also the first vehicles anywhere to feature dual-view 'infotainment' screen technology. The touch screen in the centre of the dash used Parallax Barrier Technology to allow the front seat passenger to watch TV while the driver was using the satnav; looking at the screen from different angles, they saw different displays and could not see each other's display. That satnav was also no longer DVD-based. Instead, its data was uploaded to a dedicated on-board hard drive,

Parallax Barrier Technology on the 2010 Range Rovers allowed the passenger to watch TV while the driver saw only a screen displaying driving information.

The facia was also overhauled quite extensively for 2010. The back-projected instruments allowed more information to be displayed, but only when the driver needed it and without introducing unnecessary clutter.

and annual updates were to be made available through Land Rover dealers for uploading to the vehicle.

Announced at the Frankfurt Motor Show in September 2009 for January 2010 sales were two further luxury options. One was electronically adjustable reclining rear seats, intended mainly for chauffeur-driven vehicles. These were controlled by the rear seat passengers and could be had with both heating and cooling, four-way adjustable lumbar support and airline-style winged head restraints. Laminated rear-door privacy glass also reduced noise levels in the rear. The second enhancement was the optional availability of the harmon/kardon Logic 7 1200-watt High Dynamics audio system, with fifteen independent channels driving nineteen premium quality speakers.

... And Onwards

At the time of writing in late 2009, the L322 Range Rover was expected to remain in production until 2013 or 2014, and its replacement (then being developed as project L405) was anticipated in late 2013. It seemed unlikely that there would be any major changes to the model in its final four years, although a strong possibility was the introduction of an entry-level variant using the new 3.0-litre TDV6 diesel engine with its twin sequential turbochargers. The attraction of this would be to bring down the base price of the Range Rover at a time when sales were slow as the world recovered from recession. There was also a strong possibility that an enlarged 4.0-litre derivative of the TDV8 would be introduced, perhaps in a 40th Anniversary special edition.

One thing, however, was very clear. The growing importance of environmental concerns meant that the L322 would almost certainly be the last of the big Range Rovers. Land Rover was working on drastic weight reductions and on downsizing, although that was likely to be achieved through more efficient packaging rather than through reductions in the passenger space so important in a Range Rover. The new model would have to be more fuel-efficient and also incorporate some kind of hybrid powertrain. So the fourth-generation Range Rover was likely to be a very different machine from the L322 as it took the respected brand towards its half-century of achievement.

The 2010 model-year also brought new 5-litre versions of the V8 engine. One was unsupercharged; the other had the latest twin-vortex supercharger.

CHAPTER TEN

Building the L322

Ford pumped a huge amount of money into the Solihull plant to ensure that the third-generation Range Rover would be manufactured and assembled to the very highest standards. The dedicated facilities for the model's production had cost nearly £200 million by the time production began late in 2001. In addition, the new model benefited from a series of earlier changes at the Solihull site, many of them funded by BMW, and from a number of new working practices which had been introduced during the later 1990s – in both cases largely associated with the start of Freelander production in 1997.

Among the changes in working practices, it is important to highlight the major increase in automation on the assembly lines, which was mainly brought about in order to deliver more consistent quality. Land Rover had traditionally been wedded to a great deal of hand assembly, and nowhere was the change more evident than in Block 1, the old South Block, where the highly automated assembly lines for the new Range Rover ran alongside those for the Defender, which still depended heavily on traditional methods of assembly.

The increased automation also allowed for high production volumes. Although Solihull was turning out only 353 Range Rovers a week as production got under way in 2001, from the beginning of 2002 volume was ramped up to 760 vehicles a week.

For L322, Land Rover also brought a number of manufacturing operations in-house, largely in order to save costs. In particular, body panels were now pressed on-site at Solihull, although this change was to a degree counter-balanced by the increased number of drivetrain components – engines and transmissions – which were brought into the factory by road as complete assemblies. In addition, the new Range Rover no longer depended on Solihull's own Trim Shop for interior trim and fittings. Instead, the seats and, quite strikingly, the dashboards were brought into the factory as complete assemblies from outside suppliers. A computer-controlled Just-In-Time system reduced the need for large storage areas full of parts waiting to be assembled into new vehicles; instead, there were

The massive panel press installed for L322 manufacture made Land Rover almost wholly independent of outside pressings suppliers. Seen here in the first picture is a batch of freshly stamped left-hand inner body frames; the second picture shows a batch of right-hand outer body frames.

There was a vast increase in automation in the L322 assembly process. These bodyshells are passing along the Framing Line in the Body-In-White plant; the robot arms are welding machines.

small buffer zones where components were held until called forward to the assembly lines.

It is also worth highlighting the sheer complexity of the assembly operation for the L322. The third-generation Range Rover was built up from more than 6,000 parts – over twice as many as had been used in the assembly of its predecessor.

The Stamping Plant

Land Rover was particularly proud of its new stamping plant, which had cost £60 million to build and began producing new Range Rover panels in late 2000. The new plant was also earmarked for the production of panels for the new BMW Mini – which would be assembled in the UK at the Cowley plant near Oxford – and after Land Rover was sold to Ford it continued to fulfil that function.

The new plant was officially opened by HRH the Duke of Kent in December 2000, and at the time contained the largest press (in terms of bed size) anywhere in Europe. The press itself was manufactured by Müller Weingarten, and was a five-station 8300-tonne crossbar transfer type that was capable of producing a maximum of 58,000 panels per week. It was mounted on a gigantic damped concrete block which absorbed noise and vibration when the press was in action.

Most importantly for the Range Rover, its pressings were of exceptional accuracy, which contributed to top-quality fit and finish for L322. Among its products, the Range Rover's bonnet was thought to be the largest single pressing of its kind anywhere in Europe.

So every new L322 Range Rover body started life here as a series of metal blanks, which were turned into

Despite the high degree of automation in the Body-In-White plant, there was still some hand checking and hand-finishing to ensure bodies were completed to the highest possible standards.

Paint Shop 21 had been in operation since the late 1990s and had been configured to cope with Land Rover's anticipated twenty-first century requirements. This picture shows it when it was new; some modifications were necessary to cope with the size of the L322's bodyshells.

Painted bodyshells – at this stage with their doors in place – move by conveyor out of the Paint Shop and into the Final Assembly hall.

shaped panels and were then shipped onward to the Body-In-White plant.

Body-In-White

The Body-In-White plant was built on the site of some earlier buildings within the East Works at Lode Lane, and the new facility cost a further £80 million. Its function was to turn the pressings and panels turned out by the stamping plant into complete Range Rover bodyshells, and when production began it was capable of producing ten complete Range Rover bodies every hour.

The BIW plant was one area where the step-change to automated assembly was most obvious. A very large percentage – 73% – of the process was fully automated, and a total of 128 robots provided 6,350 welds for each Range Rover body. Nevertheless, BIW still employed 344 people on a two-shift system.

The Paint Shop

From BIW in the East Works, the bodyshells passed to Paint Shop 21

The Range Rover's underpinnings take shape on the Powertrain Sub-Assembly line. There were three separate sub-frames to carry the suspension, engine and transmission. These are early models with the BMW petrol V8 engine.

Here's why those tilt slings were necessary: a great deal had to be fitted to the underside of the bodyshell at this stage, before it met up with its powertrain and suspension. Visible here are the saddle-type fuel tank and some of the underbody sound-deadening and insulation panels.

The doors were removed from the bodyshells and moved to a separate sub-assembly line. The bodyshells were then mounted in 'slings' which both transported them along the overhead conveyor line and allowed them to be tilted for better access.

(the number simply identified the building and its location). This had actually been built in the mid-1990s to accommodate the then new Freelander. At the time, it was the largest of its kind in Europe, and it was built to cope with anticipated Land Rover requirements well into the twenty-first century. It was also designed to meet existing and anticipated environmental legislation, and to minimize energy

consumption. Water-borne paint technology reduced volatile organic compound material, while emissions from the paint curing ovens were treated by a five-canister regenerative oxidizer which drew a significant proportion of its energy needs from the oxidation of the very fumes it was de-toxing.

Even so, the Paint Shop had to be modified to the tune of £15 million to cope with the weight and size of the new Range Rover's bodyshell, which was then thought to be the largest monocoque construction in the motoring world. An upgrade to the electrocoat oven was also incorporated to ensure the best possi-

ble finish, and a revised cavity wax insulation booth was added. This enabled Land Rover to offer an extended corrosion warranty on the vehicle of up to six years for anti-perforation cover and three years for cosmetic cover.

The Assembly Process

From the Paint Shop, fully painted bodyshells were taken by conveyor into the assembly hall in Block 1. Here, Range Rovers were assembled on a dedicated line.

Block 1 was actually the oldest assembly area on the Lode Lane site, having opened for business in 1945. It was also the building where the first Land Rovers had been assembled in 1948, and even though it had been quite comprehensively extended since then, traces of the original building and its layout were still visible on the inside walls. However, the requirements of the L322 assembly lines had led to a massive refit, which had cost £40 million. Much of the floor area which was taken over for the L322 lines was originally the site of such things as the Jig Shop and the Experimental Shop, while the 'marketplace'

The L322 depended heavily on electronic systems, and as a result its wiring harness was enormously complex. A sample was displayed – in two sections – next to the Trim and Final Assembly line, in order to remove any doubts about what went where!

ABOVE: More work is being done here on the underside of a bodyshell on the Pre-Body line in Trim and Final Assembly.

RIGHT: This was the 'marriage' of bodyshell and sub-frames. Note that the doors had still not been re-united with the body. The cradle carrying the sub-frames, suspension and powertrain was lifted up to meet the bodyshell as it came in on an overhead conveyor. Once everything was correctly lined up, automatic nut runners would bolt the two together and the semi-completed vehicle would pass on its way. The long strip of paper hanging from the bonnet is the vehicle's build specification.

at the end of the lines where new Range Rovers were handed over from the Production Department to the Despatch Department was on the site of the now-demolished Product Investigation Department and Service Department.

The new assembly lines in Block 1 were designed to allow for a peak capacity of 35,000 Range Rovers a year at a rate of ten vehicles every hour on two shifts. Key to their function was a new overhead track which carried the bodyshells from each station to the next. It was this which had accounted for a large proportion of the rebuilding costs, because the whole building had to be stripped of its original roof, which was then replaced by one that was strong enough to support the over-head track. A completely new floor was also installed, along with more modern ventilation.

The Range Rover lines were also designed to incorporate the latest thinking about working practices and staff welfare. So the assembly line staff were provided with large enclosed rest areas which were integrated with the offices of what Land Rover called 'process leaders' but would probably have been known as section foremen in the days when the South Block was built. The assembly stations on the line had the latest ergonomic lifting aids and power tools, and a special feature was the inclusion of several tilt slings which allowed the body to be rotated to give better access to the underside. Working conditions were comfortable, too: these lines were not plagued by constant noise from the traditional pneumatic assembly tools, because all the tools used here were electrically powered.

There were ninety stations on the assembly line, which began as the powertrains (shipped in from outside suppliers) met up with the sub-frames which were to carry them. The rear sub-frame was also assembled into a cradle and the suspension, braking and steering components all gradually came together as the line progressed.

Meanwhile, the painted bodyshells were fed into the assembly area from the Paint Shop, arriving by overhead conveyor. They first passed along a 'pre-body' line where the doors were removed to a line-side assembly area where they were built up with window winding mechanisms, locks,

LEFT: *Still with the doors off, to allow assembly staff better access, the half-finished Range Rovers passed down the Trim line. The dashboard assembly and windscreen have already been fitted to this example, and work is being carried out to fit elements of the rear trim.*

ABOVE: *The doors had been removed not only to improve access to the interior but also because they had their own complicated assembly operation. Here the right-hand front and rear doors from one vehicle are fitted out on the Door Sub-assembly line.*

and so on. Meanwhile, additional work on the underside prepared the bodyshells for the meeting with their designated running-gear. To make this work on the underside easier, the shells were turned in their tilt slings to a convenient angle. Other items fitted at this stage included some of the soundproofing, such as the underbonnet insulation pad. Doors were then reunited with their parent bodies before the completed assemblies passed on to the next stage.

Traditionally, every car assembly line had a 'body drop' area where the body was lowered onto the running-gear, and this had been the case with both earlier models of Range Rover. However, the process was reversed for the L322 lines. The running-

gear on its three sub-frames was in fact lifted up to meet the body, and the platform which carried it could not be lowered until every mounting point had been tightened to the correct torque. This was achieved by means of a series of nut runners, which were automatically operated but were also guided by assembly line staff. Land Rover used a new term to describe this part of the Range Rover assembly process: rather than the 'body drop', this was known as the 'marriage' area.

The part-finished Range Rovers now passed to the Trim and Final Assembly area of the line, where interior trim panels, headlinings, carpets, dashboard assemblies and seats were added as they progressed slowly

down the line. All this part of the process was dependent on the computer-controlled Just-In-Time delivery system, which ensured that the correct configuration of dashboard, the correct colour of seats, and so on, arrived in time. Then windscreen and rear side glazing were applied by robot after another robot had applied the coating of glue.

Right at the end of the assembly process was an electrical station, where two important functions were carried out. One was the programming of the various on-board ECUs, which had been fitted as 'blanks' but were now configured to suit the electrical equipment built into the vehicle. The other was a full electrical check, which was indispensable

Powered lifting devices reduced the risk of injury for the assembly line staff, and one of their uses is seen here. In the first picture, two wheels have already been fitted to a 2009 model as it nears the end of the line. In the second picture, taken some years earlier, an associate double-checks the tightness of a wheel nut by hand.

for a vehicle with an electrical system that was as complex as that built into the L322. In setting up this part of the assembly lines, Land Rover had probably been acutely aware of the electrical problems that had afflicted the 38A Range Rover, and had done their very best to ensure that the L322 would not suffer from the same maladies.

Finally came the 'buy-off' line where each vehicle was examined for faults. Those which passed all checks were then moved to the 'market-place' to await collection by the Despatch Department, who would send them on to dealers or overseas sales companies as appropriate.

End of the line. A completed Range Rover – in this case an early BMW V8-engined model destined for the USA – gets a final appraisal.

CHAPTER ELEVEN

Range Rover Sport: Design and Development

Just as the first-generation Range Rover lent its chassis to the new Land Rover Discovery in 1989, so a planned new Discovery lent its chassis – and many other elements – to a new model branded as the Range Rover Sport in 2005. It was, however, a much more complicated story than that simple statement suggests.

The story of the Range Rover Sport can be traced back to the second half of 2000, just a few months after Ford had bought Land Rover from BMW. As an early priority, Ford reviewed Land Rover's future-model strategy, and as part of that review asked everyone then working on a new project to take a fresh look at what they were doing.

At that stage, the project that was intended to deliver a new Discovery centred on two separate but closely related vehicles. The model then code-named L50 was intended to be a sporty five-seater variant to meet US tastes; Land Rover North America were asking for what was in effect a smaller Discovery with a flat roof – 'a sort of Discovery Sport', as designer Dave Saddington explained it. Meanwhile, L51 was a long-wheelbase seven-seater to suit the Discovery's traditional 'family' market.

As far as possible, the two were to share common elements, and to minimize cost and complication they were to be built on a separate chassis which would be made with two different wheelbases. At BMW's request, there were to be beam axles (which would ensure the new Land Rovers did not challenge BMW's own X5 with its all-independent suspension), and the power units were also to come from BMW.

However, L50 and L51 had run into problems and the project had begun to drift. The biggest difficulty was with the five-seater model, where it was difficult to keep manufacturing costs in check so that the vehicle could be sold at Discovery price levels. As designer Mike Sampson remembered, 'We struggled with it enormously in Design, Engineering and Marketing terms. Nobody really knew what it was!' Dave Saddington recalled the same uneasiness about the vehicle's definition: 'The seven-seater had a clear business case but nobody could nail down any sales volumes for the five-seater. It was going to be first into a new market.'

That fresh look which the new Ford management had called for bore fruit. Dave Saddington put one of the full-size models between a Range Rover and a Discovery Series II, and with skilful use of black tape masked off some elements of the design. 'I tried to get people to think of it as a baby Range Rover rather than as

Early thinking about L320 envisaged a design with what Mike Sampson called '1.5 doors' on each side. It would have given the vehicle a sporting appearance without losing the practical appeal of a four-door layout. The cockpit-style interior is already in evidence here.

The year was still 2000, and Mike Sampson was exploring the '1.5-door' idea further. The edge-pull door handles were deliberately intended to recall the original 1970 Range Rover. Note that the name of Range Rover Sport had already been suggested by this stage, although it had not been formally adopted.

a Discovery-minus,' he explained. 'This automatically put it into a higher price bracket, so there was no longer any need to bring it down to a price. That made for a better business case!'

This proved an important turning-point. Ford management picked up the idea and decided to run with it, possibly influenced by the knowledge that other manufacturers already had plans for sporty SUV models such as this 'baby Range Rover' could become. So although L50 and L51 were formally abandoned late in 2000, some of the work that had gone into them was carried over into a pair of projects which had a similarly symbiotic relationship. Under the Ford project numbering system, these became L319 (which would deliver the new Discovery with its long wheelbase and seven-seat configuration) and L320 (which would be the sporty 'baby Range Rover').

As a first stage, all the requirements for the new models had to be fed into a chassis design programme, and Land Rover's Steve Haywood was appointed to lead this in autumn 2000. Ford was keen on building L319 and L320 on the 'platform' (chassis and suspension) of the then unreleased new Ford Explorer (model U152), and in September 2000 Haywood and a group of chassis and packaging engineers began a three-month stint in Dearborn when they examined this option very thoroughly.

But the Explorer proved unsuitable. 'It was too low to the ground,' explained Steve Haywood.

More conventional, but still a Range Rover: this is a Mike Sampson sketch which presents L320 as a two-door model, more like the original Range Rover.

**L.320
RANGE ROVER** *SPORT*

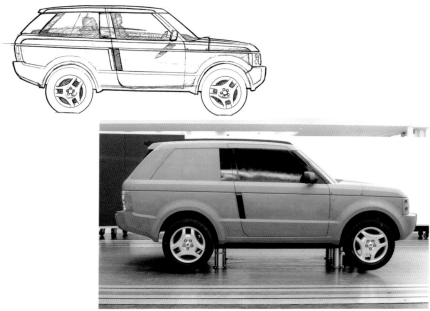

CENTRE: The two-door L320 was progressed to a full-size clay. Here it is being built in the Design Studio; the darker line around the roof area is the outline of a slightly different treatment that was being portrayed on the other side.

RIGHT: The completed two-door clay carried Range Sport badging on its bonnet. Once again this was simply what the designers were calling it at the time; officially, it had no name other than Project L320. The rear end looks rather odd from this angle because of the alternative designs on each side of the model.

The TDV6 and TDV8 Diesel Engines

The origins of the TDV6 and TDV8 diesel engines used in the Range Rover Sport can be traced back to 1998, two years before Ford bought Land Rover from BMW. That was when Ford and PSA Peugeot-Citroen signed an agreement known as Gemini to develop a new family of diesel engines for joint use. Part of the plan was to develop a turbocharged V6 engine that would be suitable for transverse installation in Peugeot and Citroen models while also being suitable for north–south installation in Ford's Jaguar saloons; Ford knew it as the Lion engine, apparently in honour of Peugeot's lion logo.

In practice, the V6 engine project was a lot more difficult than the two companies had originally hoped, but it did deliver a world-class diesel engine that appeared first in 206bhp twin-turbo form in the Jaguar XJ saloon in summer 2004. In Jaguar form, it was known as an AJD-V6 type and was built at Ford's Dagenham engine plant.

The AJD-V6 was the first to use a block made of Compacted Graphite Iron, which gave high strength, stiffness and durability, so allowing the block to be smaller and therefore lighter. Its density also helped to minimize noise transmission. There were aluminium cylinder heads set at an angle of 60 degrees, four valves per cylinder, and belt-driven twin overhead camshafts.

While the V6 diesel engine was still under development in summer 2000, Ford bought Land Rover. Examination of Land Rover's engine product plans immediately made clear that the BMW engines around which the forthcoming Range Rover had been designed would have to remain in the programme for the time being: its development was too far advanced for them to be changed before production began. However, Ford did not want to buy in BMW engines for any longer than necessary, and so a new and very refined large-capacity high-performance diesel engine was a must for the Range Rover. An important factor was that this engine had to be ready to meet the EU4 emissions regulations that would come into force on 1 January 2007.

First thoughts were to use the new 2.7-litre V6 diesel in the Range Rover. With twin turbochargers, as in the Jaguar installation, it was already a long way down the development road and looked like a natural choice for Land Rover's flagship. Using a single-turbo version in the L319 (Discovery 3) and L320 (Range Rover Sport) models whose development was initiated at about this time would ensure satisfactory model differentiation while minimizing manufacturing costs and complication.

However, it quickly became apparent that the twin-turbo V6 would not fit into the Range Rover. The problem was that the Range Rover had its differential attached to the structure, and that this arrangement would have compromised the engine mountings for the V6. For the Discovery 3 and Sport, there was no such problem, and so that installation went ahead as planned. For Land Rover use, the engine was built with a single turbocharger and a 190bhp power output. Known as the TDV6, it differed from Jaguar derivatives in having a single-piece front cover, a special sump with baffle-plates, and an engine-driven cooling fan.

The obvious next step was to create a special version of the engine for the Range Rover. From the early days of the Gemini programme, the Ford team had kept in mind the possibility of one day developing a V8 version of the new engine. As a V8 derivative was of no interest to PSA, it had not been part of the Gemini agreement, but Ford was free to draw on technology from that agreement and incorporate it in other engines as it saw fit. A V8 diesel would be absolutely ideal for the Range Rover, and so outline planning work soon began at Ford's research centre in Aachen, Germany, on the engine known as the Lion V8.

At this stage, the engine was very much a Ford project, even though it was being drawn up specifically for the Range Rover. The Ford team did look at other potential applications – among them the Jaguar XJ and XK cars – but decided not to pursue them. This single-application requirement simplified the task of preparing the engine for production, remembered Grant Horne, who was appointed Land Rover's Programme Manager for the Lion V8 engine in March 2001.

Although the Lion V8 was very closely related to the Lion V6, the differences between the two engines in fact outnumbered the similarities. The key carry-over feature was the combustion chamber design – the most expensive and time-consuming element in designing a modern diesel engine – and for this reason the bore and stroke dimensions of the two engines were also the same. This commonality would in due course allow for the V6 and V8 diesels to be assembled on the same lines at Ford's Dagenham engines plant.

Later, a new combustion chamber would be designed for the 3-litre TDV6 engine that was announced for the 2010 model-year, leading to speculation that a 4-litre TDV8 using the same modified bore and stroke dimensions would follow.

Despite these common elements, there would be fundamental differences in the design of the two engines from the start. The 6-cylinder was designed with a 60-degree angle between the cylinder banks, which gave the best balance and refinement in a V6 configuration. However, V8s need a 90-degree angle to get the best balance, and ultimate refinement was of course one of the drivers in the Range Rover programme. So the Lion V8 was designed from the start with a 90-degree angle between its cylinder banks.

This in turn created some extra challenges associated with the oil drain for the twin turbochargers, which were to be mounted low down. The solution was to use a scavenge pump, as this was the only way to guarantee satisfactory performance at some of the peculiar operating angles associated with Range Rovers in off-road use. Meanwhile, the Lion V8 was also given a chain-drive for the camshafts in place of the V6's belt drive, to cope with the greater stresses in the larger engine. The injection pump was also mounted at the front of the engine instead of the rear, mainly for packaging reasons.

The single-turbo 2.7-litre TDV6 had started life as Jaguar's AJD-V6 with twin turbochargers, but was adapted for the Range Rover Sport.

Once the design had been completed, the Aachen Research centre handed the Lion V8 over to Land Rover as a CAD package to begin the development phase of the engine. This was carried out at Ford's Dunton research centre in the UK by a joint team of Land Rover and Ford engineers. 'We were trying to learn from the V6 and to feed in the Land Rover

---

The TDV6 and TDV8 Diesel Engines *continued*

requirements,' recalled Grant Horne. 'At this stage, the Ford people had little knowledge of Land Rover products and of their special needs.'

The Dunton phase lasted for some six or eight months, and after that the programme was transferred to Dagenham. 'Ford put in an engine programme manager to oversee development,' says Grant, 'a chap called Roland Ernst who was a very good guy.'

With just two years left before the engine was needed in production, the normal Ford process of three prototype stages had to be telescoped down to two. Here, the experience gained from the Lion V6 proved invaluable. No major problems showed up, but several changes were made between the first 'Batch 1' prototypes and the improved 'Batch 3' engines. This development phase ended in early 2005, and over the next nine months the new tooling was prepared. Everything was ready by the engineering sign-off target date of November 2005, and the first 250 engines built on the production tooling (and assembled on the same line as the V6 diesels at Dagenham) were used for testing and to establish and check build processes. Engine Job 1 – the first proper production engine – was built in April 2006, and over the next four months production engines were tested in vehicles. Then finally, Range Rover Job 1 – the first production Range Rover TDV8 – left the lines on schedule during August.

By this time, the TDV8 engine had also been earmarked for the Range Rover Sport, and the V8 diesel Sport was announced shortly after the 2007 Range Rover. To suit the Sport installation, the TDV8's sump had to be redesigned to suit the different differential mounting of the T5 chassis. Then the turbochargers had to be relocated about 100mm further back to suit the different engine bay packaging. Finally, and most obviously, the front-end drive had to be redesigned to accommodate the pump for the anti-roll suspension on the Sport. This pump was fitted in underneath the alternator, so the alternator had to move up and the Sport version of the engine wound up with two belt drives instead of the one of the Range Rover engine. In addition, the Sport's exhaust was specially tuned 'to give more of a rasp,' explained Grant Horne.

The approach and departure angles were inadequate, and there was insufficient suspension travel. So it would have needed too much new hardware. We also studied the interior package, and the Command Driving Position just wasn't there. Those two fundamentals were too far from the brand DNA, and the platform was too important for Land Rover's future. So we convinced management that we needed a new platform.

Work on that new platform, which was coded T5, began at the very end of 2000. Just one important design element survived from Land Rover's brush with the Explorer. This was the 'portholes' in the rear chassis side members, which allowed the driveshafts to run through rather than under the chassis rails. Freed of the earlier BMW requirement to use beam axles, the T5 team decided also to incorporate the latest cross-linked all-independent air suspension that Land Rover had developed for the still-secret L322 Range Rover. Also in the design stages was the system which later became known as Terrain Response (*see* sidebar, page 129) and when it became clear from customer clinics that buyers wanted features

that would make their lives easier, the T5 team decided to incorporate this into the new platform as well.

The basics of the T5 platform were clear by the middle of 2001; most importantly, some of the traditional load-bearing function of a chassis was to be transferred to the body structure so that the chassis itself could

be lighter. Weight was to be minimized by having the chassis members made by the then new hydro-forming process, and GKN Dana started work on a new joint-venture factory at Telford in Shropshire purely to turn out these new chassis for Land Rover. With all the key elements in place, Steve Haywood changed jobs

The four-door body became policy, but there was still no firm decision on the name. This sketch by Mike Sampson shows a design quite close to the one chosen for production, but the bonnet badge is still the rather uncomfortable 'Range Sport'.

Geoff Upex (left) had been appointed Design Director for Land Rover under the Ford regime, and he oversaw the design of L320. Studio Director with direct responsibility for the L320 team was Richard Woolley (right).

to become Chief Programme Engineer for the new L319 Discovery.

At this stage, L320 had no other name – although the Gaydon engineers knew it as the Baby Range Rover and early drawings by Mike Sampson show that the Range Rover Sport name was around from the start. But it did have its own Chief Programme Engineer. John Hall, who was then in charge of Advanced Vehicle Design and had run the L50

and L51 programmes, stepped in to give the programme a kick-start himself. Only after things had got properly under way did he hand over the reins to Tom Jones.

An important issue right from the start was defining what this new vehicle was. The benchmarks were seen as the BMW X5, the Porsche Cayenne, and some derivatives of the Mercedes-Benz ML-class. 'Our brief was to create an all-new product for Land Rover that embodied Range Rover style in a more compact, sporty package,' remembered Richard Woolley, who was appointed Chief Designer from the start. Stuart Frith, who later became Chief Programme Engineer, pointed out that agility was seen as a key element in the vehicle's make-up. 'Land Rover had developed the phrase 'sports tourer' to align the project team behind a clear concept,' he remembered.

Door Experiments

The initial design sketches for L320 were done in late 2000, before the engineering programme started in earnest. Among those first sketches were some by Mike Sampson which envisaged L320 as a two-door model with a number of design cues from the original Range Rover. These included edge-pull door handles,

a clamshell bonnet, and even a mock-up of the twin fans behind the grille! Richard Woolley believed that the two-door configuration 'could epitomize the sporty aspect I was looking for, and help reinforce L320's individuality among its stablemates.'

However, the two-door idea did not last long. Customer research fed into the L320 programme made quite clear that buyers wanted a four-door layout, and so the programme embraced that. But this was to be a very different kind of Land Rover product, and so Mike Sampson proposed what he calls a one-and-a-half door layout for each side. There would be a long front door, to give the appearance of a sporty coupé, with a rear-hinged half-size back door. This looked like a flyer for a time, and in fact an engineering package prototype was built on the chassis of a 38A Range Rover.

However, the idea was not pursued. 'The major problem was building enough strength into the body,' according to Mike Sampson. 'It was too risky and would have been too high an investment for the then predicted volumes.' So the design team went back to a conventional four-door configuration during 2001. The basics of the L320 programme had probably been settled by October 2001, the date that Richard Woolley associates with the start of the programme proper.

Divergence

Meanwhile, the T5 chassis team had assembled their first prototypes, and had sent them out on the road as 'mules' under the bodies of Ford Explorers and Mercury Mountaineers. Some

Several of the prototypes had the V-prefix registrations current in 1999–2000, which made them look slightly older than they really were. It was customary to paint such vehicles black by this time, and this example has mock-up light units made of a black rubberized material, a mask over the grille, and some of its camouflage sheets rolled up on the bonnet.

Terrain Response

Land Rover's Terrain Response system became possible because so many sub-systems on Land Rover's vehicles were now electronically controlled. In essence, it linked all these systems together through a common control interface, so that they worked in harmony to deliver the best performance. It also simplified the driver's tasks by reducing the number of separate controls in the vehicle.

A single rotary control on the centre console allowed the driver to select a setting appropriate to the driving conditions, and the electronic systems then did the rest. Terrain Response was initially focused on off-road driving conditions, but was later expanded to include on-road driving dynamics as well.

The system development team, led by engineer Jan Prins, analysed the characteristics of nearly fifty different types of off-road surface to determine the vehicle system inputs necessary to optimize the performance across those surfaces. They then reduced these to five 'programmes', described as General Driving; Grass, Gravel and Snow; Mud and Ruts; Sand; and Rock Crawling. Each one had its own setting on the rotary control, which automatically defaulted to General Driving mode after the ignition was switched off.

Terrain Response co-ordinated and controlled a number of key sub-systems on the vehicle. These included the engine management system, the automatic gearbox, the electronically controlled front and rear differentials (when these were fitted), and the air suspension height settings. In addition, Terrain Response was linked to the slip control or traction systems – ABS, ETC, DSC and HDC – and would make use of these if appropriate.

So, for example, in the Grass, Gravel and Snow setting, which was designed to cope with slippery surfaces, the throttle map was altered to give a more progressive torque delivery and reduce the risk of sudden heavy throttle applications which would induce slip. The gearbox shift points were optimized to reduce torque at the wheels and so prevent slip by selecting higher gears with early upshifts and late downshifts. And the electronic differentials would be pre-loaded to respond faster at the first indication of loss of traction.

The Terrain Response system was operated by a simple rotary control on the centre console.

For the 2010 model-year, Range Rover Sport models had an additional Dynamic setting on the Terrain Response Control. This was designed to give more sporting handling on the road, and controlled the electronic damper settings as well as the vehicle's other systems.

Terrain Response was previewed on the Range Stormer concept vehicle in 2004. It entered production later that year on the new Discovery 3, and became available for the Range Rover Sport in 2005. It finally reached the Range Rover (L322) in 2006 on 2007-model vehicles.

---

of these were Attribute Prototypes (incorporating proposed elements of the future vehicle) for L319, and others for L320. Although the two had a great deal in common, L320 was going to be a very much more sporty vehicle and its chassis would later be tuned to give the appropriate characteristics.

A key difference between L319 and L320 would also lie in their engines. Although both would have the new Jaguar-derived 4.4-litre petrol V8 and the 2.7-litre TDV6 diesel, only L320 would also take on the supercharged V8 and the TDV8 diesel, while only L319 would have the Ford petrol V6.

At this stage, Stuart Frith was running the Prototype Division at Gaydon, and had overall responsibility for Jaguar as well as Land Rover prototypes. His team had assembled

the Explorer 'mules', and was testing them from 2002 to meet a cut-off point of late 2003. By that date, both body and chassis elements of L320 had to be ready so that the first Confirmation Prototypes – which would use the production body design, chassis and running-gear – could be constructed.

The need to meet rather earlier deadlines for the Discovery meant that the chassis was ready before the body, which was signed off at the end of 2003. The plan was to fine-tune the L320 chassis on the Confirmation Prototypes. Then, just as the first Confirmation Prototypes were being assembled, L320 Chief Programme Engineer Tom Jones left. Stuart Frith found himself as the natural replacement because he had been so closely involved with testing the chassis prototypes, and became

Chief Programme Engineer that summer.

Meanwhile, the public had already been softened up for the introduction of a new, sporty Range Rover by the showing of the Range Stormer concept in January 2004. The proposed production body design had also been clinic'd (shown to groups of potential customers) during 2003 in Europe and North America. 'The results were the same and conclusive,' said Richard Woolley. 'They loved it!'

Fine-tuning

There was still plenty of work to do before the planned start to production in early 2005, however. Stuart Frith remembered that the first Confirmation Prototypes didn't have the body control that the L320 team

The Range Stormer

'The main intention of the Range Stormer was to gauge public reaction to the idea of a sporty Range Rover,' confirmed Land Rover designer Richard Woolley. The concept-car which wowed the world's media on its introduction at the Detroit Show in January 2004 was planned as a stand-alone project, and was neither an evolution of the L320 programme nor an early iteration of it – although it did have input from some of the L320 team. Design Director Geoff Upex has said that it was an indication of the way the Sport's design might have gone if it had not been subject to constraints.

The Range Stormer design was overseen by Richard Woolley as Studio Director, exterior design being led by Sean Henstridge with Paul Hanstock in support. The interior was done by Mark Butler aided by Ayline Koning, who was responsible for the striking leather-covered seats that appeared to float inside the cabin.

The concept-car was built on the chassis of a 4.6-litre second-generation Range Rover, which shared its 108-inch wheelbase with the forthcoming Range Rover Sport. It was driveable to the extent that was needed for a show car, although the hydraulically-operated scissors-type doors were always intended to add to the drama of its announcement at Detroit and were never seriously considered for production.

The car has subsequently been handed over to the Heritage Motor Centre at Gaydon, where it is regularly on display.

wanted. Steering was also too quick at speed and didn't have the required agility at low speeds.

They dealt with this in several ways. Body control was improved by fine-tuning the body mounts themselves, of which there were ten conventional rubber mounts and four miniature damper units. Steering response was improved by scrapping the existing system and asking ZF to come up with a variable-ratio, speed-proportional system. Experience with Jaguar programmes, says Stuart, had taught him that ZF could deliver to fairly short time-scales.

The final stages involved tuning the dampers and selecting the right tyres to give the on-road characteristics that the L320 team wanted. They worked closely with various tyre manufacturers on this, but Stuart remembers that Continental was particularly good because it was able to turn changes around in five or six weeks, half the time it took other manufacturers.

All the time, the off-road characteristics of the vehicle were high on the agenda, too. Most of the basic work had already been done for the Discovery 3, but the on-road requirement for L320 was very different and it was important not to lose sight of the off-road performance.

Another Mike Sampson sketch, this time again showing the four-door in almost final form. However, the wing vents are different, and although the position of the tailgate badge has been settled, it reads Land Rover rather than Range Rover.

These Mike Sampson sketches were done specifically for the launch, and were designed to emphasize the links between the Range Stormer concept vehicle and the production Sport – hence the orange colour and the deliberate vagueness of the dead side view in showing how many doors the Sport would have!

In developing the Discovery 3's off-road package, Land Rover had used the Toyota Land Cruiser as a benchmark ('although,' said Stuart, 'we knew we were already that good!'); so the benchmark for L320's off-road ability became Discovery 3.

Naming

Naming the vehicle was the responsibility of the Marketing Department, and although some members of the L320 team did have an input to the debate, the final result was out of their hands. 'Range Sport', which had been touted as early as 2000, somehow didn't roll off the tongue very easily. Names such as RS300 and RS400 had been registered with the appropriate authorities, and would have given the new model a very sporty and technical image. However, in the end it became Range Rover Sport, despite continued misgivings in some parts of the company that this might devalue the Range Rover name. The decision reflected Land Rover's

The Range Stormer was a 'tease', intended to gauge public reaction to the idea of a sporty Range Rover rather than to reveal much about the actual vehicle.

new orientation, as explained by Managing Director Matthew Taylor in September 2003 during his speech at the Frankfurt International Motor Show: 'It is the Range Rover, even more than the original Land Rover, that is now the inspiration for this company's future,' he said.

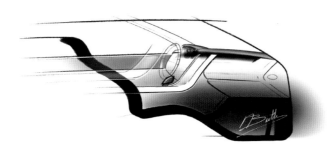

This Mark Butler sketch for the Range Stormer's interior did show the 'cockpit' design in something like its production form.

The seats in the Range Stormer were deliberately futuristic and probably neither very practical nor very comfortable – but they did create the right aura of excitement for the concept vehicle.

CHAPTER TWELVE

The Life and Times of the Range Rover Sport

'It takes us into the growing performance SUV market but is different from all its rivals,' said Land Rover Managing Director Matthew Taylor at the time of the Range Rover Sport's launch.

> We see it as a less frenetic, more re-fined alternative to existing perform-ance SUVs. It is ideal for fast, comfort-able, long-distance driving and practical enough for everyday use. Yet it is also exceptional off-road, offering better all-terrain ability than any competitor. Like all Land Rover products, it offers the broadest range of capability in its class.

And, heading off questions about the use of the Range Rover brand name on this new model positioned below the L322 in the Land Rover pecking order, he added: 'It also perfectly complements the existing Range Rover – the luxury SUV. Range Rover Sport is more compact and will be priced to fit between Discovery 3/LR3 and the Range Rover in the Land Rover product range.'

Exact pricing was announced later, but it was November 2004 when the Range Rover Sport was announced to the media and Land Rover dealers opened their order books. Actual availability would not begin until mid-2005, after a public debut at the North American International Auto Show in Detroit during January, and after a media ride-and-drive event in Scotland in April 2005.

In fact, Land Rover had been building up to the launch of the Sport for well over a year before any customers were able to take deliv-ery of one. As this was a new model in the Land Rover line-up – a fifth 'nameplate', as the company liked to describe it – and as it was some-what controversially going to wear Range Rover badges, it was very important to get the launch right. So the first indications of what was afoot had been made clear as early as January 2004 at that year's Detroit motor show. There, in a dramatic presentation featuring dry ice, Matthew Taylor had presented the Range Stormer concept vehicle, a 'taster' intended to allow Land Rover to judge public reaction.

The reaction, predictably, was overwhelmingly enthusiastic. There had, perhaps, been a growing public perception that the Range Rover was becoming just a little too solemn and serious, a little too divorced from everyday reality and maybe even a little staid. Linking the revered name (even if only half of it) to this excit-ing, dynamic concept for a sporting SUV to rival the likes of the Porsche Cayenne and BMW X5 went down a storm.

In fact, the Range Stormer was only distantly related to the

Early publicity pictures of the Sport showed this Vesuvius orange supercharged model, to tie in with the similarly-coloured Range Stormer concept car. The colour was available only on the First Edition models in the 2005 model-year.

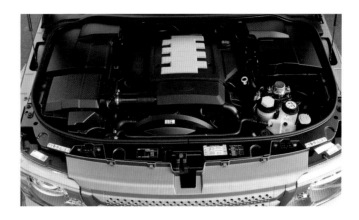

LEFT: The core power unit for Europe was the 2.7-litre TDV6 that was shared with the Discovery 3. Frugal and refined, its main weakness was disappointing response at higher speeds.

ABOVE: For the USA, the entry-level engine was the 4.4-litre Jaguar petrol V8. As was usual by now, there was not much of it to be seen under the bonnet!

production Range Rover Sport. The concept vehicle had been deliberately built as an attention-grabber, and its only real links to the forthcoming production model were its size and its sporting intent. It did, though, sensitize the public to what was coming.

The Real Thing

The headline news when the real Range Rover Sport was announced was of course the 396bhp supercharged engine, which powered the model to 60mph in 7.2 seconds and on to a top speed of 140mph. No matter that most buyers would not be driving this most expensive variant home from the showroom; the lesser models basked in its reflected glory. Below it in the model hierarchy came a variant with the 306bhp naturally-aspirated Jaguar V8, and at entry level was a variant with the 'cooking' 2.7-litre TDV6 and 190bhp. That would prove the most popular variant in Europe: affordable, frugal and yet stylish, it tapped into a latent customer demand.

Even so, the supercharged Sport sold very strongly to a particular clientele, often caricatured as Premier League footballers and those who emulated them. What was quite certain was that the Sport was selling to a new group of customers, people

The flagship engine was of course the supercharged 4.2-litre V8. It made the Sport a rapid performer on the road, and helped to justify its name. These pictures show what it was really like, and the underbonnet view.

The tailgate badge was the easiest way of recognizing a supercharged model, although these also had different wheels from other Sports.

The Range Rover name was carried on a textured plastic plinth at the bottom of the lower tailgate – an interesting departure from Land Rover practice.

who had never even considered owning a Land Rover before but were attracted by the charisma of the new model.

This was precisely what Land Rover had wanted, although it did bring with it certain risks. Cars which have a very strong 'fashionable' appeal sometimes reach their sales peak early and then become unfashionable and unwanted. Solihull was well aware of this and was prepared to keep the model alive with new features if necessary but, to the company's great surprise, it just kept on selling. There was no need to introduce major updates and, as it was cheaper not to do so, Land Rover kept its powder dry.

In fact, the Sport's sales debut was little short of sensational. World-wide, it sold 30,356 examples in its first six months, and during 2006 it became Land Rover's best-selling product, taking some sales away from its Discovery 3 sibling. Sales just went on increasing, and in 2007, though eclipsed by sales of the new and considerably cheaper Freelander 2, it was a major factor in Land Rover's all-time annual sales record of 226,395 vehicles – a 17.6 per cent improvement over 2006.

There were, of course, different specification levels, although all models came with automatic transmission and leather upholstery. The entry-level models were available only with the TDV6 diesel engine and were known (but not badged) as S types. Above these came SE and then HSE variants, both available

with the TDV6 and naturally-aspirated petrol V8 engines. Then right at the top came the Supercharged model with its own specification level that added certain items to the HSE specification. The Supercharged variants also had distinctive black Land Rover oval badges and 20-inch wheels with 275/40 R 20 tyres in place of the 19-inch wheels and 255/50 R 19 tyres on other models. Optional, and at this stage unique to the Sport, was Adaptive Cruise Control, which used radar to maintain a set distance from the car in front by adjusting the accelerator and brake settings as necessary.

The awards began to come in, too, although the Sport was never quite as heavily decorated as its Discovery 3 contemporary. It was voted Scottish SUV of the Year in October 2005 and *Top Gear* SUV of the Year that December.

The Need for Individuality

Land Rover knew how important it was to keep the Range Rover Sport fresh and exciting for its target buyers, and the model had been on sale for just about nine months when the first 'refresher' was announced. It was, somewhat predictably, a bodykit. In Britain, this was made public at the end of March 2006 during the Goodwood Festival of Speed, and was used to create a new model called the

The interior was a major success, even though it shared many elements with the related Discovery 3 model. The swept lines of the centre console enhanced the 'cockpit' feel and suited the car's sporty pretensions. Different colour and trim combinations enabled buyers to choose between a luxury ambience (the Ivory leather with Cherry Wood trim) and a harder, more sporty ambience (the Aspen grey leather with Rhodium silver-grey trim).

The Sport was also a very practical vehicle, with a tailgate split to allow either the upper section or the full panel to open. A sliding load bay floor was available to make loading easier, too.

Range Rover Sport Supercharged HST. In other countries, however, the bodykit only became available as a kit of parts to be added by dealers.

The bodykit consisted of angular front and rear aprons, a larger tail spoiler and rectangular tail-pipes. It was supposedly inspired by the Range Stormer, although there was probably more public relations wishful thinking in that description than there was fact. On the UK-market HST model, it was accompanied by a very full specification that included an electric sunroof, privacy glass, body-colour lower doors and lower tailgate, a rear e-diff, limed oak trim, 20-inch Stormer alloy wheels and chromed aluminium side-vents. The HST was available only in five colours (Bonatti Grey, Cairns Blue, Java Black, Rimini Red and Zermatt Silver) and was an expensive proposition at £63,000.

There were those at Land Rover who freely admitted that they did not like the HST kit at all, but they were happy to bow to the demands of the market. And there was no doubt that Land Rover had correctly anticipated what would happen: within the next

few months, a number of aftermarket specialists brought their own Range Rover Sport bodykits to market to meet a growing demand for a Sport that looked different.

The launch of the bodykit was simply Land Rover marking time, though, because a second and much more important 'refresher' for the Sport line-up was going to be announced just a few months later. For the 2007 model-year Land Rover announced availability of the new TDV8 diesel engine as a fourth option alongside the TDV6, the 4.4-litre petrol V8 and the 4.2-

litre supercharged V8. The new 3.6-litre diesel engine became available in the showrooms from November 2006, and was an immediate hit. In Europe (it was not made available in the USA or the Middle East), it rapidly became the engine of choice and more or less demolished sales of the naturally-aspirated petrol V8, which was thirstier and could not match its torque and acceleration.

The 2008 model-year was characterized in the UK and certain other markets by the withdrawal from sale of those models powered by the 4.4-litre naturally-aspirated V8 petrol

Yet in spite of all its on-road sporty pretensions, the Sport had the same off-road capability as its siblings. It was certainly the best off-road performer in its class, and by a wide margin.

Limited Editions: UK Market

All the special and limited editions were hand-finished by Land Rover Special Vehicles.

Model-year	Designation	Characteristics
2005 (Sep 2004)	First Edition	Unknown quantity, based on supercharged HSE. Vesuvius orange paint (as on Range Stormer), perforated Sports Leather upholstery and Limed Oak wood trim
2009 (Mar 2009)	Stormer	300 examples, based on TDV6 S. Alaska White, Santorini Black or Stornoway Grey with bodykit and 20-inch wheels
2010 (Mar 2010)	Autobiography	500 examples, based on TDV8 or supercharged V8. Bodykit, special finish for grille and side vents, 20-inch diamond-turned alloy wheels

US Market

In addition to the limited editions listed here, 2009 brought two special-value editions designed to promote flagging sales. These were known as the Stormer Alloy Wheel Value cars; there were 500 of the first batch and 499 of the second.

Model-year	Designation	Characteristics
2006	First Edition	643 examples, based on supercharged model. 450 with Vesuvius orange paint
2008 (Aug 2007)	Sport Stormer	250 examples, based on supercharged model. Bodykit, luxury interior package with audio-visual system; Adaptive Cruise Control
2009	HST	314 examples, with bodykit

Optional from the beginning was Adaptive Cruise Control, which automatically maintained a set distance from the vehicle in front. When fitted, its presence was revealed by this panel in the apron air intake.

engine. Displaced by the excellent new TDV8 diesel, this engine nevertheless remained available for the USA, the Middle East, and some other countries.

The UK was treated to another HST edition, slightly cheaper than the earlier one at £59,895. Once again the bodykit and 20-inch Stormer wheels were the main distinguishing features, together with body-colour lower sides and tailgate, privacy glass, limed oak wood interior trim, premium carpet mats and the latest Logic 7 ICE system. And then came 2009, which should have been a quiet year before the planned major range overhaul of the 2010 model-year.

The 2009 model-year was severely affected by the world-wide recession which had been gathering pace, and sales of non-essential vehicles such as the Sport ran into trouble. In Britain, there were very few Range Rover Sports registered with the 09 and later 59 plates, although Jaguar Land Rover did register a larger than usual quantity themselves for use as company cars to be sold into the market after a year's use by JLR employees.

Meanwhile, in an attempt to stimulate sales, Land Rover announced a 300-strong Stormer Edition at the Boat Show in January 2009. It was designed as a value-for-money prospect, with a lot of extra equipment loaded onto an entry-level S-specification TDV6 model. That extra equipment included the HST bodykit with its associated 20-inch wheels, body-coloured side mouldings and lower tailgate, leather upholstery, front and rear parking sensors and pre-wiring for a Bluetooth mobile phone installation. Available from March 2009 in just three colours (Alaska White, Santorini Black and Stornoway Grey), the car cost £43,550 – still an awful lot of money at a time when the market was badly depressed.

The 2010 Changes

The motor industry always has to plan well ahead for major new-model introductions, and Land Rover had been planning for some time to announce a series of major upgrades for the Range Rover Sport in autumn 2009 for the 2010 model-year. As things turned out, it was hardly an auspicious time to do so: most buyers were already thinking about downsizing for their next car, if they could afford one at all, and many were probably hoping to hold out until the promised new generation of hybrids and electric-powered vehicles was on the market. The last thing on their minds was a luxury, high-performance Range Rover Sport that cost even more than the previous year's model.

However, Land Rover was locked into its new-model cycle and took the decision to go ahead with the

The line-up was expanded for 2007 with the new TDV8 diesel engine, which delivered far better performance than the TDV6.

planned 2010 Range Rover Sport. The new models were introduced in July 2009 with a range of three engines. Entry-level types, available with SE or HSE trim levels, were powered by the new 3.0-litre TDV6 engine; the mid-range models had the TDV8 diesel engine and came only with HSE trim; and the top model had the new 5.0-litre supercharged petrol V8 and came as an HSE. For non-European markets, there was also a 5.0-litre naturally-aspirated petrol V8. The V8 engines were essentially the same as the ones announced for the 2010-model Range Rovers; the TDV8 diesel was already familiar; but the new 3.0-litre TDV6 was an important development that was shared with the Discovery 3.

This new engine featured twin turbochargers in addition to its enlarged capacity, but these had a parallel sequential arrangement, the first of its kind to be fitted to a V engine. Most of the time, the engine used only the larger primary turbocharger, which was a variable-geometry type, and the smaller secondary turbo remained out of circuit. However, above 2500rpm, the secondary turbo-charger was brought into play within 300 milliseconds, seamlessly boosting the power delivery in the upper rev ranges where the earlier 2.7-litre engine had been disappointing. The engine would also meet the EU5 regulations due in 2011 when fitted with a Diesel Particulates Filter.

Even though the Sport had been the most successful of Land Rover's products, customer feedback suggested that it needed to be given a more distinct identity. So the changes for 2010 added sophistication and sporting flavour, but retained the Range Rover brand characteristic of restraint.

Land Rover also believed that it was important to reduce the model's

In 2006, Land Rover introduced a bodykit, partly as a way of keeping customers away from aftermarket specialists who were planning similar modifications. It found a ready market, and in the UK was used to create the HST variant.

G4 Challenge Range Rover Sports

Land Rover prepared a small number of Range Rover Sport models for the second G4 Challenge adventure sports event, held in 2006. They were based on 4.4-litre V8 HSE models and were painted in the event's Tangiers Orange. The Sports were used in the South East Asia section of the event.

The G4 Challenge was a massive promotional event as far as Land Rover was concerned, and so examples of the new Sport had to feature among the vehicles used on the 2006 event. Even the snorkel, on the far side of the vehicle, had been styled to look sporty!

apparent size at a time when large vehicles had suddenly become politically incorrect purchases, and so Gerry McGovern's designers had restyled the front end, with a larger apron air intake and a slimming two-element grille that also helped to distinguish the Sport from the Range

Rover with its new three-element grille. The lights had LEDs incorporated into their bezels, in anticipation of a daytime running light requirement but also reflecting a trend that had already been cleverly exploited by Audi, and there was a range of new alloy wheels. The two-element theme of the grille was continued into the lamp units, around the sides onto the air intakes, and all the way through to the rear light units as well.

Key to the 2010 changes, however, were several which emphasized the model's sporting character. The new and more powerful engines were just the start. Stiffer front suspension bushes gave better steering response, while the supercharged model went to new Brembo six-pot front brake callipers on ventilated discs and the TDV8 diesel took on the four-pot Brembo set-up from the outgoing supercharged car. Both models had ventilated rear discs with lightweight aluminium, single-piston callipers, but the discs on the supercharged car were larger. Land Rover claimed a better pedal feel, too.

All new was Adaptive Dynamics, a system that integrated with the existing Dynamic Response to demonstrate that a refined ride and sharp handling were no longer mutually exclusive. Central to the system were new DampTronic dampers, made by Bilstein but actually developed in-house by Land Rover, which incorporated continuously adjustable valves. Damper pressure on each wheel was monitored 500 times a second, and predictive technology enabled the system to be prepared for the road ahead rather than having to react to it. A refinement to the Stability Control System also helped to

The supercharged model remained the flagship of the Sport range. Large numbers of buyers in the UK chose silvers, greys and blacks instead of strong colours like this red, which suited the shape so well. Conventional wisdom was that vehicles in these 'inoffensive' colours were easier to sell on.

The 2010 model-year changes were designed to give the Sport a clearer identity of its own, and to add to its capability, equipment levels, and luxury. Alaska White, as here, certainly showed off the new shape, but to some eyes it also made the vehicle look strangely bland.

However, the 2010 interior changes were a major success, removing much of the fussiness of the original design while retaining the sporty nature of the 'cockpit' style. Changes in materials also brought a more up-market feel.

Annual Production Figures

Figures relate to calendar year, not to model-year.

2005	39,250
2006	58,126
2007	61,701
2008	45,693
Total (to end 2008)	204,770

slow the vehicle automatically on a bend taken too fast.

The Terrain Response system was also upgraded, with revised Sand and Rock Crawl settings and a new sixth setting that was unique to the Sport. Known as Dynamic (and actually previewed on the Terrain Response control of the Range Stormer concept car back in 2004), this setting made adjustments to the Adaptive Dynamics system, the accelerator pedal mapping, the Stability Control system and the gearchange settings to give a more sporty drive.

According to Design Director Gerry McGovern, Sport customers wanted the interior to be 'more Range Rover', and so the 2010 models got the full luxury treatment. The basic 'cockpit' design with its high centre console was retained, but there was much more leather throughout, with a new and wider choice of colours. On the new steering wheel it also had paddle-switches

LEFT: The new 3.0-litre twin-turbo TDV6 was another exceptional engine, which removed the weaknesses of the older 2.7-litre variant and delivered performance almost equal to that of the TDV8.

BELOW: The 2010 models also added a new Dynamic mode to the Terrain Response system. Its symbol, seen here, was a winding road.

Specifications for Range Rover Sport Models

Layout and chassis

Four-door estate with horizontally split tailgate
Box-section ladder-frame chassis

Engine

TDV6 2.7-litre diesel (2005 on)
 2720cc (81mm × 88mm) Ford-Peugeot ohv V6 diesel with four valves per cylinder, common-rail injection, turbocharger and intercooler (early versions EU3 compliant; EU4 versions from January 2007)
 Siemens PDC2 engine management system
 18:1 compression ratio
 190bhp at 4000rpm
 325lb ft at 1900rpm

4.4-litre Jaguar V8 (2005–2009)
 4394cc (88mm × 90.3mm) Jaguar AJ-8 petrol V8 with four camshafts and four valves per cylinder
 Denso EMS generation 1 engine management system
 10.75:1 compression ratio
 300bhp at 5500rpm
 315lb ft at 4000rpm

4.2-litre Supercharged V8 (2005–2009)
 4197cc (86mm × 90.3mm) Jaguar AJ-8 petrol V8 with four camshafts and four valves per cylinder plus Eaton supercharger and intercooler
 Denso EMS generation 1 engine management system
 9.1:1 compression ratio
 390bhp at 5750rpm
 410lb ft at 3500rpm

TDV8 diesel (2006 on)
 3630cc (81mm × 88mm) Ford-Land Rover OHV V8 with diesel four valves per cylinder, common-rail injection, twin turbochargers and intercooler
 17.3:1 compression ratio
 268bhp at 4000rpm
 472lb ft at 2000rpm

TDV6 3.0-litre (2009 on)
 2993cc (84mm × 90mm) Ford-Peugeot OHV V6 diesel with four valves per cylinder, common-rail injection, twin parallel sequential turbochargers and intercooler (EU5 compliant)
 Bosch Gen 3 engine management system
 16:1 compression ratio
 245bhp at 4000rpm
 442lb ft at 2000rpm

5-litre Jaguar V8 (2009 on)
 5000cc (92.5mm × 93mm) Jaguar-Land Rover LR-V8 petrol V8 with four camshafts and four valves per cylinder
 9.5:1 compression ratio
 375bhp at 6000rpm
 375lb ft at 2500rpm

5-litre Supercharged V8 (2009 on)
 5000cc (92.5mm × 93mm) Jaguar-Land Rover LR-V8 petrol V8 with four camshafts and four valves per cylinder plus Eaton twin-vortex supercharger and intercooler
 9.5:1 compression ratio
 510bhp at 6000rpm
 460lb ft at 2500rpm

Transmission

Permanent four-wheel drive with centre differential incorporating viscous coupling to give automatic locking; Terrain Response traction system standard; optional locking rear differential
Final drive ratio: 3.73:1 (V8 petrol models)
                    3.54:1 (TDV6, TDV8 and V8 supercharged models)

Specifications for Range Rover Sport Models *continued*

Primary gearbox

Six-speed ZF 6HP26 automatic (2005–2009 models); ratios 4.171:1, 2.340:1, 1.521:1, 1.143:1, 0.867:1, 0.691:1, reverse 3.403:1
Six-speed ZF 6HP28 automatic (2010 and later models); ratios as for 6HP 26 gearbox

Transfer gearbox

Separate 2-speed type with 'active' centre differential; High ratio 1:1, Low ratio 2.93:1

Suspension

Independent front and rear suspension with height-adjustable electronic air suspension and telescopic dampers; double wishbones front and rear

Steering

ZF Servotronic speed proportional power-assisted rack and pinion

Brakes

Four-wheel disc brakes with dual hydraulic line, servo assistance and Bosch four-channel ABS
Ventilated front discs with 317mm diameter (2.7-litre TDV6), 337mm diameter (4.4 V8) or 360mm diameter (supercharged V8), with four-piston callipers (2005–2009); 360mm diameter with twin-piston sliding callipers (TDV6 and TDV8, 2010 models), or 380mm diameter with six-piston fixed callipers (supercharged V8, 2010 models)
Ventilated rear discs with 325mm diameter single-pot callipers (TDV6 and V8 models, 2005–2009) or 350mm diameter and four-piston callipers (supercharged V8s and TDV8, 2005–2009); 350mm diameter with single-piston sliding callipers (TDV6 and TDV8, 2010 model-year) or 365mm diameter with single-piston sliding callipers (supercharged V8, 2010 model-year)
Servo-operated parking brake operating on drums within the rear discs

Vehicle dimensions

Wheelbase:	108.1in (2745mm)
Overall length:	188.5in (4788mm)
Overall width:	75.9in (1928mm); 85.4in (2170mm) over mirrors
Overall height:	71.5in (1817mm) at standard ride height

Unladen weight (for typical UK-market models):

2.7-litre diesel models:	5412lb (2455kg)
4.4-litre petrol models:	5468lb (2480kg)
4.2-litre supercharged V8 models:	5670lb (2572kg)
3.6-litre TDV8 models:	5855–6076 lb (2656–2756kg)
3.0-litre TDV6 models:	5588–5886 lb (2535–2670kg)
5.0-litre supercharged V8 models:	5710–5906 lb (2590–2679kg)

Performance

2.7-litre TDV6 models:
Maximum speed: 120mph (193km/h)   *0–60mph:* 11.9secs

4.4-litre petrol V8 models
Maximum speed: 130mph (209km/h)   *0–60mph:* 8.2secs

4.2-litre V8 supercharged models
Maximum speed: 140mph (225km/h)   *0–60mph:* 7.2secs

3.6-litre TDV8 models
Maximum speed: 130mph (210km/h)   *0–60mph:* 8.6secs

3.0-litre TDV6 models
Maximum speed: 120mph (193km/h)   *0–60mph:* 8.8secs

5.0-litre petrol V8 models
Maximum speed: 130mph (210km/h)   *0–60mph:* 7.2secs

5.0-litre V8 supercharged models
Maximum speed: 140mph (225km/h)   *0–60mph:* 5.9secs

for rapid gear changing, a feature borrowed from high-performance cars and one that reinforced the car's sporting nature.

The facia had been considerably cleaned up, with 50 per cent fewer switches, and shared its new instrument pack with the Discovery 4. Most welcome was the new analogue clock that replaced the barely-legible digital read-out on the centre console of the earlier Sports. The new main instrument dials were much less cluttered than before, and between them was a five-inch driver information screen which delivered key information very effectively and replaced the earlier message centre screen. But the Sport retained its unique char-

acter, with new seats front and rear that were more shape-hugging than before, and electrically adjustable side bolsters on the options list.

There were also several new features shared with other models in the range for 2010. A remote 'key' allowed both keyless entry and a keyless start when receivers in the vehicle sensed its proximity, while High Beam Assist in the new LED headlights both switched the lights on when the ambient light fell below a certain threshold and dipped the headlights automatically when it detected the lights of an oncoming vehicle. Tow Assist made hitching up to a trailer easier by displaying the view to the rear of the vehicle onto

the dashboard screen with an overlay of guidance lines, and there were five cameras in the Surround Camera system which made low-speed manoeuvring easier with a clear on-screen view of the area immediately around the vehicle. The latest hard-drive navigation system was fitted, and Gradient Release Control was added to the existing Hill Descent Control to prevent a sudden lurch as the vehicle's brakes were released on a steep downhill stretch off-road.

Yet the performance, equipment and luxury upgrades were not the full story. Land Rover also incorporated some of its new 'environmental' technologies on the 2010 Sport. Notable was the introduction of

Prominent twin exhaust outlets and a plate badge reading 'Supercharged' were key distinguishing features of the 2010 Range Rover Sport.

an Intelligent Power Management System that included Smart Regenerative Charging. The alternator charged the battery when the vehicle was coasting rather than when it was accelerating, so reducing drag on the engine and therefore fuel consumption. Drag on the engine was also reduced by the clutch on the new air conditioning pump, which now disengaged when the air conditioning was off. There were more fuel savings in other areas, each one of them small in itself but contributing to an overall improvement. There was less slip in the torque converter of the new ZF automatic gearbox, for example, while the higher torque from all engines allowed taller overall gearing which again reduced fuel consumption. In addition, a lower idling speed for the new TDV6 engine and faster warm-up for the petrol V8s ensured minimum fuel wastage.

... and the Future

Land Rover had originally expected sales of the Range Rover Sport to peak after a couple of years and then to decline as the model's fashionable appeal wore off. The company anticipated a production life of about six years, which would have suggested an end to sales in about 2011. However, those plans were revised in the light of the model's sustained sales success.

As this book went into production in 2009, it appeared that work had begun on the second-generation Sport under the project code of L494. The T5 platform was expected to go out of production in 2014, and L494 would reach the showrooms the same year. Instead of being developed on the same platform as the next Discovery, the second-generation Sport was expected to use the same aluminium space-frame architecture as the fourth-generation Range Rover (project L405), which was likely to enter production a year earlier.

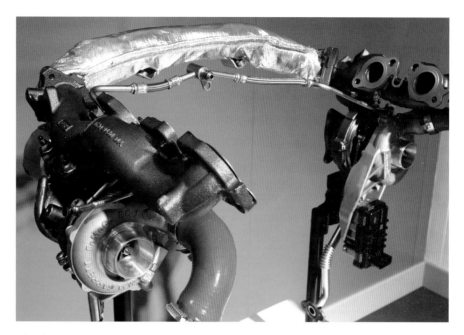

This demonstration cutaway shows how the two turbochargers were interlinked to give the parallel sequential arrangement which brought additional boost in when it was needed at higher speeds.

For 2010, the flagship models were powered by the new 5.0-litre supercharged V8 engine. Clearly visible here is the characteristic sump shape used for the Range Rover Sport.

CHAPTER THIRTEEN

Building the Range Rover Sport

As Chapter 11 explains, the Range Rover Sport was designed from the outset as one of two vehicles to be built on the same platform, the other being the Discovery 3. Part of the thinking was that the two vehicles could also be built on the same assembly lines instead of having a dedicated line each, and as a result the Range Rover Sport assembly operation had some very significant differences from the assembly operations for all of the other three models that had worn the Range Rover badge. Nevertheless, that assembly operation also had a number of similarities to the one established for the L322 Range Rover and described in Chapter 10.

Land Rover invested heavily in new assembly buildings for the Range Rover Sport and its twin brother the Discovery 3. The largest investment went into the T5 Trim and Final building at the eastern end of the Solihull site, but there was also huge investment in a new Body In White plant which assembled the bodyshells for both models. The first ground for this was broken in July 2002, after a number of older buildings had been demolished. The new assembly areas became operational early in 2004, and initially produced only Discovery 3s, which were introduced around a year before the Range Rover Sport.

As usual, many Range Rover Sport components were manufactured off-site and were brought into the Solihull factory by road. A computer-controlled 'Just In Time' system ensured that there was no need for large component storage areas alongside the assembly lines. Instead, there were 'buffer zones' where small stocks of items were kept – just enough in each case to cater for fluctuations in line speed. It was the responsibility of Land Rover's suppliers to deliver the items required on time, and there were penalty clauses in their contracts to discourage defaulters.

Chassis and Powertrain

Among the major components brought into the factory from outside were the engines, which came from the Jaguar plant at Bridgend and the Ford plant at Dagenham; gearboxes, which came from ZF at Freidrichshafen in Germany; and chassis frames, which came from a Wolverhampton factory owned jointly by GKN and the American Dana Corporation. This factory was specially built to use the hydro-forming process developed by Dana, where malleable steel is put into a mould and forced into shape by liquid injected at very high pressure. The process delivered very accurate results and also allowed weight to be saved through the use of thinner metal sections in some areas.

All these components were delivered to the T5 Trim and Final building, and at the start of the build process each chassis frame was put onto a moving assembly line that snaked its way up and down the length of the vast assembly hall. Suspension units were bolted on, brake lines were put in, fuel tanks were added, and before long each chassis was ready to receive its major hardware of engine and transmission.

Both Discovery 3 and Range Rover Sport variants of the T5 chassis went down the same lines, and to ensure that there was never any confusion about what the chassis was to become or which of the many engine and gearbox options it was to receive, each one had a coded 'build sheet' attached to it. As it passed each assembly station, the associate in charge checked the code for that station and fitted the correct part – which, of course, had been delivered to the line-side with very

Door panel pressings for the Range Rover Sport in stillages within the BIW plant.

precise timing thanks to the computer control systems in place.

Body In White

Meanwhile, bodies were taking shape in the Body In White plant. Their construction began with front, middle and rear 'ladder' sections being welded together to make the complete underframe structure of the body. The gaps were then filled in as the floor panels were welded on, making a strong sandwich construction. Next to be added was the front bulkhead – a very important item because all the main dimensions of the Sport's body were taken from it.

CENTRE AND RIGHT: Overhead slings, different from those used on the L322 Range Rover assembly lines, carry the Range Rover Sport bodyshells along the Trim and Final line. Many of the bodies are silver, grey or black – all popular colours in the middle of the decade when the Sport was launched.

On the Trim and Final Assembly line, carpeting and other interior items are assembled into the painted bodyshell of a Range Rover Sport.

Sport bodyshells – silver again – are lifted up into the roof of the assembly hall to be moved on to the next stage of the line.

In the meantime, the body sides and the rear end were being put together. Robot arms were used to swing huge side panels into position for spot-welding, and in each case, the joining of inner and outer panels made another very strong sandwich construction. Roof panels were made by the same principle.

Further down the line, the 'box' of sides, tail panel, headers (bracing the body sides) and roof came together, and its joints were carefully sealed. At this point, the shape of the body became recognizable for the first time. With all the main dimensions now fixed, it was then possible to mount the doors, an operation which was computer-controlled to ensure absolute consistency of panel gaps. Front wings were then jig-fitted to the bulkhead, and the bonnet was added, followed by the front panel.

The now-complete shell did not stay that way for long. Each shell had its doors removed before being whisked away by conveyor up into the roof of the building and out of the BIW plant into the Paint Shop. Those doors would eventually meet up with their original body on the Trim and Final Line, and the perfect fit which the robot assemblers achieved was guaranteed by leaving the hinge halves in place on the door and body, and removing the hinge-pins.

Final Assembly

From the Paint Shop, the newly painted bodies were brought by overhead conveyor into the main assembly hall. Here, they began their journey along a first-stage trim line, where dashboards, interior panels and carpets were added, and where glass was fitted by robot arms in a special cell.

Window glass is added to bodyshells by robots on a glazing cell. Note that the doors are still off the vehicle at this stage.

Each body was then taken back onto a high-level conveyor in preparation for being mated to its appropriate chassis automatically. In earlier times, the Body Drop was always one of the most interesting elements of the assembly operation, but for the Sport and its Discovery 3 (and later, Discovery 4) sibling, the body was not dropped onto the chassis.

Instead, the chassis was hoisted aloft on its assembly cradle until it met the body on the high-level conveyor. This was a precision operation, which saw the two units very accurately aligned by computer control. The body was then released from its conveyor cradle and the whole assembly was lowered again, moving a stage forward at ground level to make room for the next pairing. The ten bolts securing body to chassis were done up automatically, and that precise lining up of body and chassis achieved by computer control ensured that bolts and holes lined up first time, every time.

The body-and-chassis assembly was now picked up in a cradle suspended from another overhead conveyor line and moved slowly down the Final Trim line. Seats and residual interior trim were installed and, then, thanks again to the computer systems controlling the assembly process, the right set of doors for each vehicle materialized alongside the track and was re-fitted.

Still suspended by its cradle, each vehicle then moved forwards to be fitted with its wheels, themselves already fitted with tyres. The now-complete vehicle was then carried forward towards a rising ramp where the wheels met the ground for the first time. At the top of this ramp, with the vehicle now standing on its own wheels, the cradle detached itself and returned to the start of the assembly line to pick up another body. The vehicle was then rolled off the ramp to the ECU calibration area, where the appropriate settings for its destination country and specification were downloaded. Visual quality control checks were also carried out here.

With a battery, water and fuel added, each Sport was started up and driven onto a rolling road, where a number of engine and transmission functions were checked. It then went through a water-spray test and was driven to a 'sign-off' area where it awaited collection by the Despatch Department, whose job was to send it on its way to the supplying dealership or direct to a customer.

Body has met chassis – which was lifted up to meet it in the same way as on the L322 lines – and the seats are installed. Clearly visible on the assembly line trolley are the nut runners which tightened the bolts holding the chassis and bodyshell together. The nearly completed vehicle is now on its way to the final line, where it will be reunited with its doors, fitted with wheels, and 'bought off' by the Despatch Department.

CHAPTER FOURTEEN

First-generation Range Rovers
and the Aftermarket

The basic simplicity of the original Range Rover and its low equipment levels contrasted strongly with its obvious potential as a sophisticated high-performance luxury car. From very early on, customers and aftermarket specialists alike recognized that potential. British Leyland, meanwhile, made no more than token upgrades in the Range Rover's first few years and, reassured that their efforts were not going to be nullified by changes to the standard model, the first aftermarket specialist companies began to develop improvements.

Body Conversions
and Enhancements

Probably the first to bring a major Range Rover improvement to market was FLM Panelcraft, a small London coachbuilder which had earlier developed an estate-car conversion for the Rover P6 (2000 and 3500) range of cars. Panelcraft's four-door Range Rover conversion appeared in 1974 and was actually granted Land Rover Approval by the Special Projects Department at Solihull, which meant that converted

vehicles would still be covered by the standard Land Rover warranty.

The timing was critical: when the Range Rover was launched in 1970, Land Rover (as part of British Leyland) was still on the boycott list established after the 1967 Arab–Israeli War and its products could not be sold in Arab countries. However, BL was making strenuous efforts to have the boycott lifted and from 1975 the Range Rover went on sale in the Middle East. George Adams, then BL's Middle East Sales Director, remembered that it became a

The four-door conversion was pioneered by FLM Panelcraft to meet demand from the Middle East. Note how the interior door handles were all modified versions of the standard two-door type.

Not every conversion added extra doors or more luxury equipment. This was a camper conversion from Carawagon, which dated from 1973. Very few were built.

Another conversion for the Middle East, this troop carrier was a conversion by Wood & Pickett.

ABOVE: *This Panther four-door conversion was built in 1976, probably for the Middle East. The roof rails and running-boards enabled security staff to ride on the outside of the vehicle. The spare wheel was relocated on the bonnet to make room for a rearward-facing bench seat in the back.*

The Wood & Pickett Sheer Rover sloping front end is seen here. In this case there is a twin headlight conversion; often, rectangular units from a Rover SD1 would be fitted in a special black housing, and the grille bars would be continuous all round the front. The four-door conversion, wide wheelarches and running-boards were all Wood & Pickett's work, too.

When Land Rover tried to get a grip on the Middle East conversion market, FLM Panelcraft was one of the companies that provided a 'standardized' four-door model. This example dates from 1977, and was probably painted in light blue with a dark blue stripe and blue upholstery. The interior featured four individual Recaro seats.

The Custom Specialists

Carmichael

Fire appliance specialists Carmichael developed the three-axle Range Rover with Land Rover engineers and used it for their Commando airfield crash rescue vehicle. From 1980, the company formed a separate division, Carmichael Custom Vehicles, to exploit this chassis for custom bodywork. Two types were available, called the Clansman and the Highlander, but they had probably disappeared by the middle of the 1980s.

Chameleon

Chameleon traded from an address in London's Park Lane, and appear to have been a marketing company. They offered a variety of conversions, many of which were probably built by A.E. Smith, but appear to have ceased trading by the mid-1980s.

Elektiar

Very little is known about Elektiar, who had offices in London's New Bond Street and a showroom in Riyadh, Saudi Arabia. Their only known conversion was a long-wheelbase six-door model with twelve seats, dating from approximately 1984.

FLM Panelcraft

Originators of the four-door conversion in 1974, this company continued to convert Range Rovers, mainly for Middle Eastern customers, into the 1980s. There were both luxury conversions and special-purpose conversions, such as open troop-carriers on the two-door Range Rover for use by royal bodyguards.

Glenfrome Engineering

Glenfrome was well-known for its bespoke conversions of all kinds on Range Rovers. In 1980, the company developed a desert buggy conversion with a GRP body called the Facet, and another one called the Profile. These failed to meet their sales targets and were ultimately responsible for the company's closure in the early 1980s.

JNR Motors

Aston-based JNR Motors developed a three-axle Range Rover conversion which was offered as a complete vehicle with a basic estate-type body. However, most of the JNR three-axle chassis were probably supplied to other specialists.

Overfinch

Shortly after the original Schuler division was renamed Overfinch (see below), the company was sold to new owners. It was briefly renamed Overfinch 2, but the name then reverted to the simpler Overfinch. The company continued to develop the 5.7-litre Chevrolet conversion, changing from the Voith transfer box and FF Developments' anti-lock braking system when Land Rover introduced its own ABS system in 1989. Handling improvements were added to the menu, and from 1994 there were cosmetic improvements as well. Overfinch continued to build bespoke Range Rovers right through the production life of the second-generation model, and at the time of writing was still offering its own highly exclusive versions of the third-generation type.

Panther Westwinds

Better known for its modern recreations of classic designs such as the Panther DeVille and the Panther Rio, this company also developed a four-door Range Rover conversion in 1976. Although the company did produce sales literature for its Range Rover, the original contract appears to have been for a fleet intended for a Middle Eastern customer, and it is not clear whether any more were made.

Rapport Automotive

Rapport began by offering performance conversions in the shape of the Australian-built 4.4-litre V8 engine and Allard turbochargers. Their association with Chris Humberstone Design enabled them to develop a variety of custom Range Rovers for the Middle East, which were marketed through offices in Park Lane, London. Rapport ceased trading in the early 1980s, transferring their operations to Symbol.

Schuler

Schuler was a new company in 1975, established as an offshoot of the UK arm of Schuler Presses, a German machine-tool manufacturer. It ran with limited backing from the parent company and an enormous amount of enthusiasm from Arthur Silverton, Managing Director of the UK division, whose idea it was. Schuler concentrated on dynamic enhancements – more powerful engines, better transmissions, handling and brakes. The company was renamed Overfinch in 1985 to avoid embarrassment to the parent Schuler Presses company, which was making machine presses for the Range Rover's rival Mercedes G-Wagen.

Scottorn

Scottorn Trailers had developed a powered-axle trailer conversion with Land Rover during the 1960s, and at the end of the 1970s they worked with Solihull on six-wheel drive conversions for both Land Rovers and Range Rovers. Their known Range Rover conversions were all simple estate-type vehicles. The company was absorbed into the Boughton Group during the 1980s.

SMC Engineering

Bristol-based SMC Engineering developed a three-axle conversion with selectable drive to the rear axle in the early 1980s. Some of their chassis were fitted with distinctive bodywork by Longwell Green Coachworks, also of Bristol, but it is probable that many SMC chassis were supplied to other Range Rover specialists under sub-contract.

The Custom Specialists *continued*

A.E. Smith

A.E. Smith was a long-established vehicle body building company based in Kettering, Northamptonshire. The company worked mainly as a sub-contractor to some of the better-known names in the bespoke Range Rover business, but also delivered a few basic body conversions under its own name.

Alvin Smith Range Rovers

Alvin Smith's company carried out most of the development work for Schuler in the 1970s and early 1980s, and by 1981 was offering elements of the Schuler conversions under its own name. These included the automatic transmission and Schuler FF transfer gearbox, the twin rear damper conversion, twin-headlamp grilles, and others.

Symbol

Symbol was another company within the same group as Rapport, and took over the Rapport operations in about 1982. It also traded from the same offices in London's Park Lane. The conversions it offered were the same, but the company ceased trading in approximately 1984.

Townley Cross-Country Vehicles

Townley was a Land Rover franchised dealer in Eltham, south London, and in the early 1980s was the only authorized export dealer in the UK. Dealing with export orders, the company received many requests for custom-finished Range Rovers, and turned over part of its workshops to building such vehicles. Although it ceased conversion work in 1988, it did manage to build some quite extraordinary vehicles in the few years of its operation.

Vantagefield

Vantagefield was established in London in 1982 by two former employees of earlier Range Rover specialists. Its first conversions were similar to those already on offer, but over the years the company developed a reputation for building bespoke Range Rovers, primarily for the luxury market in the Middle East. Diversifying into other bespoke coachbuilding areas enabled Vantagefield to stay in business when demand for Range Rover conversions tailed away, and the company was still functioning in 2010, still delivering to order a variety of conversions of the current Land Rover range.

Wood & Pickett

Wood & Pickett was established in 1947, and during the 1960s gained a name for its luxury conversions of the Mini. The company turned to building four-door Range Rovers in 1976, gradually developing luxury interior conversions and other distinctive specialities. Among these was the sloping-nose front end that was always known as the Sheer Rover (*sheer* or *Shir* is the Arabic word for lion). Wood & Pickett was among the most prolific and best-known Range Rover specialists before selling out to the Henley Group at the end of the 1980s. The company finally closed down at the end of the 1990s.

A.E. Smith of Kettering built a number of special Range Rovers both under its own name and under contract to other companies. This 135-inch stretch was built in the late 1970s; note the rear air conditioning vents between the two front seats. The vehicle was pictured in A.E. Smith's workshops where some minor bodywork problems were being rectified; note the bare metal on the rear wing panel.

This six-wheeler was another Wood & Pickett creation, and dated from around 1980. In the rearmost window pillar is a filler for the long-range fuel tank.

The original six-wheel chassis was built by Carmichael for their Commando airfield crash-rescue tender. By 1980, they were also building straightforward six-wheel estate conversions with four doors, and more elaborate custom-bodied versions such as the Clansman. Its raised rear roof gave headroom for passengers in the rear.

cult overnight. Not only did it have a combination of desert driving ability with suave city presence; it also brought respectable road performance to the party and somewhere in the background (thanks in no small part to connections with the British Royal Family) it had top-drawer appeal. It was, in a nutshell, exactly what the newly oil-rich upper-crust in the Middle East wanted as their additional revenues rolled in after the major oil price rises of 1973–1974.

For the wealthier buyers who were prepared to pay, FLM Panelcraft's four-door conversion fitted the bill perfectly. By later standards, though, it was relatively crude. Its front doors were simply shortened versions of the standard items, while the rear doors were made up from modified fronts with sliding rather than wind-down windows. The standard edge-pulls were retained front and rear, the rear one being almost unusably small. In basic form, it was not luxurious, but buyers soon began to demand such things as Recaro orthopaedic seats, special upholstery, air conditioning, electric windows and a refrigerator for cold drinks.

As far as the UK market was concerned, the Panelcraft four-door was virtually non-existent. However, its success overseas prompted other specialist converters to get in on the act, and by 1976 there were competing four-doors (with a broadly

Glenfrome was probably the first to build a full convertible, and this example of its Ashton model was pictured when new in June 1981. Note the chromed bumpers – nearly ten years before Land Rover made them available – and the rear end treatment, which uses a Rover P5 number-plate light and chrome finisher.

Townley were Land Rover dealers who did their own conversions and supplied them to mainly Middle Eastern customers. This group, pictured in the early 1980s, shows a selection from the huge variety of options available.

similar configuration) from Wood & Pickett of London and from Glenfrome Engineering of Bristol. As the demand for luxury conversions grew, so it became clear that there was neither lounging room nor room for additional luxury fittings within the standard Range Rover body. So the converters responded to that by developing longer wheelbases. The 110-inch Range Rover chassis already available from Land Rover showed the way forward, but within a few years the aftermarket specialists were building chassis with wheelbases of 109, 118, 124 and 136 inches as well.

Demand soon became too great for the major companies to cope on their own, and so they turned to subcontractors. These companies ended up working for more than one of the majors, and sometimes for all of them: a typical example was A.E. Smith of Kettering, who carried out basic chassis and body extensions. These would then be delivered to other specialists, who were sub-contracted to create bespoke interiors or fit special equipment to suit the customer's requirement. This

There was, of course, always room for one-offs. Townley built this six-wheel 'Desert Ranger' for a member of the Saudi Arabian Royal Family, widening it and adding a 5.7-litre Chevrolet V8 engine. The interior was very special indeed – but note the use of cloth wearing surfaces for a hot climate.

Glenfrome designed and built the Facet and the similar Profile, but poor sales of these futuristic-looking desert buggies ultimately led to their demise.

system allowed several more companies to spring up, some of them no more than co-ordinators who took an order for a bespoke vehicle, had it built by a number of sub-contractors, and then put their name on it. There were healthy profits to be made.

Among the customers, it was inevitable that there should develop a degree of competition. Each individual customer wanted to out-do his neighbour in the specification of his individualized vehicle. Demand for bespoke Range Rovers continued throughout the second half of the 1970s and into the 1980s, and was only enhanced by further increases in the price of Middle Eastern oil in 1979. There were some outrageously showy creations, many of which offended British ideas of good taste and some of which had dubious engineering integrity.

Other Range Rovers were painstakingly adapted to suit the demands of their users, being fitted with such things as hydraulically elevating seats which lifted their occupants through a sunroof and enabled them to follow through binoculars the flight of sporting birds in the desert. Some were adapted for military or semi-military purposes, being turned into open troop carriers and typically used for bodyguard and escort duties.

Between 1975 and 1977, British Leyland could barely keep up with orders from the Middle East. But it

Land Rover's own Special Vehicles division also built some modified Range Rovers to order. This one was built for the British Ambassador in Moscow in 1992, and was based on a 3.9-litre Vogue SE.

soon became apparent that a large percentage of Range Rovers going to Arab countries were being converted in one way or another, and BL quickly recognized that this had disadvantages. First, BL had no real idea of what was being sold in the Middle East with the Range Rover badge, and there was a risk that a poor conversion might damage the vehicle's image and reputation in those markets. Second, a great deal of extra money was being channelled through the coachbuilders – money that BL wanted for itself.

So a decision was made to try to control the market. The key aims were to regularize the supply chain and market pricing, deliver quality control from Land Rover, and provide a proper parts and service back-up. BL reached agreement with its Middle Eastern distributors to divert some of their Range Rover allocations to a group of 'approved' converters, who would turn them into four-door models with a common specification. None of this, of course, would prevent an individual client having additional work done on his vehicle, if that was what he wanted.

Land Rover, on behalf of British Leyland, appointed three converters to do the job – Panelcraft, Wood & Pickett, and Glenfrome. It was George Adams who persuaded the principals of these companies to bury their differences and to agree on a common specification for a four-door Range Rover. So around twenty vehicles a month from the Middle East allocation were held back in a special compound, and from there they were sent to one of the three converters. There were minor variations among their products, but the special Middle East specification four-door was known as the HL or Hi-Line. It was painted in opalescent

One of the best-balanced 'stretch' conversions was the 118-inch chassis, which gave front and rear doors of the same size. This one was built in the late 1980s by Vantagefield, who knew it as their Westminster conversion. The interior was also fully re-trimmed to suit the client's wishes.

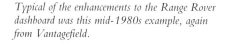

Typical of the enhancements to the Range Rover dashboard was this mid-1980s example, again from Vantagefield.

Vantagefield also built convertibles on the four-door Range Rover, but the two-door was more popular.

light blue with a blue stripe down the side and up the E-post. The interior featured blue leather and electric windows, and a fridge in the back was standard. BL carried out quality inspections, looked after the vehicle allocations and kept the order bank at its overseas sales division in London. Eventually, this strategy enabled it to control about 80 per cent of the market.

None of this, of course, prevented some specialists from creating ever more outrageous Range Rovers. When the East German leader, Erich Honecker, wanted some long-wheelbase Range Rovers for hunting, he by-passed BL altogether and had them built by the established Berlin coachbuilder Rometsch. Glenfrome developed two futuristic body styles made from GRP (glass-reinforced plastic) which they called the Facet and the Profile, and which turned the Range Rover into a desert buggy. Sadly, demand did not match the company's expectations, and this project led to their demise.

Yet there was still demand for more space inside Range Rovers, and the early 1980s saw Carmichael establish a special division to build passenger-carrying bodies on the three-axle chassis they had originally developed for airfield crash tenders. On the long-wheelbase four-door chassis, six-door models with three rows of seats appeared, while elegant convertibles appeared on the standard wheelbase.

The arrival of a factory-built four-door Range Rover in 1981 inevitably took some of the market away from the specialist converters. However, Land Rover once again acted as a referee, and brokered an agreement under which Wood & Pickett and Glenfrome produced specially-trimmed models, now with a blue side stripe on white paintwork, for the Gulf States. Gradually, though, the Middle Eastern market for customized Range Rovers died away. By the end of the 1980s, buyers had had their fill of Range Rovers (which had, of course, been around for a very long time) and were moving on to other large 4 × 4s such as the Toyota Land Cruiser 80-series and the Nissan Patrol.

Land Rover was also catering far better for demand by offering more luxurious production models, more powerful engines, and higher levels of equipment. Many of the specialist converters turned to other business; others had already shut up shop for one reason or another. None of the

There were just two of these Vantagefield Sceptre conversions, which turned the Range Rover into a three-box saloon with a conventional boot.

original Range Rover bespoke conversions specialists survived except for Vantagefield, a relative late-comer to the scene which had been established in 1982.

Dynamic Enhancements

While expensive body conversions and chassis stretches grabbed the limelight in the 1970s and 1980s, they were not the only aftermarket activity centred on the Range Rover. It was in 1975, just a year after Panelcraft produced their first four-door conversion, that Schuler began to develop high-performance conversions.

Schuler conversions were always rare, expensive, and way ahead of their time. They were probably sold mainly in the UK. Most were built for Schuler by Alvin Smith Garages, a Surrey specialist which also aided in Schuler development by campaigning an off-road racing Range Rover that acted as a test bed for new ideas. The Schuler focus was on dynamics, and

This rather interesting picture dates from 1988 and shows a Vantagefield conversion in a typical scene from the Middle East. The vehicle is keeping pace with a racing camel, and the camel's owner is watching (and probably shouting encouragement) from the back while his chauffeur drives alongside the track.

the company's basic 350HE conversion had a 200bhp tuned 3.5-litre V8 engine with four Dellorto 40 DHLA carburettors and a hotter camshaft. Also available was an engine conversion using the Australian-built 4.4-litre derivative of the Rover V8 engine.

The 350HE had wider wheels and tyres and stiffer suspension to improve handling. Many had an air dam below the front bumper to improve the aerodynamics, and twin headlamps to give safer illumination for high-speed driving at night. Schuler

Universal Sunroofs in the UK offered their Cabana targa-top convertible in the early 1980s, but it seems to have remained rare.

As turbocharging became popular, so specialists began to apply it to the Range Rover. This was a twin-turbo conversion by Janspeed on a carburettor V8 Range Rover.

At the end of the 1980s, Dennis Priddle Racing developed the Sprintex supercharger for Range Rover applications. It is seen here fitted to the engine of an injected 3.5-litre Range Rover belonging to a Scottish police force.

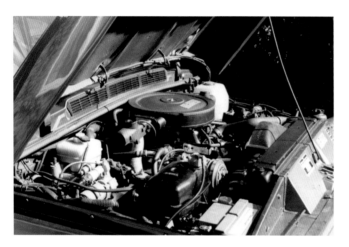

Overfinch were always the leading performance specialists, and from the early 1980s their stock-in-trade was the General Motors 5.7-litre V8 engine. Examples are seen here in 1994 guise (with carburettors) and 1998 guise (with petrol injection); the company continued converting first-generation Range Rovers for several years after these had gone out of production.

also offered 3-speed automatic transmission and 5-speed manual gearbox conversions. The automatic was initially a Borg Warner Type 65, and later a Chrysler A727; the 5-speed used the British Leyland LT77 gearbox. Some Schuler conversions had additional instrumentation such as a rev counter, and also had Recaro sports seats for driver and passenger. As these were again individually-specified conversions, in theory the sky was the limit.

Further development led in 1980 to the Super Ranger, which had a new chain-driven transfer box developed in conjunction with the German truck transmissions specialist Voith.

Unlike the equal front-to-rear torque split which the standard transfer box provided, the Schuler transfer box had a 40-60 front-to-rear split to improve handling. It also had a viscous-coupled centre differential. The Super Ranger came with a remarkably advanced anti-lock braking system made by FF Developments and derived from the Dunlop Maxaret system used on aircraft landing gear.

Thinking outside the box, Schuler experimented with a Range Rover powered by a 5.3-litre Jaguar V12 engine in 1980, but the length of the engine demanded a lengthened chassis, and this experiment was abandoned as too costly. In 1982,

however, the company turned to the new 5.7-litre (350cu in) small-block Chevrolet V8. That engine was also used by some of the other conversions specialists – with or without Schuler's participation – to provide much-needed power for some of their larger, heavier or armoured Range Rover 'specials'.

The Schuler company was re-named Overfinch in 1985, and continued to offer high-performance conversions for the first-generation Range Rover based on the Chevrolet V8 engine until the late 1990s. Switching from carburettor to fuel injection when the parent company did so, the engine gradually became more and more powerful, and by the time of the last Overfinch conversions of the first-generation Range Rover, it was developing 330bhp and could power a Range Rover to 60mph in 6.3 seconds. Overfinch went on to use the same engine in their conversions of the 38A Range Rover. From 1994, the Overfinch performance conversions were backed up by a range of interior and body enhancements, which in due course developed into a complete bespoke vehicle package.

There were of course others in the high-performance Range Rover market. The Rover V8 had swiftly become a favourite among performance enthusiasts in the UK, and a wide variety of tuning components had become available. Not all were suitable for the Range Rover, of course, which needed low-down torque to overcome its weight rather than top-end power which was nullified by its barn-door aerodynamics.

However, some specialists worked on Range Rover applications of the engine. Turbocharged engines were briefly popular in the 1970s and 1980s, from specialists such as Janspeed and, later, Turbo Technics. Both single- and twin-turbocharger conversions were available. By the end of the 1980s, Dennis Priddle Racing had developed a supercharged conversion, using the Sprintex supercharger that was made in Scotland, and in 1988 the Fife Police tried one out on one of their motorway patrol Range Rovers.

However, probably the best-known builder of high-performance Range Rover engines was John Eales, who called his company JE Motors (later JE Development). Eales developed the first 3.9-litre engines, which were used in rally-raid Range Rovers in the later 1970s and early 1980s; he then developed the 4.2-litre engine, a 4.3-litre, a 4.5-litre and even a 5-litre derivative of the original V8. John Eales engines were used in most of the factory-sponsored rally-raid Range Rovers, and in due course he sold the rights to his 4.2-

From 1994, Overfinch also focused on bespoke interior and exterior fittings. This is a 1999 570 HSi conversion, based on a 1995 Range Rover. Note the special 'Nevada' wheels with high-speed road tyres, the colour-coded bodykit, mirror heads and door handles, and other custom-finishing touches. The special paint colour was from the Overfinch palette and the interior had been completely re-trimmed in top-quality leather.

litre design to Land Rover, who used it in the long-wheelbase LSE models and in some special standard-wheelbase models as well.

Fuel Savers

Diesel engines did not enter the picture until the very end of the 1970s, although there was quite a strong demand for them from continental Europe, where diesel power gained acceptance for cars long before the same happened in the UK. Some of the first conversions used Peugeot 2.5-litre turbocharged diesels; from 1982, Janspeed Engineering offered the Italian VM 2.4-litre turbodiesel, as used in the Rover 2400SD Turbo car that was introduced that year; and from about 1985 a favourite was the new 2.4-litre 6-cylinder BMW turbocharged diesel – although this was always expensive.

Several other diesel conversions were developed for the first-generation Range Rover, even after Land Rover introduced its own Turbo D model in 1986 with the 2.4-litre VM engine. In the forefront of the specialists were Motor and Diesel Engineering, who offered the 6-cylinder 3.6-litre VM engine, as well as the 3.5-litre 4-cylinder Mazda type which was available both with and

without a turbocharger and associated intercooler.

Learning Curve

Unable to develop their own production specification because of a lack of funds, the Land Rover engineers nevertheless kept a close eye on these custom-built vehicles. Although they were too expensive to represent the demands of a wide variety of buyers, they did indicate very clearly how the basic Range Rover could be developed, and there is no doubt that later Range Rover production improvements 'piggy-backed' on them.

Although the demand for high-performance Range Rovers held up extremely well – and eventually led to the development of the Range Rover Sport and the use of the supercharged engine – the Middle Eastern market for customized Range Rovers gradually died away. Many of the specialist converters turned to other business; others had already shut up shop for one reason or another. Only two companies remained active: these were Vantagefield and Overfinch, the former still focused on Middle Eastern markets and the latter primarily on high performance and on bespoke interior work.

CHAPTER FIFTEEN

Later Range Rovers and the Aftermarket

As the previous chapter shows, there had been a very wide diversity of aftermarket 'improvements' for the original Range Rover. But by the time the second-generation Range Rover went on sale, the market for expensively customized conversions had almost vanished. Most of the companies who had made a killing in the heyday of the customized first-generation models had gone out of business or moved on, and the electronic complexity of the 38A discouraged others from catering for a strictly limited demand.

By contrast, the market for performance improvements widened. One reason was that the electronic engine management systems used on all the 38A's engines could easily be modified to deliver better acceleration, and as a result several companies that specialized in 're-chipping' offered performance improvements that were readily available to the man in the street. 'Sports' exhaust systems helped a little, too.

Most common were improvements for the BMW diesel engine; this could be re-chipped to deliver 177–180bhp with a corresponding increase in torque, and it could also be fitted with a bigger intercooler to improve the performance even further. As the engine was widely perceived to be under-powered for the Range Rover, performance enhancements of this kind became very common.

Just two UK companies continued to build the type of major conversion that had been characteristic of the 1970s and 1980s. These were Jankel – the group which had owned Panther Westwinds in the 1970s – and Vantagefield. However, their 38A conversions were built in small numbers and to individual order, and were of course hugely expensive.

Jankel was receiving its first enquiries about custom-built 38As by 1995, and to meet requests for more space within the body developed a three-axle conversion for the 38A, with selectable drive to the rear axle. On the extended chassis that resulted from this, it built both closed passenger-carriers with three rows of seats (and a raised rear roofline to provide headroom) and roofless models with elevating seats as chase vehicles for desert falconry. The additional weight of these conversions probably led in some cases to a demand for additional power, and no doubt Jankel sometimes fitted uprated engines from some of the specialists discussed later.

The JE S500 conversion added a supercharger to the 4.6-litre V8 engine in the second-generation Range Rover. The vehicle could accelerate to 60mph in 7.4 seconds.

Also available from Jankel by mid-1998 was a long-wheelbase two-axle conversion, with an extra 42in (107cm) in the wheelbase. Once again, this allowed the body to contain three rows of seats, so that the vehicle became an eight-seater. An extra pair of side doors meant that each row of seats had its own access, which suited clients who did not want to clamber past a folding middle row to get into the rear seats on the four-door six-wheeler conversions. However, the two-axle models were necessarily less capable in desert conditions than the three-axle types, and were designed primarily for use as town limousines.

Vantagefield built a small number of 38A conversions for some of its long-standing Middle Eastern customers, but in the beginning the scope of these conversions was severely limited. Some customers asked for steel springs in place of the air suspension that was somewhat mistrusted in the Gulf States; others wanted elevating seats and large opening sunroofs to create traditional falconry chase vehicles; and some chose uprated engines as well. In mid-2001, just a few months before the third-generation Range Rover was announced, Vantagefield also completed a six-wheel power-roof convertible with

Among the special accessories available for the 38A from Overfinch was this rearward-facing folding bench seat.

selectable drive to the third axle for a member of a Middle Eastern royal family – but this was a unique and exceptional conversion.

Bespoke interior enhancements were of course also available from Overfinch as a complement to its high-performance conversions of the 38A Range Rover. By their nature, these were much more limited in their scope than the major body and chassis conversions from Jankel and Vantagefield. Typically, an interior upgrade from Overfinch would consist of a re-trim where the new upholstery matched the style then

used in the Bentley Turbo saloon, the instruments took on white faces with black numerals to resemble contemporary sports car practice, and chromed interior door handles, padded armrests and extra wood trim increased the luxury ambience.

These enhancements gradually broadened the scope of Overfinch's work during the 1990s, but at the heart of the company's business was still high performance. The introduction of its 570 HSE model was delayed until May 1998 because of difficulties in modifying the 38A's complex electronic systems, but once again the

Overfinch celebrated twenty-five years of creating bespoke Range Rovers with a limited edition of the 38A that featured a 6.3-litre derivative of the General Motors V8 engine.

ABOVE: *The wife of a UK Vantagefield customer refused to buy an ordinary MPV to transport her children to school, so she asked Vantagefield to stretch a 38A Range Rover and add an extra row of seats.*

The boom in converted Range Rovers for the Middle East was over, but some clients still came back for more. Vantagefield created this example to special order, with a 5.0-litre John Eales V8 engine, a built-in rollover cage, and steel coil springs in place of the air suspension that some Middle Eastern clients mistrusted.

BELOW: *This three-axle 38A cabriolet with selectable six-wheel drive and power-operated top was another Vantagefield creation for a Middle Eastern client. The vehicle was also equipped with a winch at the front.*

5.7-litre Chevrolet small-block V8 was pressed into service. This third-generation Overfinch version of the engine was initially available with 330bhp at 4700rpm and 425lb ft at 3150rpm and powered the 570 HSE to 60mph in 7.2 seconds and on to more than 130mph.

Later versions delivered more power and torque, but the most powerful Overfinch engine was the 400bhp 6.3-litre long-stroke derivative of the Chevrolet V8 that was offered in the limited-production 630R Anniversary model announced in December 2000. The 'Anniversary' was Overfinch's own twenty-fifth anniversary in business (the total included their years as Schuler), and the 630R could reach 60mph in 6.61 seconds and a maximum of 138mph.

All these Overfinch conversions came with stiffer suspension for better handling, and with uprated braking and reprogrammed automatic gearboxes where necessary. The company had also developed an electronically controlled active ride system by mid-2001, but this was so expensive that it attracted only a handful of orders.

By this stage, JE Motors had evolved into JE Engineering and was looking beyond pure engine work to the development of complete vehicle packages. The company's most powerful naturally-aspirated engine was a 5-litre version of the Rover V8, and this was certainly used in some conversions by Vantagefield. However, in autumn 1996 the company announced a supercharged and inter-cooled derivative of the 4.6-litre V8 that delivered around 360bhp. Packaged with brake and suspension upgrades as the JE 'S' conversion, it was too expensive to find many

buyers, and so in February 1998 the company introduced its more accessibly priced S500 conversion. This had a 315bhp supercharged 4.6-litre V8 with 368lb ft of torque (500Nm, which was where the S500 name came from) and could reach 60mph in 7.4 seconds. Top speed was over 130mph. JE also offered supercharged versions of the 4.0-litre engine, which of course delivered less power and torque.

The first L322 modifications from Arden were cosmetic ones. The chromed exhaust pipes are most obvious on this vehicle, which also has wider wheels and tyres.

The German tuner Hamann drew on its expertise with BMW engines to create faster Range Rovers, and added a variety of cosmetic alterations as well.

The Mayfair long-wheelbase Range Rover was announced in 2006 and was made available with either a 300mm or a 600mm increase in wheelbase. There were interior enhancements, too, and a full-length glass roof.

At the end of the 1990s, ADI Engineering also developed a supercharged 4.0-litre V8 conversion, with 243bhp and 292lb ft. Its take on the 4.6-litre engine was a turbocharged and intercooled version with 380bhp at 4900rpm and 466lb ft at 3670rpm, but the company unfortunately ceased trading before these engines could make much impact on the market.

Not Much Scope

Land Rover had planned the scope of the third-generation Range Rover very thoroughly: there were so many equipment options and such a wide range of additional choices through the Autobiography scheme that there was relatively little left for aftermarket specialists.

Nevertheless, the two BMW engines available in the first L322

When the 38A illustrated on page 162 was getting a bit long in the tooth, its owner asked Vantagefield to build a replacement on the basis of an L322 Range Rover.

*The Overfinch Holland & Holland limited edition
was created in tandem with the famous sporting
gun manufacturer and was introduced in 2009.*

models were a prime target for additional work, not least because many German tuners had already developed performance upgrades for the BMW cars that had these engines. Rechipping these engines was relatively straightforward, and adding a larger intercooler to the turbocharged diesel delivered yet more performance, and several companies that specialized in performance enhancements generally rather than in Range Rovers specifically, had upgrades on the market very quickly.

Notable among the German specialists was BMW specialist Hamann Motorsport in Hüttisheim, who already had its HM 5.0 5-litre development of the BMW V8 available for BMWs that used the engine. By mid-2002, the engine was available in the L322 Range Rover, promising 360bhp at 5800rpm and 520Nm at 4400rpm with a maximum speed of 139mph and a 0–60mph time of 8.8 seconds. With a long-stroke crankshaft and a bigger bore, the swept volume of this engine was 4941cc. Hamann were also quick off the mark with an upgrade for the 6-cylinder diesel engine, which delivered 220bhp and 468Nm after they had worked on it.

Customers for these performance upgrades often wanted some cosmetic enhancements to their vehicles, if for no other reason than to make them look different, and among Hamann's offerings were some 22-inch five-spoke alloy wheels – a size that was outrageous for the time, when the largest wheel available from Land Rover was an 18-inch size. Also in Germany, Arden of Krefeld announced a range of cosmetic enhancements for the L322 models, but these were mainly small items and were probably intended to edge Arden into the Range Rover market in preparation for its later upgrades on the Jaguar engines that would be

The Range Rover Sport lent itself to sporty improvements, and Project Kahn went the whole hog with a racing stripe for its Pace Car.

In Germany, Loder 1899 boosted the performance of the Sport and also added its own bodykit and wheels.

introduced in 2005. As a long-time Jaguar aftermarket enhancement specialist, Arden was well placed to work on those forthcoming new engines.

Overfinch, meanwhile, worked on a more comprehensive upgrade, and by 2003 had developed their own 380bhp 5-litre (4930cc) conversion of the BMW V8 with a bigger bore and a longer stroke, the latter using the long-throw crankshaft from BMW's own M5 engine. This was called the 580S (5 litres, 8 cylinders, a zero for good measure and the S for Sport) and came with a modified automatic transmission with more closely-spaced gear ratios. Subtly modified front and rear aprons, plus chrome-tipped exhausts, new 20-inch alloy wheels and interior trim changes with an optional rearward-facing bench seat for two children made the 580S stand out from the crowd. The 0–60mph time was a creditable 7.1 seconds.

The 580S, however, was something of a stop-gap model, intended to tide Overfinch over until the new Jaguar engines were available. The company kept customer interest alive by announcing a new 'aero pack' of body styling addenda in July 2005, and then by March 2006 was ready with its own 440bhp, 475lb ft derivative of the supercharged Jaguar V8 engine. This was released in tandem with a restyled 'Aero II' bodykit, 22-inch multi-spoke 'Tiger' alloy wheels, and a range of interior enhancements that included a rearward-facing seat divided into two so that one half could be folded up when not in use, to increase load space. When the TDV8 diesel was announced a year later, Overfinch swiftly introduced a performance enhancement package for this as well.

However, the Overfinch marketing plan was clearly to become firmly established at the highest level of the bespoke vehicle market, and

Built in the USA but operated by a hire company in the north of England, this was a 'stretch limo' conversion based on the Range Rover Sport. The interior looked more like the inside of a nightclub than that of a car.

to that end the company developed what it called the Country Sports Concept. This was previewed at the Hurlingham Club in autumn 2008, and by autumn 2009 the idea had been adopted by gun manufacturers Holland & Holland, who put their name to a limited edition of 100 such vehicles. These were available with either the supercharged petrol V8 or the TDV8 diesel engine, in each case as enhanced by Overfinch.

Other aftermarket specialists also developed performance tunes for the Jaguar V8 engine, and among them were Arden in Germany, who announced the AR7 (2007 model), AR8 (2008 model) and AR9 (2009 model) derivatives, each slightly different from the last. JE Engineering developed a 5.1-litre derivative of the supercharged engine, but this was still-born when Land Rover announced their own supercharged 5-litre for the 2010 models. Meanwhile, it was already apparent that there would be a big demand for performance-tuned TDV8 diesel Range Rovers and so JE turned their attention to that engine as well. A variety of chip-tuning specialists also began to offer upgrades for the TDV8, and some of the more serious ones also offered upgraded intercoolers to deliver even more power and torque.

This six-wheel, six-door Sport was another Vantagefield creation for a Middle Eastern client. There was an additional row of seats, and all upholstery was in cloth rather than the usual leather.

Meanwhile, the more traditional upgrades were not entirely neglected. From October 2004, eighteen of Land Rover's franchised dealers in the UK began to sell a rearward-facing fold-away bench seat known as the Range7, which provided two extra child seats for the L322. In January 2006, the entrepreneurs behind this accessory then announced a long-wheelbase Range Rover called the Mayfair Edition. Available only through Land Rover dealer Stratstone in London's Mayfair, this came as the Mayfair 300 (with 300mm/11.8in stretch) or the Mayfair 600 (with 600mm/23.6in stretch). The conversion featured a panoramic glass roof, various interior upgrades including electric reclining aircraft-style rear seats, and could be armoured on request. However, the

The two-door LSE Coupé was based on the Sport and was an attempt to emulate the looks of the Range Stormer concept car. The proportions worked very well.

cost ensured that the Mayfair models would remain rare.

An Alternative Focus

While the L322 Range Rover remained popular enough to attract the aftermarket specialists, the real focus of aftermarket work after 2005 switched to the Range Rover Sport. It appealed to a different market, typically a younger buyer, and typically somebody who wanted both high performance and an individualized vehicle that reflected his or her personality or image. As the L322 and the Sport shared engines after autumn 2005 (although the Sport also had the TDV6 diesel, which was not available in the Range Rover), it was easy for tuners to offer their upgrades for both models and so to attract a wider customer base.

So from the start, aftermarket specialists focused on performance enhancements for the supercharged petrol V8 and for the TDV6 and (later) TDV8 diesel engines. The unsupercharged 4.4-litre V8, however, attracted little attention. Chip-tuning

A special show version of the LSE Coupé was created in conjunction with New York jeweller Tiret, and featured diamond-studded instruments. The front end had also undergone development since the prototype was first seen.

was the favourite, was available from a wide variety of companies, and at a few hundred pounds was affordable to a wide spectrum of owners. Only those with a little more money to spend and a little more understanding of the possibilities visited specialists who extracted more performance by fitting larger intercoolers as well. As an indication of what was available, from December 2008 JE Engineering offered their Stage 1 tune for the TDV8 engine which gave the Sport a 0–60mph acceleration time of 7.1 seconds.

Cosmetic enhancements were also important to the Sport's target customers, and in the USA Land Rover whipped up enthusiasm for the possibilities by having a supercharged Sport customized by Troy Lee Designs and displaying it at the SEMA tuning show in November 2005. Many specialists developed bodykits and large-diameter alloy wheels with attention-seeking designs. To established players Overfinch, who offered engine upgrades, 22-inch wheels and an 'Aero' bodykit from March 2006, were added companies new to the market.

The German specialist Loder 1899 of Odelzhausen announced a Range Rover Sport Black Edition in April 2006, with a striking bodykit of front and rear aprons and side sills, wheels up to 23 inches in diameter, and a 220bhp TDV6 upgrade. In June 2006, Project Kahn, a Bradford company already working on Mercedes-Benz upgrades, announced its Pace Car conversion. Finished in orange with a broad black stripe, this had the company's Stage 2 power conversion and

Wolf Design in the UK introduced a bodykit for the Sport, with wide wheelarches to cover some of its more radical wheel and tyre options from its parent company, wheel-and-tyre specialists Wolfrace.

22-inch wheels. Project Kahn went on to offer a variety of additional enhancements for the Sport. Then in September 2008, Wolf Design in the UK announced its bodykit for the Sport, with new front and rear aprons, fat wheelarches and new side sills designed to cover some extra-wide wheel-and-tyre options available from parent company Wolfrace Wheels, based at Maldon in Essex.

Meanwhile, the impact of the Range Stormer concept car shown at Detroit in January 2004 had not been forgotten. In February 2008, LSE Design, a new company established specifically for the purpose, announced its LSE Sport Coupé. This was a two-door conversion of the Range Rover Sport, without the expensively impractical scissors-type doors of the Range Stormer but with a number of other design cues that

reflected the concept car's influence. The company promised an exclusive run of just 150 cars in 2008, of which the twenty for the UK would be sold only through Stratstone of Mayfair.

Although the prototype did appear and was shipped across to the USA to take part in the annual Cannon-ball Run, LSE Design's timing was unfortunate, because the western world was hit by an economic recession in spring 2008. Undeterred, the company nevertheless got together with New York jeweller Tiret to produce a special show car which featured a diamond-studded instrument panel. The LSE Design Tiret Coupé was displayed at the Basel-world watch and jewellery exhibition in March 2009. Whether the project would be taken any further was not clear as this book went into production.

APPENDIX

VIN Codes

Range Rover chassis numbers and VIN codes (first-generation models)

Between 1970 and 1979, the old Rover Company chassis numbering system was still in use. Chassis numbers consisted of a 3-digit type identifier followed by a 6-digit serial number and a letter suffix. The letter suffix indicated major specification changes which were of importance when servicing the vehicle, and was changed sequentially.

Up to February 1975 (approximately), each type had its own serial number sequence that began at 00001. From February 1975, the serial number sequences were amalgamated into a single sequence (the first of the amalgamated numbers was 12024E). The final number was 61821G.

Example: 355-01238A
This breaks down as follows:
355	Home market	
	356	RHD export
	357	RHD, CKD
	358	LHD
	359	LHD, CKD
01238	Serial number (i.e. the 1238th vehicle within the 355 sequence)	
A	First type, before specification changes	
	B	from January 1973
	C	from November 1973
	D	from October 1974
	E	from October 1975
	F	from May 1977 approximately
	G	from September 1978 approximately

From 1 November 1979, all Range Rovers carried VIN codes to conform to internationally-agreed standards. Some vehicles built in October 1979 may also have had these. Those used for the first year (i.e. 1980 model-year) had 14 characters, consisting of an 8-character prefix code and a 6-digit serial number. From 1 November 1980, three further characters (SAL) were added to the prefix, making 17 characters in all that broke down into an 11-character prefix code and a 6-digit serial number.

Example (later type): SALLHABV1AA-123456.
This breaks down as follows:
SAL	Manufacturer code (from 1 November 1980)
LH	Range Rover
A	100-inch wheelbase
	B = 108-inch wheelbase (ie LSE)
B	Two-door body
	A = Two-door "van" body
	M = Four-door body
	R = Monteverdi four-door conversion
V	3.5-litre V8 carburettor petrol engine
	E = 2.4-litre VM diesel engine
	F = 2.5-litre 200Tdi or 300 Tdi diesel engine
	L = 3.5-litre V8 injected petrol engine
	M = 3.9-litre V8 injected petrol engine
	N = 2.5-litre VM diesel engine
	3 = 4.2-litre V8 petrol engine
1	RHD with 4-speed manual gearbox
	2 = LHD with 4-speed manual gearbox
	3 = RHD, automatic
	4 = LHD, automatic
	7 = RHD with 5-speed manual gearbox
	8 = LHD with 5-speed manual gearbox

Range Rover chassis numbers and VIN codes (first-generation models) *continued*

A	Model code (all Range Rovers to mid-1984)	
	B = 1985 model-year	H = 1991 model-year
	C = 1986 model-year	J = 1992 model-year
	D = 1987 model-year	K = 1993 model-year
	E = 1988 model-year	L = 1994 model-year
	F = 1989 model-year	M = 1995 model-year
	G = 1990 model-year	N = 1996 model-year
A	Assembled at Solihull	
	F = Shipped as KD for overseas assembly	
123456	Serial number	

Note that US models had a different system for the model-year identifier, as follows:

	H = 1987 model-year	N = 1992 model-year
	J = 1988 model-year	P = 1993 model-year
	K = 1989 model-year	R = 1994 model-year
	L = 1990 model-year	S = 1995 model-year
	M = 1991 model-year	

38A VIN codes

Models for Europe and the Rest of the World

The VIN codes consisted of 17 characters, made up of an 11-character prefix code and a 6-digit serial number.

Example: SALLPAMJ3MA-123456.
This breaks down as follows:

SAL	Manufacturer code (Rover Group)
LP	Range Rover 38A
A	Standard (108-inch) wheelbase
M	Four-door body
J	4.6-litre V8 petrol engine
	3 = 4.0-litre V8 petrol engine
	W = 2.5-litre six-cylinder diesel engine
3	RHD with automatic gearbox
	4 = LHD, automatic
	7 = RHD with 5-speed manual gearbox
	8 = LHD with 5-speed manual gearbox
M	Model-year 1995

	T = 1996	Y = 2000
	V = 1997	1 = 2001
	W = 1998	2 = 2002
	X = 1999	

A	Assembled at Solihull
123456	Serial number

Models for North America

The VIN codes consisted of 17 characters, made up of an 11-character prefix code and a 6-digit serial number.

Example: SALPA1J41SA-234567.
This breaks down as follows:

SAL	Manufacturer code (Land Rover)
P	Range Rover 38A
A	108-inch wheelbase
1	Four-door body
J	4.6-litre V8 petrol engine
	3 = 4.0-litre V8 petrol engine
4	LHD with 4-speed automatic gearbox
1	Security check digit
	(0 to 9, or X)
S	Model-year 1995

	T = 1996	Y = 2000
	V = 1997	1 = 2001
	W = 1998	2 = 2002
	X = 1999	

A	Assembled at Solihull
234567	Serial number

L322 VIN codes

Models for Europe and the Rest of the World

The VIN codes consisted of 17 characters, made up of an 11-character prefix code and a 6-digit serial number.

Example: SALLMAMA23A-123456
This breaks down as follows:

SAL	World manufacturer code (Land Rover UK)
LM	Range Rover L322
A	Standard trim
M	Standard four-door body
	K = armoured four-door body
A	4.4-litre BMW V8
	C = 3.0-litre BMW Td6 turbodiesel
	D = 5.0-litre LR-V8
	E = 5.0-litre supercharged LR-V8
	2 = 3.6-litre TDV8 diesel
	4 = 4.2-litre supercharged AJ-V8
	5 = 4.4-litre AJ-V8
	7 = 3.6-litre TDV8 diesel with Diesel Particulate Filter
2	LHD with 5-speed automatic gearbox
	1 = RHD with 5-speed automatic gearbox
	3 = RHD with 6-speed automatic gearbox
	4 = LHD with 6-speed automatic gearbox
2	Model-year 2002

3 = 2003	5 = 2005	7 = 2007	9 = 2009
4 = 2004	6 = 2006	8 = 2008	A = 2010

A	Assembled at Solihull
123456	Serial number

Models for Canada, China, Mexico and the USA

The VIN codes consisted of 17 characters, made up of an 11-character prefix code and a 6-digit serial number.

Example: SALMA61406A-234567
This breaks down as follows:

SAL	World manufacturer code (Land Rover UK)
M	Range Rover L322
A	S specification
	B = HSE without Luxury Pack
	C = HSE with Luxury Pack
	D = Limited Edition
	E = HSE without Luxury Pack, with Logic 7 and Bi-Xenon
	F = HSE with Luxury Pack, with Logic 7 and Bi-Xenon
	G = SE specification
	H = Westminster
	N = Standard trim (China only)
6	Standard body configuration (i.e. four-door estate)
A	4.4-litre BMW V8
	C = 3.0-litre BMW Td6 turbodiesel
	D = 5.0-litre LR-V8
	E = 5.0-litre supercharged LR-V8
	2 = 3.6-litre TDV8 diesel
	4 = 4.2-litre supercharged AJ-V8
	5 = 4.4-litre AJ-V8
	7 = 3.6-litre TDV8 diesel with Diesel Particulate Filter
4	LHD with 6-speed automatic gearbox
0	(Check digit; may be 0 to 9, or X)
6	Model-year 2006

3 = 2003	5 = 2005	7 = 2007	9 = 2009
4 = 2004	6 = 2006	8 = 2008	A = 2010

A	Assembled at Solihull
234567	Serial number

Range Rover Sport VIN Codes

Models for Europe and the Rest of the World

The VIN codes consisted of 17 characters, made up of an 11-character prefix code and a 6-digit serial number.

Example: SALLSAA235A-123456
This breaks down as follows:

SAL	World manufacturer code (Land Rover UK)
LS	Range Rover Sport
A	Standard trim
	J = Japan
A	Standard body configuration (four-door estate)
2	3.6-litre TDV8 diesel
	1 = 2.7-litre TDV6 diesel
	3 = 4.2-litre supercharged Jaguar V8
	5 = 4.4-litre Jaguar V8
	7 = 3.6-litre TDV8 diesel with Diesel Particulate Filter
	D = 5.0-litre petrol V8
	E = 5.0-litre supercharged petrol V8
	F = 3.0-litre TDV6 diesel
	G = 3.0-litre TDV6 diesel with Diesel Particulate Filter
3	RHD with automatic gearbox
4 = LHD with automatic gearbox	
5	Model-year 2005
	6 = 2006 8 = 2008 A = 2010
	7 = 2007 9 = 2009
A	Assembled at Solihull
123456	Serial number

Models for Canada and the USA

The VIN codes consisted of 17 characters, made up of an 11-character prefix code and a 6-digit serial number.

Example: SALSA234X5A-123456
This breaks down as follows:

SAL	World manufacturer code (Land Rover UK)
S	Range Rover Sport
A	Standard trim
	B = S trim
	D = SE trim
	F = HSE trim
	H = Supercharged
2	Standard body configuration (ie four-door estate)
	D = 5.0-litre petrol V8
	E = 5.0-litre supercharged petrol V8
3	4.2-litre supercharged Jaguar V8
	5 = 4.4-litre Jaguar V8
	D = 5.0-litre petrol V8
	E = 5.0-litre supercharged petrol V8
4	LHD with automatic gearbox
X	Check digit (0-9, or X)
5	Model-year 2005
	6 = 2006 8 = 2008 A = 2010
	7 = 2007 9 = 2009
A	Assembled at Solihull
123456	Serial number

Index

3.9-litre V8 engine   34
4.2-litre V8 engine   39
4.6-litre engine and manual gearbox   57
20th Anniversary edition   107
25th Anniversary edition   33
30th Anniversary edition   67, 72
35th Anniversary edition   106
60th anniversary (of Land Rover)   111
100-inch Station Wagon   15
109-inch chassis   153
110-inch chassis   153
118-inch chassis   153
124-inch chassis   153
135-inch chassis   34
136-inch chassis   153
200Tdi engine   54
1999 model-year (aborted proposals)   65

ABS system   36
Acocks Green   44
Active ride system   163
Adams, George   148, 155
Adaptive Cruise Control   134
Adaptive Dynamics   114, 138
ADI Engineering   164
AE Smith (coachbuilder)   151, 153
Air suspension   39, 58, 95
Alcon brakes   104
Allsopp, Bob   54, 55
Alochrome   45
Aluminium construction   95
Alvin Smith Range Rovers   151, 156
Ambulance derivatives   34
AMC air conditioning (Australia)   51
Anti-roll bars   39
Approved converters   153
Arden (tuner)   165, 167
Armoured Range Rovers   104
Assembly processes, second generation   84
Austin-Morris   11
Austin-Rover   12
Autobiography   39, 64, 101, 105, 111
Autobiography edition
   first generation   33
   third generation   106
   Range Rover Sport   136
Automatic choke   23
Automatic gearbox   20, 28, 31, 51, 79, 98, 104, 105, 109
Automatic In Vogue edition   28, 33
Automation (on assembly lines)   117
Axe, Roy   92
Axles, second generation   58

Bache, David   16
Bangle, Chris   89, 90, 92
Bannock, Graham   15
Barton, Tom   15
Bashford, Gordon   14, 16
Berger, Wolfgang   87, 99
Bertone   55
Bilton, John   54
Blenheim leather   110
Block 1   44, 117, 120
Block 7   61
Block 38A   59
BMW   13, 62, 86
BMW 2.4-litre diesel engine   159
BMW 2.5-litre diesel engine   54, 64, 79
BMW 3.0-litre diesel engine   96
BMW 3.5-litre V8 engine   65
BMW 3.9-litre V8 diesel engine   98
BMW 4.4-litre V8 engine   65, 96
BMW 5.3-litre V12 engine   65
BMW 6.0-litre V12 engine   97
BMW Design (department)   92
BMW diesel engine improvements   160
BMW X5   86
Body Drop   48
Body In White plant   78, 119, 144, 145
Bodykits   39, 135
Boeschel, Gerhard   89
Bolderstone, Frank   55
Bordeaux edition   72
Borg Warner transfer box   34
Borrego edition   67
Braemar edition   72
Brembo brakes   105, 109, 138
Bridgend (Jaguar engine plant)   144
British Aerospace   12
British Leyland   11
British Motor Corporation   10
British Trans-Americas Expedition   26
Brooklands edition ("in Brooklands Green")   33
Brown, Joe   18
Buick V8   15
Build faults   62
Butler, Mark   130

Cadillac Escalade   95
Callaway edition   67
Cairngorm edition   72
Camel Trophy   36
Cameron, Ian   93
Carawagon   149
CARiN edition   71
Car magazine   60

Carmichael   25, 34, 150
Chalmers, Peter   52
Chameleon   150
Chassis-and-body structure   14
Chevrolet 5.7-litre V8 engine   158
Chevrolet 6.3-litre V8 engine   162
Chip-tuning   168
CKD   see Overseas Assembly
Classic name   43
"Classic" derivative of 38A (proposal)   75
Comet wheels   75
Comsteel programme   49
Concept Oyster   16
Contour seats   101
Convertibles   156
Country Sports Concept   167
County edition (UK)   71
County SE edition   71
Crathorne, Roger   16, 18, 88
Crompton, Geoff   16
Crush cans   43
CSK edition   33
Custom-building specialists   150

Dagenham engine plant   126, 127, 144
DampTronic   138
Dana Corporation   144
Dennis Priddle Racing   159
Design Bible   90, 93
Design Research   91
Designworks (BMW)   90, 92
dHSE edition   71
Diesel engines, first generation   28
Dietsch, Murray   111
Discovery   8, 36, 52, 73, 120
Discovery 3   144
Disguise panels   60
Drayton Road (styling studio)   55
DSE+ edition   71
Dunlop Maxaret   158
Dunton reseaech centre (Ford)   126, 127
Dynamic Response   138

Eales, John   159
Eastnor Castle   16, 87
East Works   78, 119
Eaton supercharger   see Supercharger
Edis, Alan   52, 54
Edmonds, Noel   43
Electrical faults   62
Electronic Park Brake   110
Elektiar   150
Elsey, Dick   99
Ernst, Roland   127

Facet (by Glenfrome) 156
Fast throttle system 64
Ferraiolo, Paul 86
FF Developments 158
Fire engine variants 34
First Edition (Range Rover Sport) 136
First production models (of 38A) 61
First Range Rover 21
FIZ 89, 99
FLM Panelcraft *see* Panelcraft
Floating roof 26
Four-cylinder engine proposal 20, 21
Ford 13, 100, 125
Ford Explorer 100, 125, 128
Freelander 9, 94, 97, 99, 117, 120
Freelander 2 134
Frith, Stuart 128, 129
Fuel tank 96

G4 Challenge
 Range Rovers 108
 Range Rover Sports 138
Gearbox, LT95 four-speed 17
Gebler, Berndt 99
Gilroy, Tony 28, 29, 54
GKN 144
Glenfrome 26, 150, 153, 155, 156
Gloster Saro 34

Hall, John 54, 55, 59, 77, 128
Hamann Motorsport 165
Hanstock, Paul 130
Hartley, Gavin 90, 93
Haywood, Steve 125, 127
HCB-Angus 34
Henstridge, Sean 130
H-gate transmission selector 60
High Line models 24
Hi-Line models 155
Hill Descent Control 102
HL models 24, 155
Hodgkinson, Mike 29
Holland & Holland edition 67, 72
 by Overfinch 167
Holland, Jim 100
Honda 61, 85
Honecker, Erich 156
Horne, Grant 126, 127
HSE+ edition 71
HST derivative
 for UK 135
 for USA 136
Hurricane alloy wheels 65, 75
Hydro-forming process 127, 144

Independent front suspension 58
Independent suspension, all-round 95
"Infill" building 44
Interior design, first generation 18
International Scout 7
In Vogue

first edition 28, 33
 second edition *see* Automatic In
 Vogue
 third edition 33

Jaguar 100, 126
Jaguar engines 103
Jaguar Land Rover 13, 136
Jaguar-Rover-Triumph 11
Jaguar V12 conversion 158
Jankel 160
Janspeed 159
JE Development 159
JE Engineering 163, 167, 169
Jeep Wagoneer 7
JE Motors 159
JE "S" conversion 163
JE S500 conversion 163
JNR Motors 150
John Thompson Pressings 44, 79
Jones, Tom 128, 129

Kellett, John 58
Kensington edition 67
King, Spen 7, 14, 15, 19
Koning, Ayline 130

Lxx LGL registrations 61
Land Rover brand 8
Land Rover Ltd 12, 29, 44
Last-of-line vehicle
 first generation 43
 second generation 77
Launch, first generation 23
 second generation 61
 third generation 100
 Range Rover Sport 132
Leather upholstery 33
Leyland 10
Limited editions
 first generation, UK 33
 second generation, UK 71
 third generation, UK 106
 third generation, USA 107
 Range Rover Sport, UK 136
 Range Rover Sport, USA 136
Lincoln Navigator 95
Line Rectification 48
Linley edition 66, 67, 71
Lion engine 126
Loder 1899 169
Lomas 34
LR-V8 engines 111
LSE Design 169
LSE models (first generation) 39
LSE Sport Coupé 169
LT230 transfer box 28

Mxxx CVC registrations 61
McGovern, Gerry 111, 138, 139
McWilliams, Bruce 15

Mackie, George 24
"Made for me" concept 101
Magna Steyr 98
Manufacturing statistics, Range Rover
 Sport 145
Martin-Hurst, William 14
Mayfair edition 167
Mazda diesel engine 159
Mercury Mountaineer 128
Michelin dual-purpose tyres 23
Milberg, Joachim 100
Miller, Geof 15, 19, 21, 24
Mobberley, Alan 90
Mondial alloy wheels 64, 65
Monteverdi 27, 28
Monocoque 94
Morris, Bill 54

Nasser, Jac 100
New Vehicle Projects (department) 14,
 15, 16
North America 11, 15, 23, 32, 63
North American models
 first generation 35
 second generation 67
North Works 27, 44, 78
NXC xxxH registrations 23

One-and-a-half door layout 128
Overfinch 103, 150, 159, 161, 166, 169
Overseas assembly 49, 50, 51
Oxford edition 107
Oxford leather 75, 101, 110

Paint Shop 78, 80, 119, 145
Panelcraft 26, 148, 150, 152, 155
Panther 150, 160
Patrick, Alastair 86
Pendry, Mike 55, 60
Permanent four-wheel drive 19
Peugeot diesel engine 159
Pischetsrieder, Bendt 65, 99
Police vehicles 34, 73, 104
Poole, Tony 18, 22
Premier Automotive Group 100, 105,
 111
Pressed Steel Corporation (Australia) 51
Prices in the UK
 first generation 40
 second generation 74
 third generation 114
Prins, Jan 129
Prodrive 104
Production figures
 first generation 39
 second generation 77
 third generation 111
 Range Rover Sport 139
Product Planning Department 27
Profile (by Glenfrome) 156
Project Achilles 62

Project Discovery 54
Project Ibex 52
Project Iceberg 28
Project Inca 52
Project Jay 52, 54
Project Kahn 169
Project L30 87
Project L50 124, 125, 128
Project L51 124, 125, 128
Project L319 125, 128
Project L320 125
Project L322 100
Project L405 116, 143
Project L494 143
Project Pegasus 55, 59
Prototype, four-door (1972) 24
Prototype, van 24
Prototypes
    first generation 18
    second generation 60, 61
    third generation 99
    Range Rover Sport 129
PSA Peugeot-Citroen 126

Quality control 63

Rack-and-pinion steering 96
Range7 seat 103, 167
Range Rover name 21
Range Stormer 129, 130, 131, 135, 139
Rapport 150
Recession 111, 136, 169
Reitzle, Wolfgang 65, 86, 90, 92, 93, 99, 100
Rhino edition 67
Riva power boat 91
Road-Rover 18
Rometsch 156
Ross, Steve 100
Rover 3-litre engine 14
Rover Company 9, 14
Rover Group 12
Rover P6 saloons 14, 148
Rover R17 project 60
Rover-Triumph 11
RS300 name 131
RS400 name 131
Ryder, Don 11
Ryder Report 12

Saddington, Dave 120
Safety seats 20
Sales debut, Range Rover Sport 134
Sampson, Mike 65, 90, 124, 128
Schuler 26, 28, 150, 156
Scottorn 150
Self-levelling system 20

Servotronic steering 96
Shaw, Frank 19
Sheer Rover (Wod & Pickett) 149
Sheppard, Alan 93
Silvers, Graham 57, 61
Simmons, Phil 91, 92
Simultaneous engineering 55
SMC Engineering 150
Sneath, David 86, 87, 95, 100
"Soft dash" (first generation) 43
South Block 44
South Works 78
Spartanburg, proposed assembly in 89, 99
Specialist Cars Division 11
Special Projects Department 24, 26, 34, 148
Specifications
    first generation 37
    second generation 69
    third generation 112
    Range Rover Sport 140
Spencer Abbott 25, 34
Sport Stormer edition, USA 136
Sprintex supercharger 159
Stability Control System 138
Stage 2 funding 44
Stamping plant 118
Status symbol (Range Rover as) 7
Steptronic 98
Stokes, Sir Donald 11, 21
Stormer edition (Range Rover Sport) 136
Sub-frames 95
SU carburettors 33
Sunroof 33
Supercharger 57, 105, 133, 164
Swindon pressings plant 79
Symbol 151

T5 chassis 127
T5 Trim and Final building 144
TACR-2 34
Tata Motors 13
Taylor, Matthew 9, 131, 132
Td4 engine 97
Td5 engine 97
Td6 engine 97
TDV6 engine (2.7-litre) 108, 126, 133
TDV6 engine (3.0-litre) 116, 126, 137
TDV8 engine 108, 126, 135
Terrain Response system 109, 127, 129, 139
Testing
    first generation 18
    second generation 60
    third generation 94

Test track (at Solihull) 48
Thomson, George 59, 90
Thor V8 engines 64
Tiret Coupé 169
Torsen differential 98
Townley 151
Transmission plant 78
TreK edition 67
Trim and Final Assembly area 122
Trim levels, second generation 66
Troy Lee Designs 137, 169
Turbocharged engines 159, 164
Turbo Technics 159
Two-wheel drive proposal 20
TWR 39
Tyre pressure monitoring system 99, 108

Upex, Geoff 111, 130

VANOS 96
Vantagefield 151, 156, 159, 160, 161
Van variants 30
Velar 18
Venezuela (assembly in) 50
VIN codes
    third generation 115
    Range Rover Sport 142
Vitesse edition 67
VM diesel engines 32, 159
Vogue 50 edition 71
Vogue trim level, second generation 66
Vogue SE editions, second generation 71, 72
Vogue SE model, first 33
Voith transfer box 158

Wabco 36
Wadham Stringer 34
Warranty 63
Westminster editions (UK) 72, 106
Westminster editions (USA) 67, 107
West Works 45
Wilks, Maurice 14
Wilks, Nick 16
Wilks, Peter 19
Windsor leather 110
Wolf Design 169
Woolley, Richard 128, 129, 130
Wood, Alan 16
Wood & Pickett 26, 27, 151, 153, 155, 156
Working practices, second generation 85
Wyatt, Don 86, 89, 91, 92, 93, 99

YVB xxxH registrations 23